W9-BBO-011

BY CALVIN TRILLIN

KILLINGS

KILLINGS

CALVIN TRILLIN

RANDOM HOUSE | NEW YORK

Published in the United States by Random House, an imprint
and division of Penguin Random House LLC, New York.

RANDOM HOUSE and the HOUSE colophon are registered trademarks of
Penguin Random House LLC.

Originally published in hardcover in the United States by Ticknor & Fields,
in 1984, in different form.
The pieces in this book first appeared in *The New Yorker*.

Hardback ISBN 978-0-399-59140-2
Ebook ISBN 978-0-399-59141-9

Printed in the United States of America on acid-free paper

randomhousebooks.com

2 4 6 8 9 7 5 3 1

Book design by Victoria Wong

To the *New Yorker* reporter who set the standard—
Joseph Mitchell

Contents

Introduction

––––––

Reporters love murders. In a pinch, what the lawyers call "wrongful death" will do, particularly if it's sudden. Even a fatal accident for which no one is to blame has some appeal. On a daily newspaper, in fact, an accident is one of the few news events whose importance can be precisely measured by the editors who decide how much space and prominence each story is worth. In general, the space it is assigned varies directly with how many people were killed. Sufficient loss of life can elevate an accident story into a category of news that is almost automatically front-page—a disaster.

I have always been attracted by stories of sudden death. For fifteen years, starting in the fall of 1967, I traveled around the United States to do a series of reporting pieces for *The New Yorker* called "U.S. Journal"—a three-thousand-word article every three weeks from somewhere in the country. (Magazine writers asked, "How do you keep up that pace?" Newspaper reporters asked, "What else do you do?") Once or twice every year I found myself at the scene of a killing. When I began writing somewhat longer pieces, the attraction continued. Several of those longer pieces are included in this edition of *Killings,* along with a 1986 profile of Edna Buchanan, whose job as the *Miami Herald's* homicide specialist called upon her to approach the subject from a different angle.

What attracts me to killings is not importance as a newspaper editor might measure it—the number of people killed, for instance, or how closely they resembled the readers ("According to airline officials in New Delhi, there were no Americans aboard the plane"), or the prominence of the victim in the community or in the nation. A magazine like *The New Yorker* does not have the record-keeping function that a newspaper has. If a federal judge is assassinated in Texas or twelve people are killed by floods in the West, *The New Yorker* is not responsible for registering the event for the record. By the same token, it can—and did in some of these pieces—record the death of a single unimportant person without feeling the need to justify its interest the way a newspaper might in what reporters sometimes call a "nut graf" ("The Iowa murder is part of a growing national trend toward vaguely disreputable people in small towns killing each other").

While I was in the South working on one of the stories in this book, I happened to meet some reporters for the local newspaper, and they couldn't imagine why I had come all the way from New York to write about a death that probably hadn't even made their front page. Only one person had died, and she had not been an important person. Her family was not particularly important, and neither was the person accused of causing her death. The way she had died did not reflect any national trends. Her death had been the central event in what struck me as a remarkable family drama, but it seemed trivialized by the old newspaper phrase used to describe such dramas—a human-interest story. The best I could manage was "It sounded interesting."

I often wished that I could come up with something grander than that, particularly when I was asked by relatives of some victim why I was pursuing a subject that caused them pain to discuss. Not having to justify your interest is a great luxury for a reporter, but it is also a small burden. At times, I would have welcomed the opportunity to say "The public has a right to know" or "This story could prevent something like this from happening again." I couldn't even claim that I was an innocent party who had been assigned the story by the callous city editor of newspaper legend ("Hey, champ, get on your roller skates and get out to Laurel Avenue and talk to this lady whose husband just shot himself—and don't come back without their wedding picture"). I've chosen which stories to do for *The New Yorker* myself, mostly on the basis of what sounded interesting.

What I've been interested in, of course, is writing about America—or, as I realized a few years after I began "U.S. Journal," in writing about America without an emphasis on politics and government. Some ways of doing that didn't suit my needs. I wasn't interested in doing what is sometimes called Americana—stories about people like the last fellow in Jasper County, Georgia, who can whittle worth a damn. I didn't want to do stories about typical or representative Americans—stories about, say, the struggles of a Midwestern Farm Family to make ends meet. Although I was interested in places, I wasn't comfortable writing about a city or a state or a region in general terms; I didn't do stories that could be called "Boston at Three Hundred" or "Is the New South Really New?" I went every three weeks not to a place but to a story—to an event or a controversy or, now and then, a killing.

A killing often seemed to present the best opportunity to write about people one at a time. There were occasions, of course, when I found myself treating a killing as an element in a controversy that involved blocs of people rather than individuals. I once did a piece in Seattle after a white policeman had shot and killed a black armed-robbery suspect: in the controversy that followed the shooting, they both became so enveloped by their roles that the incident could have been described in just that way—a White Cop had killed a Black Suspect. There were occasions when not knowing the identity of someone involved in a killing meant writing about a sort of person rather than a person—the sort of person who might get killed that way or the sort of person who might do the killing. Once, in the early seventies, I went to the west coast of Florida to do a piece that involved efforts by the authorities to learn the identity of a body that had been found in a trunk left in the woods next to a restaurant on the interstate. The body was that of a twenty-five- to thirty-five-year-old woman. She had bad teeth. She had no scars. She had a bolo tie pulled tight around her neck It turned out that a lot of twenty-five- to thirty-five-year-old women were considered missing by someone. In the first few days after the trunk was discovered, fifty people called the St. Petersburg Police Department to say that they thought they knew who the dead woman might be. A man in his late forties phoned from central Florida to say that he thought the woman in the trunk was his wife, who had run off, with several hundred dollars of his money, in the company of a man in his thirties who drove a truck for a fruit company. A woman in Tampa said that her daughter had left home on October 28—wearing a white blouse, pink pants, and green flip-flops—and had not been in touch since, although it had been said that she met some men in a bar in Tampa and went with them to the dog races in St. Petersburg. A twenty-six-year-old woman had been missing from Wimauma, Florida, ever since her father threatened two men who had been staying with her. A man in St. Petersburg phoned to say that the woman in the trunk might be the daughter he had thrown out of the house three months before. She had been carrying on with several different men while her husband was in Vietnam, the father said, and only the intervention of his wife had kept him from killing her himself on the day he threw her out. The man became so angry talking about what he would do if he ever got his hands on his daughter that he had to be warned that he could be considered a suspect and that anything he said might be used against him.

The reports called into the St. Petersburg Police Department could conjure up a composite of the victim, but the stories of sudden death that most interested me were not those in which the people involved could be thought of as a type of person or a representative of what the lawyers call "others so situated." When someone dies suddenly, shades are drawn up, and the specificity of what is revealed was part of what attracted me. In London, in the summer of 1970, I accompanied an employee of the American consulate to a

drab hotel room in Paddington where he had to collect the possessions of an American who had died suddenly, without any known
relatives or friends in the area. The man had left nothing in the hotel
room except the contents of a couple of cheap suitcases, some half-
eaten sweet rolls, and three empty Coca-Cola bottles near the bed.
At the consulate, an inventory was taken. There was twenty-one
dollars in cash. There was an old membership card for the Screen
Actors Guild. There was an outdated passport, issued in the fifties,
listing the man's occupation as car salesman. There was a letter, dated
1961, from an MGM executive in New York: the executive said he
was sorry to hear about the man's having been under the weather
and regretted that he couldn't provide the World Series tickets the
man was looking for. There was another letter, dated 1968, from a
Las Vegas men's store telling whomever it might concern that the
man had been a courteous and responsible employee and had been
let go only because of a business slowdown. There was a card indicating graduation from a bartender's school in Los Angeles in 1968.
There was a form letter from the governor of Louisiana expressing
appreciation for the interest shown in investment opportunities in
that state. There were a lot of disposable syringes and an insulin
bottle. There were a couple dozen boxes of false eyelashes and an
invoice listing their wholesale and retail prices and some U.S. Commerce Department booklets on how to set up small export businesses. The inventory, of course, provided some hints as to how the
man had come to be alone in that dreary hotel room, with a supply
of both insulin and Coca-Cola. It also provided me with another
reminder of the appeal sudden death has for reporters: it gives us an
excuse to be there, poking around in somebody's life.

Reporters also tend to love trials. It may be that we are transfixed
by a process in which the person being asked a question actually has
to answer it. He cannot say he would rather not comment. He cannot tell an anecdote on a different subject. He has to answer the
question—under oath that he is telling the truth. I associate trials
with killings. I think of a trial as one of the principal illumination

devices switched on by sudden death. I suppose I carry around a kind of composite murder trial in my mind, along with a composite trunk murder victim. The prosecutor is a cautious young man—an assistant district attorney—who wears wingtip shoes and works methodically out of a loose-leaf notebook. The defense attorney is a bit flashier, and perhaps indiscreet enough to hint to reporters that his client is, in fact, guilty—the assumption being that a defense attorney who wins acquittal for a guilty client must be particularly brilliant. A defense lawyer can afford the style of a man not haunted by the prospect of having a victory reversed on appeal; there being no appeal from not guilty, he has to win only once. The caution of an assistant district attorney comes not only from the danger of reversible error but also from the conditions of his employment: a defense lawyer is engaged in private enterprise, and an assistant district attorney is a man who works for the government.

Of course, I've been to a lot of trials in which the lawyers didn't fit my composites—Daniel Boone Smith, the commonwealth's attorney of Harlan County, Kentucky, was nothing at all like a cautious assistant DA—and a lot of trials that were not particularly illuminating. Over the years, I spent a lot of courtroom hours wishing the testimony would move away from bullet trajectory and toward some accounts of how the victim liked to spend his time or some speculation on why the defendant might have wanted him out of the way. Even so, I remain fascinated by trials. I even like the examination of the jury. In fact, I particularly like the examination of the jury. When I'm in a public place among strangers—on a bus, say, or in an airplane—I sometimes have a sudden urge to make an announcement: "All right, we're going to go right down this aisle and have everyone state his name and address and occupation and then answer a few questions I have about your immediate family and your background and your prejudices." In jury selection, that actually happens—and everybody is under oath to tell the truth.

The techniques of jury selection vary widely from place to place. In Eastern Kentucky, the jury-picking method of Daniel Boone

Smith leaned heavily on what he knew about most of the families in the county—including how they felt about one another. In Brooklyn, I once sat through jury selection on a wrongful-death case with a plaintiff's lawyer whose strategy was based partly on a kind of informal ethnic sociology. The victim was a young woman—a thirty-two-year-old college teacher who had been killed in an auto accident. The lawyer for her family was looking for jurors who might be expected to place a high value on the life that was lost. To some extent, he was hoping for a personality type that he could describe only vaguely—open rather than closed, warm rather than cold. In another sense, though, he had his perfect juror specifically in mind: a fairly well-educated Jewish male in his sixties who had put two or three children through college.

Obviously, an interest in the ways that thoroughly American places like Brooklyn and Harlan County differ was one reason I started on my travels. In these stories, the place was the context for the killing, and the killing was an opportunity to write about the place. I sometimes read murder mysteries, and the ones I find absorbing are those that evoke a specific place. I'm more interested in what life is like in a Boston hospital or on the Navajo reservation or in South Africa than I am in who done it. The pieces in this book are nonfictional whodunits only in the sense that they are concerned with setting. Writing about, say, the murder of a prominent Miami criminal lawyer seemed to me inseparable from writing about the high life in South Florida.

At times during my travels, I may have become more interested in the community where the killing took place—or at least in the effect the killing had on the community—than I was in the victim. I was never much interested in the violence involved. Only a couple of these stories go into much detail about how someone was killed. This is not a book about the level of violence in America, except insofar that in this country a large selection of sudden deaths is taken for granted by a reporter looking for a story; I suppose someone doing "British Journal" or "Swedish Journal" would have to find another excuse for his presence. These stories are meant to be more about how Americans live than about how some of them die. If the old newspaper phrase didn't bring to mind an item about a motherly cocker spaniel adopting orphaned ducklings, I would be comfortable with calling them human-interest stories. Their appeal was that they were about specific humans, and I chose to tell them, of course, because they sounded interesting.

Author's Note

———

I am grateful to the late William Shawn, who, as the editor of *The New Yorker*, encouraged the "U.S. Journal" series. I am also grateful to the late Robert Bingham, who edited most of the pieces in that series, and to the other *New Yorker* manuscript editors and fact-checkers who, week after week, did their level best to keep me from embarrassing myself.

Except for some minor corrections, the stories in this book are printed as they appeared in *The New Yorker*. With one exception, they appear in chronological order and in the tense they were written in, because I think their settings include the times as well as the place. These stories are obviously not meant to reflect a statistically balanced picture of how or where Americans meet sudden death. There is no story about a storekeeper killed during an armed robbery. There is no story about a carload of teenagers wiped out by a drunken driver. There are three stories that take place in Iowa. As it happens, I have always thought of Iowa as a relatively peaceful state—all in all, an unlikely place for a killing.

KILLINGS

A Stranger with a Camera

O n a bright afternoon in September, in 1967, a five-man film crew working in the mountains of Eastern Kentucky stopped to take pictures of some people near a place called Jeremiah. In a narrow valley, a half-dozen dilapidated shacks—each one a tiny square box with one corner cut away to provide a cluttered front porch—stood alongside the county blacktop. Across the road from the shacks, a mountain rose abruptly. In the field that separated them from the mountain behind them, there were a couple of ramshackle privies and some clotheslines tied to trees and a railroad track and a rusted automobile body and a dirty river called Rockhouse Creek. The leader of the film crew was a Canadian named Hugh O'Connor. Widely acclaimed as the co-producer of the Labyrinth show at Expo 67 in Montreal, O'Connor had been hired by Francis Thompson, an American filmmaker, to work on a film Thompson was producing for the American pavilion at HemisFair in San Antonio. O'Connor went up to three of the shacks and asked the head of each household for permission to take pictures. When each one agreed, O'Connor had him sign the customary release forms and gave him a token payment of ten dollars—a token that, in this case, happened to represent a month's rent. The light was perfect in the valley, and the shooting went well. Theodore Holcomb, the associate producer of the film, was particularly struck by the looks of a miner, still in his work clothes and still covered with coal dust, sitting in a rocking chair on one of the porches. "He was just sitting there scratching his arm in a listless way," Holcomb said later. "He had an expression of total despair. It was an extraordinary shot—so evocative of the despair of that region."

The shot of the coal miner was good enough to be included in the final version of the film, and so was a shot of a half-dozen children who, somehow, lived with their parents in one of the tiny shacks. After about an hour and a half, the crew was ready to leave, but someone had noticed a woman come out of one of the shacks and go to the common well to draw some water, and she was asked to repeat the action for filming. As that last shot was being completed, a woman drove up and told the filmmakers that the man who owned the property was coming to throw them off of it. Then she drove away. A couple of minutes later, another car arrived, and a man—a thin, bald man—leaped out. He was holding a pistol. "Get off my property!" he shouted again and again. Then he shot twice. No one was hit. The filmmakers kept moving their equipment toward their cars across the road while trying to tell the man that they were leaving. One of them said that the man must be shooting blanks. "Get off my property!" he kept screaming. Hugh O'Connor, who was lugging a heavy battery across the highway, turned to say that they were going. The man held the pistol in both hands and pulled the trigger again. "Mr. O'Connor briefly looked down in amazement, and I saw a hole in his chest," Holcomb later testified in court. "He saw it and he looked up in despair and said, 'Why did you have to do that?' and, with blood coming from his mouth, he fell to the ground."

Whitesburg, a town about twelve miles from Jeremiah, is the county seat of Letcher County—headquarters for the county court, the sheriff, and assorted coal companies and antipoverty agencies. Word that someone had been killed reached Whitesburg quickly, but for a couple of hours there was some confusion about just who the victim was. According to various stories, the dead man had been a representative of the Army Corps of Engineers, a VISTA volunteer, or a CBS cameraman—any of whom might qualify as a candidate for shooting in Letcher County. The Corps of Engineers had proposed building the Kingdom Come Dam across Rockhouse Creek, thereby flooding an area that included Jeremiah, and some opponents of the dam had been saying that the first government man who came near their property had better come armed. Throughout Eastern Kentucky, local political organizations and coal-mining interests had warned that community organizers who called themselves Vistas or Appalachian Volunteers or anything else were nothing but another variety of Communists—three of them had been arrested on charges of attempting to overthrow the government of Pike County—and even some of the impoverished people whom the volunteers were supposedly in Kentucky to help viewed them with fear and suspicion. A number of television crews had been to Letcher County to record the despair that Holcomb saw in the face of the miner sitting on the front porch. Whitesburg happens to be the home of Harry M. Caudill, a lawyer who drew attention to the plight of the mountain people in 1963 with an eloquent book called *Night Comes to the Cumberlands.* Television crews and reporters on a tour of Appalachia are tempted to start with Letcher County in order to get the benefit of Caudill's counsel, which is ordinarily expressed in a tone of sustained rage—rage at the profit ratio of out-of-state companies that take the region's natural resources while paying virtually no taxes, rage at the strip mines that are gouged across the mountains and at the mudslides and floods and pollution and ugliness they cause, rage at the local merchants and politicians who make a good living from the trade of welfare recipients or the retainers of coal companies and insist that there is nothing wrong with the economy, and, most of all, rage at the country that could permit it all to happen. "Look what man hath wrought on *that* purple mountain's majesty," he will say as he points out the coal waste on the side of a mountain that had once been beautiful. "A country that treats its land and people this way deserves to perish from the earth."

In the view of Caudill and of Tom Gish, the liberal editor of *The Mountain Eagle,* a Letcher County weekly, the reactions of people in Jeremiah to the presence of O'Connor's film crew—cooperation by the poor people being photographed in their squalid shacks, rage by the man who owned the shacks—were characteristic of Letcher County: a lot of people who are still in Eastern Kentucky after years of welfare or subsistence employment have lost the will to treat their situation as an embarrassment, but outside journalists are particularly resented by the people who have managed to make a living—running a country store or a filling station or a small truck mine, working for the county administration, managing some rental property. They resent the impression that everyone in Eastern Kentucky is like the people who are desperately poor—people whose condition they tend to blame on "just sorriness, mostly." In Letcher County, fear of outsiders by people who are guarding reputations or economic interests blends easily into a deep-rooted suspicion of outsiders by all Eastern Kentucky mountain people, who have always had a fierce instinct to protect their property and a distrust of strangers that has often proved to have been justified. All of the people in Letcher County—people who live in the shacks up remote hollows or people who run stores on Main Street in Whitesburg—consider themselves mountain people, and, despite an accurate story in *The Mountain Eagle,* many of them instinctively believed that the mountaineer who killed Hugh O'Connor was protecting his property from smart-aleck outsiders who wouldn't leave when they were told.

The mountaineer's name was Hobart Ison. There have always been Isons in Letcher County, and many of them have managed somewhat better than their neighbors. Hobart Ison had inherited a rather large piece of land in Jeremiah—he raised chickens and rented out shacks he himself had built and at one time ran a small sawmill—but he was known mainly as an eccentric, mean-tempered old man.

Everyone in Letcher County knew that Hobart Ison had once built and furnished a house for his future bride and—having been rejected or having been afraid to ask or having had no particular future bride in mind—had let the house remain as it was for thirty years, the grass growing up around it and the furniture still in the packing crates. He had occasionally painted large signs attacking the people he thought had wronged him. He was easily enraged by people hunting on his property, and he despised all of the local Democrats, whom he blamed for injustices that included dismissing him from a post-office job. A psychiatrist who examined him after the shooting said, "Any reference to 'game warden' or 'Democrat' will provoke him tremendously." Once, when some local youths were taunting him, he took a shot at them, hitting one in the shoulder. "A lot of people around here would have welcomed them," Caudill said of the filmmakers. "They just happened to pick the wrong place."

Streams of people came to visit Ison in the Letcher County jail before he was released on bail. Women from around Jeremiah baked him cakes. When his trial came up, it proved impossible to find a jury. The Letcher County commonwealth's attorney and Caudill, who had been retained by Francis Thompson, Inc., secured a change of venue. They argued that Ison's family relationship in Letcher County was "so extensive as to comprise a large segment of the population," and, through an affidavit signed by three citizens in a position to know public opinion, they stated that "the overwhelming expression of sentiment has been to the effect that the defendant did right in the slaying of Hugh O'Connor and that he ought to be acquitted of the offense of murder."

Harlan County is a mountain or two away from Letcher County. In the town of Harlan, benches advertising Bunny enriched bread stand outside the front door of the county courthouse, flanking the First World War monument and the Revolutionary War monument and the plaque recalling how many Kentucky courthouses were burned down by each side during the Civil War. On the ground floor of the courthouse, the men who habitually gather on the plain wooden benches to pass the time use old No. 5 cans for ashtrays or spittoons and a large container that once held Oscar Mayer pure lard as a wastebasket. In the courtroom, a plain room with all of its furnishings painted black, the only decoration other than pictures of the men who have served as circuit judge is a framed poster in praise of the country lawyer—and also in praise, it turns out upon close reading, of the Dun & Bradstreet corporation. The front door of the courthouse is almost always plastered with election stickers. In the vestibule just inside, an old man sits on the floor behind a display of old pocketknives and watchbands and billfolds and eyeglass cases offered for sale or trade.

The commonwealth's attorney of Harlan County is Daniel Boone Smith. Eight or nine years ago, Smith got curious about how many people he had prosecuted or defended for murder, and counted up seven hundred and fifty. He was able to amass that total partly because of longevity (except for a few years in the service during the Second World War, he has been commonwealth's attorney continuously since 1933), partly because he has worked in an area that gives anyone interested in trying murder cases plenty of opportunity (the wars between the unions and the coal operators in Harlan County during the thirties were almost as bloody as the mountain feuds earlier in the century), and partly because he happens to be a quick worker ("Some people will take three days to try a murder case," he has said. "I usually get my case on in a day"). During his first week as commonwealth's attorney of Harlan and an adjoining county, Smith tried five murder cases. These days, Harlan County may have about that many a year, but it remains a violent place. The murders that do occur in mountain counties like Harlan and Letcher often seem to occur while someone is in a drunken rage, and often among members of the same family—a father shooting a son over something trivial, one member of a family mowing down another who is breaking down the door trying to get at a third. "We got people in this county today who would kill you as quick as look at you," Smith has said. "But most of 'em are the type that don't bother you if you leave them alone." Smith is known throughout Eastern Kentucky for his ability to select jurors—to remember which prospective juror's uncle may have had a boundary dispute with which witness's grandfather twenty years ago—and for his ability to sum up the case for them in their own language once the evidence has been heard. He is an informal, colloquial, storytelling man who happens to be a graduate of Harvard Law School.

A lack of fervor about convicting Hobart Ison was assumed in Harlan County when he came up for trial there in May 1968. "Before the case, people were coming up and saying, 'He *should've* killed the son of a bitch,'" Smith said later. "People would say, 'They oughtn't to make fun of mountain people. They've made enough fun of mountain people. Let me on the jury, Boone, and I'll turn him loose.'" Smith saw his task as persuading the citizens and the jurors that the case was not what it appeared to be—that the filmmakers were not "a bunch of privateers and pirates" but respectable people who had been commissioned by the United States government, that the film was not another study of how poor and ignorant people were in Eastern Kentucky but a film about the whole United States in which the shots of Eastern Kentucky would take up only a few seconds, that the filmmakers had behaved properly and politely to those they were photographing. "Why, if they had been smart alecks come to hold us up to ridicule, I'd be the last man to try him," Smith assured everyone. It took Smith only a day or so to present his case against Hobart Ison, although it took three days to pick the jury. On the witness stand, the surviving filmmakers managed to avoid admitting to Ison's lawyers that it was the appalling poverty of his tenants that had interested them; they talked about being attracted by expressive family groups and by the convenience of not having to move their equipment far from the road. The defense asked if they were planning to take pictures of the Bluegrass as well as Appalachia. Were they going to make a lot of money from the film? How many millions of viewers would see the pictures of poor Eastern Kentucky people? Had they refused to move? Had they taunted Ison by saying he was shooting blanks? Did the people who signed the release forms really know what they were signing? (At least one of the signers was, like one out of four of his neighbors, unable to read.)

Except for the underlying issue of Eastern Kentucky vs. Outsiders, the only issue seriously in contention was Ison's sanity. The director of a nearby mental-health clinic, testifying for the defense, said that Ison was a paranoid schizophrenic. He told of Ison showing up for one interview with long socks worn on the outside of his trouser legs and of his altercations with his neighbors and of his lack of remorse. The prosecution's psychiatrist—an impressive woman from the University of Kentucky who had been retained by Francis Thompson, Inc.—said that Ison had grown up at a time when it was common practice to run people off of property with a gun, and, because he had lived with aging parents or alone ever since childhood, he still followed that practice. Some of Ison's ideas did have "paranoid coloring," she said, but that could be traced to his being a mountaineer, since people in isolated mountain pockets normally had a suspicion of strangers and even of one another. "Socio-cultural circumstances," she concluded, "lead to the diagnosis of an individual who is normal for his culture, the shooting and the paranoid color both being present in other individuals in this culture who are considered normal." In the trial and in the insanity hearing that had earlier found Ison competent to stand trial, Smith insisted that Ison was merely peculiar, not crazy. "I said, 'Now, I happen to like mayonnaise on my beans. Does that make *me* crazy?'" Smith later recalled. "I turned to one of the jurors, a man named Mahan Fields, and I said, 'Mahan, you remember Uncle Bob Woolford, who used to work up at Evarts? Did you ever see Uncle Bob in the winter when he didn't have his socks pulled up over his pants legs to keep out the cold? Now, was Uncle Bob crazy? Why, Mahan, I bet on many a winter morning *you* wore *your* socks over your pants legs.'"

In his summation, Smith saved his harshest words not for the defendant but for the person who was responsible for bringing Hobart Ison, a mountaineer who was not quite typical of mountaineers, and Hugh O'Connor, a stranger with a camera who was not quite typical of strangers with cameras, into violent conflict. Judy Breeding—the operator of a small furniture store near Ison's shacks, and the wife of Ison's cousin—had testified that she was not only the woman who told the film crew that Ison was coming but also the woman who told Ison that the film crew was on his property. "Hobart," she recalled saying, "there is some men over there taking pictures of your houses, with out-of-state license." Smith looked out toward the courtroom spectators and suddenly pointed his finger at Judy Breeding. He told her that he would like to be prosecuting her, that if it hadn't been for her mouth Hugh O'Connor would not be in his grave and Hobart Ison would be back home where he belonged. Later, Smith caught a glimpse of Mrs. Breeding in the hall, and he thought he saw her shake her fist at him, smiling. "You know," he said, "I believe the idea that she had anything to do with bringing that about had never occurred to her till I mentioned it."

The jury was eleven to one for conviction, but the one held out. Some people were surprised that Ison had come that close to being convicted, although it was generally agreed that the prosecution's psychiatrist had outtalked the psychiatrist who testified for the defense. Smith believed that his case had been greatly strengthened by the fact that the filmmakers had been respectful, soft-spoken witnesses—not at all smart-alecky. "If there was anything bigheaded about them," he said, "it didn't show."

The retrial was postponed once, and then was stopped suddenly during jury selection when Smith became ill. On March 24, 1969, Hobart Ison came to trial again. The filmmakers, who had been dreading another trip to Kentucky, were at the county courthouse in Harlan at nine in the morning, ready to repeat their testimony. Although Smith had anticipated even more trouble finding a jury, he was prepared to go to trial. But Ison's lawyers indicated to Smith and Caudill that their client, now seventy, would be willing to plead guilty to voluntary manslaughter, and they finally met Smith's insistence on a ten-year sentence. Ison—wearing a baggy brown suit, his face pinched and red—appeared only briefly before the judge to plead guilty. A couple of hours after everyone arrived, Caudill was on his way back to Whitesburg, where he was working on the case of a Vietnam veteran accused of killing two men during an argument in the street, and the filmmakers were driving to Knoxville to catch the first plane to New York.

The following day, the clerk of the court, a strong-looking woman with a strong Kentucky accent, happened to get into a discussion about the filmmakers with another citizen who had come to know them in the year and a half since Hugh O'Connor's death—a woman with a softer accent and a less certain tone to her voice.

"You know, I asked those men yesterday morning if they were happy with the outcome," the clerk said. "And they said, 'Yes.' And I said, 'Well, you know, us hillbillies is a queer breed. We are. I'm not offering any apologies when I say that. Us hillbillies *are* a queer breed, and I'm just as proud as punch to be one.'"

"Not all of us are like that," the other woman said. "Mean like that."

"Well, I wouldn't say that man is mean," the clerk said. "I don't guess he ever harmed anybody in his life. They were very nice people. I think it was strictly a case of misunderstanding. I think that the old man thought they were laughing and making fun of him, and it was more than he could take. I know this: a person isolated in these hills, they often grow old and eccentric, which I think they have a right to do."

"But he didn't have a right to kill," the other woman said.

"Well, no," the clerk said. "But us hillbillies, we don't bother nobody. We go out of our way to help people. But we don't want nobody pushin' us around. Now, that's the code of the hills. And he felt like—that old man felt like—he was being pushed around. You know, it's like I told those men: 'I wouldn't have gone on that old man's land to pick me a mess of wild greens without I'd asked him.' They said, 'We didn't know all this.' I said, 'I bet you know it now. I bet you know it now.'"

I've Always Been Clean

West Chester, Pennsylvania

JUNE 1970

John Mervin, a menacing-looking young man with long unkempt hair and a shaggy beard, was arrested for murder last
November, confirming the suspicions of a lot of West Chester
citizens about the kind of crimes young people who looked like that
were capable of perpetrating. The killing that Mervin was accused
of—shooting to death an unemployed nineteen-year-old named
Jonathan Henry—had taken place during what a newspaper account referred to as a "liquor and drug party." Anybody who had
seen Mervin around town knew that he wore not only a beard but
the jacket of an outlaw motorcycle gang called the Warlocks. The
lead story on his arraignment in West Chester's *Daily Local News*
revealed that at the time of the killing Mervin was out on bail on a
charge of assault with intent to kill—a charge resulting from an October shooting in front of a West Chester saloon. The paper identified Mervin as a student at West Chester State College, which might
be considered an odd thing for a Warlock to be, except that some
people in West Chester were ready to believe almost anything about
the kids at West Chester State. The type of school that used to be
known as a teachers' college, West Chester State is sufficiently conservative so that someone with a beard would not have been permitted to take classes there a few years ago, but lately the townspeople
have been concerned about what they often call "that small element" in the college, an element associated with drugs and demon-

strations and bizarre appearance and a lack of respect for accepted values. The small element at West Chester State that worries the townspeople blends easily with a small element among their own children—the most visible result being a band of students or ex-students or drifters occupying the ledges around the steps of the county courthouse, flaunting mustaches and long hair and dirty T-shirts, staring arrogantly at the respectable citizens who walk by.

West Chester has about fifteen thousand citizens, almost all of whom consider themselves respectable. Some of them commute to Philadelphia or to Wilmington or to industries in towns in surrounding Chester County, but West Chester is too self-contained to be considered a suburb. It has a few small industries of its own, plus the legal and bureaucratic machinery that goes with being a county seat. The area that surrounds it still looks rural; the fields and barns of Chadds Ford, familiar from the paintings of Andrew Wyeth, are only a few miles to the south. The law offices clustered around the county courthouse are not in modern office buildings but in brick row houses, marked with neat white shingles. There has always been a lot of talk about history in Chester County—about when the county was founded and how many covered bridges it has and how many generations it has been Republican. But in the last year or two there has also been a lot of talk about drugs and disturbance and crime. The borough council made an effort to improve the police force, buying some new equipment and hiring the chief of county detectives, Thomas Frame, as police chief, at a considerable raise in pay. But a series in the local paper last June said that marijuana was easily available a few steps from the courthouse, the black people of West Chester continued to raise questions about equal treatment, and the kids on the ledges around the courthouse steps continued to symbolize all that menaced the traditional tranquillity of West Chester. The arrest of John Mervin for shooting Jonathan Henry caused some angry outbursts about just how far things had gone with the "hippies." (Although motorcycle gangs have been known to break up peace demonstrations and harass flower children, West Chester citizens tend to bunch all oddly dressed people together as hippies.) Then, a few days after the arrest, Chief Frame held a press conference to announce that John Mervin was an undercover police officer, having been recruited from the Warlocks and secretly sworn in a couple of months before. The police arrested a dozen or so people, most of them from around the college, for having sold drugs to Mervin. Frame announced that thanks to Mervin's efforts the police force had gained possession of forty-eight thousand dollars' worth of dangerous drugs. Mervin, who appeared at the press conference in a neat business suit, said that the arrests resulting from his work would "nearly annihilate any drug distribution" in West Chester. The chief, without commenting on the details of the shootings, said Mervin had "handled himself in the best manner a police officer could" and would begin to work on regular police shifts. John Mervin became a hero.

After it was revealed that Mervin had been an undercover agent, *The Philadelphia Inquirer* decided that he was not merely a student but an honor student, as well as a former high school football star—a young man who, underneath that hippie disguise, had precisely the attributes any American parent would be proud of. In an *Inquirer* story headlined HIPPIE POLICEMAN LIVED IN DEGRADATION AND FEAR, Mervin said that the most difficult part of his assignment was not the physical danger but the frustration of not being able to tell his loved ones that he was actually a policeman. "They thought I had gotten into bad company," he said. They were, of course, right: by his own account, Mervin had been in the Warlocks, a group that takes some pride in being considered just about the worst company in eastern Pennsylvania, for two years before anybody approached him about being a policeman. But the stories in the Philadelphia papers made it sound as if practically anything Mervin had ever done was part of the hippie disguise that he had manfully suffered under until he was at last able to throw it off, the drug traffic in West Chester having finally been annihilated. "His love of his motorcycle gained him admission into the Warlocks motorcycle gang two years ago," the *Inquirer* piece said. "And that helped him in his disguise." In a later piece, Philadelphia's *Evening Bulletin* reported the assurance of Mervin's contact man in the police department that Mervin was "always polite, never using elsewhere words and actions he had to use as a hippie drug purchaser and twilight world character." Mervin told the *Inquirer* that his first action after his identity was revealed was to call his mother.

Although the initial reaction in West Chester to Chief Frame's announcement was overwhelming support of Mervin, the support was not unanimous. The October shooting outside the West Chester saloon had been investigated only perfunctorily by the West Chester police after Mervin was arraigned and released on bail. But the killing of Jonathan Henry had taken place in an apartment behind a restaurant-and-bar just outside West Chester, in the jurisdiction of the West Goshen Township police, who continued their investigation even after Chief Frame publicly expressed his confidence in Mervin's innocence. The district attorney's office made it clear that it was pursuing the murder charge, and eventually it even got a preliminary hearing held on the October shooting—a hearing that produced the testimony of a couple of witnesses that Mervin, after an argument at the bar, had shot his victim in the leg and then had stood over him and shot him in the back. Chief Frame hinted that the district attorney was sore at not having been informed in advance of Mervin's mission and that the other law-enforcement agencies in the county resented West Chester's success in arresting drug dealers. Frame supported Mervin's story that the October shooting had been in self-defense; after the man who had been shot in the back testified, the West Chester police arrested him, on a complaint by Officer Mervin.

Some people familiar with the drug scene in West Chester scoffed at the notion that arresting some college kids for offenses such as selling Mervin a Chiclets box full of LSD tablets had had any effect on the drug traffic. The college crowd began to tell anyone who would listen that Mervin, far from being an honor student, had for a couple of years been a motorcycle tough who bragged about his violence—a bully who had merely redirected his bullying toward coercing people into selling him drugs. Some conversations among West Chester citizens were not about Mervin's heroism but about why someone with his background was sworn in as a policeman and why he was allowed to continue after the first shooting and why he was getting such vigorous support from the police department. "I would like to know what line of duty Mervin was performing on both October 4 and November 19," someone eventually wrote to the *Daily Local News*. "Or who has something on whom?"

Black people in West Chester have the wariness that black people anywhere would have toward a policeman who shoots two people— in this case, two white people—within six weeks, and they have even more reason than most black people to be worried about having an armed former member of a motorcycle gang patrolling the town in a police car. Last Labor Day, during a demonstration in the Chester County town of Parkesburg, a prominent black leader named Harry Dickinson was shot to death, and three members of a motorcycle gang called the Pagans were among those accused (but not convicted) of his murder. No Warlocks had been named by Mervin as drug dealers; when the preliminary hearing on the October shooting was finally held, there were complaints that witnesses testifying against Mervin were intimidated not only by threats of arrest from the West Chester police but by the threat implied by the presence of six attentive Warlocks in the courtroom. Liberals in West Chester were concerned about what has developed in other parts of the country into a sort of alliance between the police and the motorcycle gangs, with the gangs almost in the role of police auxiliaries in the rougher dealings with peace demonstrators and black people and students. At a West Chester borough-council meeting not long after Chief Frame's press conference, the only black councilman moved that, in line with the procedure followed elsewhere when a policeman is accused of a felony, Mervin be suspended until he was exonerated. The motion failed to get a second.

Mervin continued to ride in a police car, carrying a gun, and he began to appear with Chief Frame around the county to lecture on the evils of drugs—explaining to service clubs and PTAs and high school assemblies that "popping a pill" meant taking a tablet and that "acid" meant LSD. The forty-eight thousand dollars' worth of drugs that Mervin had captured—Frame's estimate of the retail price of the drugs Mervin had purchased for twenty-two hundred dollars in borough funds—became fifty thousand dollars at some point in the lecture series. As time went on, it was quoted occasionally as a hundred and thirty-five thousand dollars. The kids around the courthouse steps began to put on mock drug-buying scenes for the benefit of passing citizens: "Hey, you got any grass to sell?" "No, but I hear there's a guy down at the police station . . ."

On January 26, a Chester County grand jury indicted Mervin for the murder of Jonathan Henry. West Chester had a new mayor by then, the first Democratic mayor in a century or so, and on the evening after the grand-jury decision he ruled that Mervin had been a special officer whose duties were at an end. There was angry reaction to both the indictment and the mayor's ruling. A number of policemen staged a brief protest in which they handed in their guns—apparently symbolically, since they took them right back when Chief Frame told them to. The police started the John A. Mervin Defense Fund. A number of letters to the *Daily Local News* said that the borough was behaving shoddily by taking away the gun and the position of a man who had saved untold numbers of the community's children from the perils of drugs and had since reported attempts on his life by the murderous elements who control the drug traffic. The borough council, overriding the mayor, voted to hire, and immediately suspend, Mervin as a regular rather than a special police officer—guaranteeing that a salary would be put aside for him while the cases were in court and that West Chester would have, among its other historical claims, the distinction of having hired as a policeman someone under indictment for two felonies, one of them murder. A few days later, Mervin reported that he had been shot in the thigh with a .22 while he lay watching television. The mayor felt compelled to write a letter to the *Daily Local News* stating that the decision to end Mervin's service and take away his gun had been made with the approval of Chief Frame and in the best interests of Mervin as well as of the borough. "The futile debate which councilmen and the mayor engaged in on Wednesday night regarding Mervin's pay fades into insignificance today in light of what occurred last night," the *Daily Local News* editorialized the day after Mervin was shot. "What are a few hundred dollars compared to the life of a man who risked everything in order to smash a flourishing drug ring in West Chester?"

"There are only two opinions in West Chester about Mervin," a local reporter said when Mervin came to trial for murder this month. "Either he's a trigger-happy thug who conned the cops or he's a dedicated police officer." People on both sides thought that public opinion was about evenly divided, the word of mouth against Mervin having partly undercut almost universally laudatory press notices. Some of Mervin's most vocal support was judged to be based on a fear of drugs ("Drugs have become such a fearful thing people want to stop the problem and they don't care how," Devere Ponzo, head of Chester County's Black Action Committee, has said. "If a couple of people get killed—tough"); some of it may have come from political considerations (it was thought that raising questions might have been insulting not only to the chief of police but to the Republican establishment that supported him); some of it was undoubtedly a matter of ideology (one group that backed the John A. Mervin Defense Fund—the Association of Alert Citizens, a group that grew out of an anti-sex-education organization called Taxpayers for Decency—based its support partly on the ground that, in the words of one of its spokesmen, "we support the police—period"). But a lot of the talk about the Mervin case in West Chester emphasizes, aside from any political or ideological or antidrug feeling, how much people *want* to believe in John Mervin. Some people in Chester County (and in the newsrooms of Philadelphia newspapers) seem to have fastened on the Mervin case as a belated sign that the threatening and inexplicable manifestations of the youth culture are not true after all—that the long-haired, arrogant-looking kids around the courthouse steps might also throw off *their* disguises and reveal themselves to be honor students and former high school football stars and battlers against the deadly menace of drugs, that other mothers who are worried about their children's having fallen in with bad company might be told, as John Mervin's mother was told, that it was all an illusion. As the pool of jurors—most of them middle-aged or elderly people, virtually all of them white—walked into the courthouse on the first day of Mervin's trial, one of the usual "hippies," a thin young man with long hair, sat cross-legged on the ledge next to the courthouse steps. He stared at them with a slight smile, occasionally taking a swig of orange juice out of a quart bottle. When any of the jurors being examined said that he already had a firm opinion about the case, both the assistant district attorney and the defense lawyer assumed the opinion was that John Mervin was innocent.

The John Mervin who appeared at the trial was clean-shaven and dressed in summer-weight Ivy League clothes—a baby-faced, somewhat stout young man who answered his elders with polite "Yes, sirs" and "No, sirs." It would have taken an extraordinary leap of imagination to envision him as a hoodlum biker, dressed in a greasy Warlock jacket, swinging a chain—except, of course, to the extent that he had to wear a costume in the line of duty. (When Mervin testified that he had joined the Warlocks two and a half years before, his attorney said, "Were you engaged in any *other* activities that made you valuable as a police officer?") Mervin testified that after being recruited by Chief Frame he had let his clothing and hair become unkempt and had started attending psychedelic and exotic parties.

Trying to show that Mervin had not had to play any role to be accepted in local lowlife, the assistant district attorney asked him if it wasn't true that as an undercover man he wore the same clothing he had worn as a private citizen, merely allowing it to get a bit dirtier. Mervin looked offended. "I've always been clean," he said. According to Mervin, Jonathan Henry had been shot as he was about to shoot a West Chester State student named Jeffrey Saltzman, whom Henry suspected of being an undercover policeman—a scene precisely like those conjured up by Chief Frame's statements that as an undercover man Mervin had constantly risked his life in "this drug jungle." Saltzman, who happens to be the son of the mayor of the tough Delaware River town Marcus Hook and the nephew of a West Chester policeman, appeared as a defense witness to corroborate the story. He turned out to be a husky, collegiately dressed young man who also said "Yes, sir" and "No, sir." When the assistant district attorney, trying to argue that Saltzman had been a prospect for membership in the Warlocks, asked him why he had had one of his ears pierced, people in the courtroom looked flabbergasted—as if someone had, for reasons too bizarre to contemplate, asked Saltzman why he had begun talking to his friends in Urdu or why he had taken up the lute.

The witnesses against Mervin made no claim to being the type of people West Chester parents would be proud of. A West Chester State student testified that he had found Mervin's Warlock jacket in his front yard, and that Mervin, saying that Jonathan Henry had worn the jacket while assaulting a girl, had sworn vengeance. The student had long hair and a mustache; the only question he was asked by the defense attorney was one eliciting the admission that he knew some of the people against whom Mervin had brought charges of dealing in drugs. The fourth person present at the scene of the shooting—Eugene Moran, the tenant of the apartment where the shooting took place—testified that Mervin, with Saltzman's acquiescence, had shot Henry in cold blood; the assistant district attorney argued that the bullet angles supported Moran's story and made the Mervin–Saltzman version physically impossible. But Moran also admitted having told the grand jury that he remembered nothing about the crime; he said he had been threatened by Mervin and Saltzman and was terrified of talking. Moran, a thin man in his thirties who was wearing a suit that seemed too large, had been to college and was said to be fond of discussing philosophy—although on the night in question he happened to be speechless from overconsumption of Southern Comfort and water. He didn't look in the least collegiate.

Jonathan Henry, as described in court, seemed even more disreputable than those who had testified that he might have been murdered. Michael Thompson, a Warlock who appeared in a kind of Hitler mustache, took the stand to describe how he and Henry spent their days. Henry would come by for him every day about three or four in the afternoon, and then they would "just ride around, get some beer and drink, do anything we wanted to, really." Thompson said they occasionally dealt in LSD, in a minor way, for gas money. The proprietor of a bar frequented by the Warlocks testified that Henry had waved a gun around, threatening people, the night before he died. Mervin testified that Henry had bragged to him about shooting someone—or, as Mervin put it, about having to "dust somebody off."

Henry, in fact, sounded remarkably like the description that West Chester State students offer of John Mervin. But after a week's testimony, the assistant district attorney was under no illusions about being able to persuade the jury that John Mervin was anything but a decent young officer who had once been obliged to pretend to be like Jonathan Henry. After reminding the jury that they were not trying "the police or police in general or the issue of Support Your Local Police," the assistant district attorney further reminded them that neither sympathy nor prejudice should affect a jury's decision—and the sympathy and prejudice he was talking about was sympathy for John Mervin, a young college student, and prejudice against Jonathan Henry, a violent drug peddler. The judge repeated the admonition in his charge: "We are not here concerned with whether Henry deserved to live."

It took the jury approximately twenty-five minutes to reach a verdict of not guilty. Afterward, in the corridor, the jurors were having a final chat with each other when Mervin walked by, holding hands with a pretty girl. A number of the jurors walked up to shake his hand and pat him on the back and wish him luck. "Thank you. Thank you, sir," Mervin said to one of them. They smiled at him as he walked on down the corridor—a nice-looking, neatly dressed, polite young man who did look as if he had always been clean.

Jim, Tex, and the One-armed Man

Center Junction, Iowa

FEBRUARY 1971

Jim Berry came to Center Junction in 1962 and didn't do much that anybody approved of from then until the time he left, rather suddenly, last June. A native of Nashville, Tennessee, he had ended up in Center Junction because a decrepit house there happened to become available sometime after he married a woman from a nearby town. He hadn't been in the house long before he was in an argument with the town council about whether he could be forced to install a septic tank. His steadiest source of support for a houseful of children and stepchildren seemed to be Aid for Dependent Children payments—a form of welfare small-town people in Iowa tend to consider a government subsidy for random breeding. Some people in Center Junction say they found Jim Berry a likable person when he was sober, but nobody liked him when he was drunk. Dorothy's Tap, the only tavern in town, wouldn't serve him. When Jim Berry drank, one citizen recalls, "he was always a-needlin' and a-pushin'." He owned a shotgun and a rifle and a pistol, and it was said that he could throw a knife well enough to take the bark off a tree. There were stories in Center Junction about people who had called Jim Berry's bluff and faced him down—the way a Western-movie hero might face somebody down in a bar—but a lot of people, aware, perhaps, that they really might not act like a Western-movie hero if Berry started needling them, feared and resented him. Someone who asks a citizen of Center Junction for an explanation of why

Jim Berry was so belligerent when drunk is likely to get a simple, direct answer. "He had Indian blood in him," the citizen will say. "Liquor makes 'em wild."

People found it irritating that Berry always seemed to get away with things. Nobody in Center Junction has ever got away with much. Most people who live in Center Junction live there because they were born there. Since there isn't any work to speak of in the town itself—it's a fading little farm town of only about two hundred people—a lot of people drive to work every day in places like Monticello or Anamosa or even Cedar Rapids, thirty miles away. Some of their children get tired of driving and move to Cedar Rapids. Jim Berry never woke up early on a cold morning to drive to the Cuckler Steel Span Company, in Monticello. He was an upholsterer by trade, but he worked at it only sporadically. After an operation on his back a few years ago, he began drawing Social Security disability payments. People in Center Junction muttered that his back seemed all right for hunting or fishing or leaning over a bar. Nothing serious seemed to happen to Berry when the deputy sheriff picked him up for drunkenness or driving without a license. People in Center Junction often say that Jim Berry once killed a child on the highway in the southwestern part of the state. In fact, a manslaughter charge against him was dismissed; he served a few months for leaving the scene of an accident. When people mention the case, they seem angry not only that a child died but also that Berry seemed to have got away with something.

Center Junction people admit that when Berry did do upholstery it was excellent work—work that made it easy to believe him when he said that in Nashville he and his brother did the jobs for the city's top four decorators. In fact, people in Center Junction say that Jim Berry was good at whatever interested him. "There ain't nothing Jim couldn't tell you; there ain't nothing he couldn't fix, or even make," one of them has said. "I don't know what his IQ was supposed to be, but something fantastic." A couple of years ago, Berry took a correspondence course in electronics. He fixed a few radios and television sets—and fixed them well—but the main result of the course was that he became an avid citizens band radio operator, installing an elaborate rig in the shed he sometimes used as an upholstery shop. He got to know citizens band slang, so that, wanting to sign off to another CBer and send regards to the man's wife, he could say, "Seventy-threes, good buddy, and a stack of eighty-eights for the XYL." He even went to a couple of CB jamborees. He was particularly proud of having the most powerful station in the area. ("Jim had to be top of the hill," one of the townspeople says.) By "skipping" signals off the ionosphere, CBers often operate at distances much greater than the hundred and fifty miles permitted by FCC regulations, and Berry boasted of being able to talk to West Germany every morning. Because skipping is against the regulations, CBers who do it identify themselves with "skip handles" rather than real names or call letters, and often use the handles even for legal conversations. Berry liked to call himself the Bald-Headed Hippie or Freddy the Freeloader for long-distance broadcasting. The skip handle he preferred locally was Buckshot.

Around June of 1969, Jim Berry got into a CB conversation with a man who had an even more powerful station than he did—a man called Tex Yarborough, who lived in Maquoketa, Iowa, about twenty-five miles east. It turned out that Tex Yarborough and Jim Berry had a lot in common—although Tex was only about thirty, a dozen years younger than Jim. Like Jim, Tex had ended up in his wife's home county, having come up from Dallas a couple of years before. He had three rifles and a pistol. Tex was a machinist by trade, but, like Jim, he didn't make a fetish out of steady work. In fact, he didn't work for the year he knew Jim Berry. (When Mrs. Yarborough was asked later how her husband managed, with no income, to support a wife, three children, a roomful of radio equipment, and three cars, each car with its own CB mobile unit, she said, "Credit. We had good credit.") Like Berry, Tex was a proud son of his home state. He ordinarily wore cowboy boots and a cowboy hat, and he apparently claimed at

times to be a cousin of Ralph Yarborough's, who was then the senior
senator from Texas. Tex had been in trouble for offenses like passing
bad checks and assault and battery, and he had been in jail in Texas.
His skip handles were Short Stuff, Tex, and Dirty Pierre.

Jim Berry and Tex Yarborough became friends. They spent a lot
of time talking on the radio—to each other and to people like Lumberjack and Blue Goose and Sparkplug and the Mustanger. That fall,
they met often to go hunting or fishing or drinking. They had their
differences. Jim believed that Tex sometimes "threw a carrier" on
him—that is, keyed his microphone so that people talking on weaker
stations would be cut off. (Center Junction people claim that Jim
was in the habit of throwing carriers himself.) One night, when Jim
and Tex returned to the Yarborough house after visiting a few taverns, they had a scuffle that consisted of—depending on which story
is believed—Tex's knocking Jim down for making an offensive remark to Mrs. Yarborough, or Jim's trying to help Tex to bed drunk
and being attacked for his trouble. But Tex put in some radio equipment for Jim, and Jim, in return, agreed to make some new cushions
and a skirt for the Yarboroughs' couch—a project that was only half-
finished when a fire in Jim's shed burned up the rest of Tex's material. According to Berry, there was even talk about a partnership: in
a building Yarborough knew about in Maquoketa, Jim would do
upholstering while Tex acted as salesman and deliverer. That was
supposedly the project Jim wanted to talk about when he asked Tex
to come by—about a year after they had met—and they went to
Lou's Place in Monticello, where they met the one-armed man.

Lou's Place, identified by a sign for Hamm's Beer on a side street in
Monticello, has a beer-company décor. There is a Schlitz clock, a
Miller clock, and three Hamm's clocks. Calendars are by Budweiser,
Pabst, and Hamm's; lamps by Pabst, Hamm's, and Schlitz. About
the only objects of nonbrewery art are three tapestries—peacocks,
mountain goats, and horses—that Lou (Louise Garrett) bought once
from a foreign-looking traveling man. In Lou's Place, people often

argue in loud voices and men use bad language in front of women, who use bad language back. But the most abusive customer can usually be put out by a barmaid, who may be only five feet two but has the advantage of being sober, of having put out a number of similarly abusive customers in the past, and of holding the power to refuse service indefinitely. Jim and Tex arrived at about noon on a Friday in June—Tex a heavyset man wearing his customary cowboy boots and cowboy hat, Jim a taller, thinner man with a small, tired-looking face. They had come in about the same time the day before, and Bonnie Balsiger, the barmaid on duty, remembered them well—particularly Tex Yarborough. "He told me, 'I don't know how I ended up in a dumpy little town like this,'" she said later. "I told him that no one drug him into the town and if he didn't like it he could get the hell out of it." At one point in that first afternoon, Bonnie, leaning over the bar to pick up a glass, had noticed that Yarborough had a knife in his lap. He was talking about using it to slice up Jim Berry.

"You're going to have to forgive me for what I'm going to have to do," Tex told Bonnie.

"Whatever you're going to do, don't do it in here," she said. She ordered Tex to put away the knife or get out, and he put away the knife. He and Jim had spent the rest of the afternoon drinking together. "He was real picky, real boisterous, real loudmouthed," Bonnie said later of Tex. "The kind you have to cool down."

On Friday afternoon, Tex and Jim spent some time drinking with a group of pipeline workers, including a one-armed man named Jim Leonard. Wet weather had stopped work on a gas line being laid near what Jim Leonard remembered as "some little ole bitty place south of Anamosa." He had come into Lou's Place to ask his boss for an advance on his wages so he could drive home for the weekend to Bald Knob, Arkansas, where he and a number of other pipeliners live between jobs—relying on two subscriptions to a pipeline newsletter from Houston to keep them informed about where the next job might be. He had stayed around for a few hours to drink. Leonard's boss, agreeing to the advance, had laid a hundred-dollar bill on the table. The hundred-dollar bill was just about the conversational high point in a long afternoon at Lou's Place that was otherwise marked by Lou's telling Tex Yarborough that he was being too argumentative to be allowed at the pipeliners' table and by a number of people present getting into an argument about something called a water dog. (Jim Berry said water dogs were very common in Tennessee—"kind of like a lizard but with skin like a catfish"—and made excellent bait for striped bass. The other side questioned not only whether a water dog made good bait for striped bass but whether there *was* such a thing as a water dog. For Lou's Place, the argument was, as Jim Berry later described it, "a regular argument—a group argument.") At one point in the afternoon, Berry had asked Jim Leonard, the one-armed man, for a ride home— Center Junction being, in a manner of speaking, on the way to Bald Knob—and at about seven they left for Berry's house, stopping on the way so that Berry could buy a pint of Jim Beam.

At Center Junction, Berry showed Leonard his radio set and his guns, and then they sat down for a drink in the living room—a room with a floor of worn linoleum and walls decorated with a three-dimensional picture of the Statue of Liberty and an operating cuckoo clock and a picture of a saucer-eyed soldier over a passage about mother love ("A mother's love is like a rose hung on your chest . . ."). Mrs. Berry was not living with her husband at the time— she and the children were in an apartment in Anamosa, the county seat—and Berry made a phone call to Maquoketa trying, fruitlessly, to find a couple of girls. Not long after that, Tex Yarborough came in the door. "I want that hundred-dollar bill," he said to Jim Leonard. There was a brief scuffle, and then Leonard ran out to the front yard, only to be caught by Yarborough and knocked to the ground. Suddenly the one-armed man kicked at Yarborough and jumped to his feet. "They're trying to kill me!" he shouted. "They're trying to rob me!" And, with a terrified look on his face, he ran down the street—at a speed he later estimated at five hundred miles an hour. Tex slowly walked back up to the house, where Jim Berry was standing in the doorway, holding his 20-gauge shotgun. Tex was only a couple of feet from the door when Jim fired the gun. Tex seemed to stand still for a moment. Then he turned and walked off the porch into the yard. "You shot me, you rat," he said. "You shot me." He walked across the street and sat down next to an old stump. Then he got up and walked back across the street and crawled into the front seat of the one-armed man's car. He was there when the ambulance arrived. The deputy sheriff came and took Jim Berry to jail in Anamosa. One of the neighbors locked Tex Yarborough's car. The motor was still running, and so was the citizens band mobile unit.

Tex Yarborough died later that evening, from the damage done by a shotgun wound in the stomach. When Jim Berry came to trial in Anamosa last fall, he said that he had shot Tex in self-defense—that Tex had been holding what seemed like a knife when he stood over the one-armed man, that Tex had muttered, "You're next, Berry, you son of a bitch," as he slowly approached the door, that Tex had reached for the gun. The way the events were seen by some people who live in a neat white house across the street—people who wouldn't have been surprised at just about anything they saw going on in Jim Berry's ragged front yard—Yarborough stepped onto the porch, the screen door flew open, and he was shot. Jim Leonard— referred to by everybody involved as "the one-armed man"—said that he, too, had seen something that he thought was a knife in Yarborough's hand, and that Yarborough had said, "Give me that money or I'll cut your goddamn throat." The prosecution pointed out that Berry had said nothing about a knife until a few hours after he was in custody—at which point the deputy sheriff had returned to look around the yard, finding only a cowboy hat. The jury failed to reach a verdict.

A lot of people in Center Junction were outraged that Jim Berry had apparently got away with something again. As his second trial approached and the news got out that the county had hired a special prosecutor from Cedar Rapids to help the county attorney, it was said around town that if Berry was found innocent and returned to Center Junction, some of his neighbors would sell their houses and leave. The second trial was held in Cedar Rapids, so not many Center Junction people could attend regularly, but a number of them showed up for the closing arguments—the men identifiable by the start of beards being grown for this summer's Center Junction centennial celebration. Berry's mother came up from Tennessee for the trial. (In answer to a reporter's question, she said that Jim's grandmother on his father's side had been part Indian; she volunteered the information that Jim, as a fourteen-year-old who had managed to join the Navy during the war, had had his picture in papers all over the country for collecting so many dimes for the campaign against polio.) The evidence was much the same as it had been at the first trial. Berry again testified that Tex had told him about past acts of violence—about pulling a man off a barstool at the Wagon Wheel in Maquoketa and stomping his face in, about beating a man's brains out with a frying pan. The jury, after two days of deliberations, failed to reach a verdict. The jurors had seemed attentive but puzzled. Why didn't Berry just lock the door if he had been threatened? But why would he shoot Tex Yarborough if he hadn't been threatened? But then why would people spend a Friday afternoon at Lou's Place arguing about water dogs?

Sergei Kourdakov

Southern California

MAY 1973

On New Year's Eve, not long after midnight, the sheriff's department of San Bernardino County sent a patrol car to Running Springs in response to the telephone call of a young woman who said that her boyfriend had shot himself. Running Springs is a tiny town in the mountains, at the point where the road up from San Bernardino splits into one highway going toward Lake Arrowhead and another toward the ski resort at Big Bear. It has an oddly temporary look, as if it had been put up absentmindedly and might someday be dismantled in the same way. The attempts at the ersatz-chalet style that sometimes distinguishes mountain resorts from supermarkets in Southern California seem halfhearted—a piece of artificial timbering here, a few loops cut out of a knotty-pine porch railing there. Running Springs has a couple of motels that catch some overflow from the resorts on a busy weekend, but they look less like modern California motels than like what used to be called tourist cabins. When the sheriff's officers arrived, a distraught young woman led them to a room at the Giant Oaks Motel. A muscular young man dressed in a T-shirt and blue jeans lay on the floor between the two beds. A champagne bottle and a glass were at his feet. There was a bottle of strawberry wine on the television set. On the desk, there was a typewriter with a partly typed page in it. A .38-caliber Smith & Wesson revolver lay on the rug. The young man had been killed by a gunshot to the head. The following day, the *Los*

Angeles Herald Examiner ran a front-page banner headline that said, RUSS DEFECTOR DEATH UNDER PROBE.

In some circles, Sergei Kourdakov had been known not just as a "Russ Defector" but as a repentant, evangelical, born-again Christian Russ Defector. Since last summer, he had been traveling to churches around the country as a speaker for Underground Evangelism, a Glendale organization that describes itself as "a ministry to the suffering church in the Communist World." The issue of Underground Evangelism's monthly magazine that had just been published carried a chapter of Kourdakov's reminiscences and an advertisement for a cassette tape, available for a donation of four dollars, of the Sergei Kourdakov story—"A Persecutor of Christians Now Witnessing for Christ." The cassette, a recording of one of Kourdakov's public appearances, has an introduction in which L. Joe Bass, the founder and president of Underground Evangelism, offers a dramatic account of Sergei Kourdakov's first twenty-one years—his triumphs as a model young Communist and Soviet naval cadet, his awful adventures as the leader of a brutal attack group that raided one hundred and fifty underground churches in the region of Kamchatka, his decision to leap from a Russian trawler off the west coast of Canada, his miraculous swim through icy waters to shore, his conversion, his amazement at discovering that a Russian-language Bible presented to him by a Canadian pastor was identical to the Bibles confiscated from the Christians he had once beaten and despised, his joy at finding in Underground Evangelism the very organization whose smuggling efforts had provided those Bibles to the persecuted Christians of Kamchatka. Underground Evangelism had featured refugee Eastern European Christians before, but never one who was a repentant persecutor of Christians as well. Orders were already coming in for his forthcoming autobiography.

Underground Evangelism was accustomed to reporting the deaths of Christians at the hands of Communist torturers; that had become, in fact, something of a specialty. The death of a Christian—Underground Evangelism's featured Christian—by his own hand while he was sharing a motel room with a seventeen-year-old girl was another matter. Within a week of the shooting, Underground Evangelism had issued a press release stating that suicide, which had been mentioned in some early press reports, was out of the question, and that the circumstances of Kourdakov's death remained "strange" and "uncertain." His life had been threatened several times by Russian-speaking men, the release said, and he had once told Bass, "If you ever hear I have had an accident or committed suicide, don't believe it. I know how the Soviet police work, because I was one of them." The problems Underground Evangelism could expect from the press became obvious immediately after the shooting when an item appeared in Toronto, where Kourdakov had lived before coming to the United States. The *Toronto Star* quoted Kourdakov's Toronto pastor as saying that Kourdakov might have succumbed to the fast pace of the American evangelism circuit—part of the fast pace being, in the pastor's view, that Underground Evangelism had been using Kourdakov and exaggerating his career and exposing him to too much publicity. A young woman who said she had known Kourdakov at George Brown College, in Toronto, was quoted as saying that, according to a letter she had received from him, Kourdakov had regretted going into evangelical work and had confessed that he did not, in fact, happen to believe in God.

The San Bernardino coroner's office had pretty much concluded that Kourdakov had killed himself accidentally while playing with the revolver, but Bass said that a county like San Bernardino did not have the facilities to deal with such sophisticated matters as the death of a Soviet defector. "What better time than midnight on New Year's Eve, and what better place than that small, tourist-packed resort area for Sergei Kourdakov to have an 'accident'?" a newsletter sent to the Underground Evangelism mailing list said. "It's a rural county, mainly desert and mountains, with a small population and a relatively small law-enforcement staff." That was not a line of reasoning that pleased the law-enforcement authorities of San Bernardino County. "Any time you have a death such as this, where there was a young man in

a motel room, a young girl, and a bottle of wine," the coroner, Bill
Hill, told the San Bernardino *Sun,* "I guess you could call it 'strange'
and 'uncertain.'"

Attacks on Underground Evangelism over its handling of Sergei
Kourdakov had begun from sources that could be expected to be
even more persistent than offended county authorities or a suspicious secular press—two neighboring Glendale organizations called
Jesus to the Communist World, Inc., and Evangelism to Communist
Lands. Glendale, a middle-class section of the Los Angeles sprawl, is
a center for ministries to the suffering church in the Communist
world more or less the way Seventh Avenue is a center for the gar-
ment industry—an industry with which the Glendale missionaries
seem to share standards of goodwill toward the competition. Glendale grew as a center for oppressed-church missions as Eastern European refugees who had moved to town to work for Underground
Evangelism took acrimonious leave of UE and formed their own
organizations. Jesus to the Communist World is run by Richard
Wurmbrand and his family—Wurmbrand being a Romanian Lutheran who wrote a book called *Tortured for Christ* and was, for a
while, best known in this country for having removed his shirt before members of the Senate Internal Security Subcommittee to il-
lustrate his testimony that the Communists had left him with
eighteen scars in their effort to make him forsake the church. Evangelism to Communist Lands is a smaller operation, run by Haralan
Popov and his family. Popov is a Bulgarian; his book, written while
he was still with UE, is called *Tortured for His Faith.*

The three Glendale missions have some difference in emphasis—
whether to concentrate on smuggling Bibles in by clandestine cou-
riers, for instance, or to float some of them toward Russia or Cuba
on appropriate ocean currents—but their literature tends to tell the
same kinds of stories about the need for Christian literature and the
need to help the families of jailed and tortured Christian martyrs.
They tend to use the same terms, and even the same martyrs. One
distinguishing feature of the Wurmbrands' discussion of mission

work to the suffering church in the Communist world is their contention that L. Joe Bass has never done much of it, at least not enough to justify the two million dollars UE collects every year for that purpose. That contention was made in a thick report that Bass answered with a counterreport denying all allegations and accusing Richard Wurmbrand of carrying on a vendetta because he was thwarted in an attempt to take over Underground Evangelism. At first, Jesus to the Communist World reacted to Kourdakov's death merely by accusing Underground Evangelism of exposing him to worldly temptations he was not prepared for in its haste to exploit him. Then it began to question parts of the story told about him—whether there actually could be one hundred and fifty raidable underground churches in Kamchatka, for instance—and his own sincerity. (According to a letter the Wurmbrands circulated, Kourdakov, after falling to the floor of a temple in Toronto and shouting that he was filled with the Holy Spirit, was asked, "With what Ghost are you filled?" and replied, "Money.") Finally, the Jesus to the Communist World literature began saying that Kourdakov not only was not in danger from the KGB but may have been a KGB plant himself. The Popovs, who ordinarily use more restrained language than the Wurmbrands in denouncing Bass, limiting themselves for the most part to charges of lying and deception, said they were saddened that Bass had used Kourdakov instead of giving him the opportunity to grow in Christ. "He was what we call a backslider," Ladin Popov, Haralan's brother, said of Kourdakov recently. "And the wages of sin are death."

Bass explains the defection of people like Wurmbrand and Popov partly as a tendency in "the Eastern European mentality" to prefer small family businesses rather than large, centralized organizations. He says that those who accuse Underground Evangelism of trying to make a martyr out of Sergei Kourdakov are themselves guilty of vilifying the boy in order to further their campaign against Underground Evangelism. According to Bass, such attacks are no more than the leader in the field should expect. "Let's face it," he said recently. "They're interested parties. They're trying to build an organization from the same pool of donors."

At the coroner's inquest, held in San Bernardino the last week in February, the star witness was, of course, the young woman who had been staying with Kourdakov at the Giant Oaks Motel—a blond high school senior who had met Kourdakov at a church camp. Her parents, also churchgoing people, had invited him to be their houseguest while he was in California. According to the testimony, the parents were aware that Kourdakov and their daughter were going to take a weekend trip together—first to Disneyland and then to the mountains, where they hoped to do some skiing while Sergei worked on the papers he had promised to prepare as part of the effort Senator Strom Thurmond and others in Washington were carrying on to win him permanent residency. A polygraph specialist for the sheriff's office testified that the girl had responded to a question about her sexual relations with Kourdakov at the Giant Oaks—a question that had been included in the polygraph test at her father's insistence—by saying that they "had come close but not completed an act." ("I might say that was the area of the greatest concern of this young lady at the time of the test, as opposed to whether or not she had shot the man," the polygraph expert said. "So I feel we have very definite ... truthful responses.") As the girl described New Year's weekend in Running Springs, she had spent most of her time watching television while Kourdakov typed away. On New Year's Eve, he had paused to watch *The Dick Van Dyke Show* and some other programs he liked, and then they had shared some champagne, and then, for no apparent reason, he had held the gun up and shot himself.

From what the investigators gathered, Kourdakov may have made a mistake about which way the cylinder turns on a Smith & Wesson .38. The previous day, it was testified, he had taken out one bullet, explaining that he was removing it for safety reasons, and the investigators surmised that he might have thought he was firing an empty chamber. The gun had been borrowed from the girl's father, an electrician, who testified that Kourdakov had his permission to borrow a weapon whenever he felt the need of one. The father had heard that some people in Washington were working on obtaining permission for Kourdakov to carry a gun—ordinarily illegal for an alien—but, he testified, "it's been my sad experience in the past that bureaucracy moves so slow that he would get killed just about the time they got papers on him."

"How many weapons do you own?" the coroner asked.

"Seven," he replied.

Bass offered depositions from churchmen in Washington attesting to what an exuberant, life-loving Christian Kourdakov had been. Some friends of the girl's parents who had met Kourdakov just before the young couple went off for the weekend testified that he had been in fine spirits and had been particularly delighted with some new custom-fitted ski boots. According to his contract with Underground Evangelism, offered in evidence, Kourdakov had no financial worries. He was receiving a salary of two hundred dollars a week, plus ten percent of the offerings collected at his speaking engagements (after expenses were deducted) and twenty-five percent of the cassette take—an arrangement that had permitted him to clear $1,688.01 for the month of October. ("He's done quite well for being a resident of our country for a short period of time," one member of the coroner's jury remarked to the court.) The future looked even brighter, since Kourdakov's contract called for him to receive fifty percent of the profits from his autobiography. He appeared to have both business and literary plans for the future. The page found in his typewriter was not documentation for Senator Thurmond but what appeared to be part of a short story.

Denying charges that Underground Evangelism had exploited Kourdakov, Bass said that the money spent on "developing Mr. Kourdakov into a well-rounded resident far exceeded any remuneration which our organization received as a result of his activities"—or, as the assistant treasurer of UE later put it to a reporter, "If you want to look on the cold, hard financial facts, we lost money on the kid." Bass said that Underground Evangelism had been mainly concerned about Kourdakov's "developing and growing into the American way of life." Much of the testimony, of course, indicated that Kourdakov had already grown into the American way of life at the time of his death: a weekend at Disneyland and at a motel, a seventeen-year-old girl more emphatic about her reputation than about murder, strawberry wine, a pair of custom-fitted ski boots, a Thunderbird in the parking lot. Where else but in America, after all, could Kourdakov find, to his ultimate misfortune, that the father of a girl he met at a church camp owned seven weapons?

After three days of testimony, the coroner's jury reached a verdict of accidental death. Bass, under questioning from the coroner, said he was satisfied with the standards of San Bernardino County police work after all. But Underground Evangelism still answers questions about the case by saying that "quiet inquiries" are being made; the last two issues of Underground Evangelism's monthly, both of them devoted almost entirely to Sergei Kourdakov, mention nothing about his gunshot being self-inflicted but talk about his insistence on continuing his work despite the danger. The inquest had, of course, brought out some information embarrassing to Underground Evangelism. The Wurmbrands ordered a copy of the transcript, and Congressman Earl Landgrebe, of Indiana—one of the sponsors of Kourdakov's visa, and a man whose own commitment to the cause is strong enough to have resulted in his being detained in Russia last year for handing out Bibles—said he believed he himself had been exploited by Underground Evangelism. Bass has said that the rank and file of Underground Evangelism supporters remained loyal despite the circumstances of Kourdakov's death—which may indicate that evangelical Christians are more broad-minded than they are usually given credit for, or that Underground Evangelism supporters depended for their information on UE literature, which gave them nothing to be broad-minded about, having mentioned alcohol not at all and sex only to say, in an early newsletter, that, contrary to rumors, "official sources completely rule out any misconduct in relation to a girl."

The April issue of Underground Evangelism's magazine announced "a fitting memorial to Sergei"—the Sergei Kourdakov Memorial Fund. Kourdakov's book is almost ready. Bass has just returned from a European trip on which he closed a deal for the German rights and began negotiation for publication in England. There have been reports that Kourdakov may have left heirs—some brothers in Russia—but they would probably have difficulty claiming his fifty percent of the book royalties even if they made their way to Glendale. Clause 11 of his agreement with Underground Evangelism said that he would not "commit any act that will reasonably tend to degrade him or to bring him or U.E. into public contempt, ridicule, or would tend to shock or offend the constituency of U.E. or the Christian church in general." Sergei Kourdakov had obviously broken his contract.

You Always Turn Your Head

Gallup, New Mexico

MAY 1973

Pete Derizotis, City Alcoholism Coordinator: *I was in the mayor's office. . . . Somebody knocked. . . . I opened the door. It was Larry Casuse and another Indian fellow.*
—Radio station KGAK live coverage, from the street in front of Stearn's Sporting Goods store, March 1

In Gallup, it was taken for granted that employees of the city government would recognize Larry Casuse on sight. A couple of years before, he had been just another one of the Navajo students at Gallup High School—a bright, husky, energetic boy who served as an aggressive linebacker on the football team and as an officer of the Indian Club. Unlike a lot of students who had grown up on or near the huge Navajo reservation that Gallup serves as a trading center, he had brought little firsthand knowledge to the Indian Club's study of Indian ceremonial costumes and Indian dances. In a city where radio advertisements for pickup trucks are in Navajo, he spoke only English; among students whose brothers returning from Vietnam were likely to have felt the need for an Enemy Way ceremony, he was accustomed to only Roman Catholic rituals. His father, a Navajo from the reservation town of Mexican Springs, had married an Austrian woman while serving in the Army and had then settled near Silver City, far from the reservation, where he

found work in the copper mines and raised his children among non-
Indians. In high school, Larry had spent a lot of time on Indian Club
work—making costumes, helping to organize the first Gallup High
School powwow—and when he went to the University of New
Mexico, in the fall of 1971, he joined the Kiva Club, an Indian cultural and social organization that had been best known for its sponsorship of an annual dance. When he became president of the Kiva
Club last fall, its interests began to turn from dances to questions
such as whether the university's history textbooks presented a true
version of Indian history and whether the advertisement of a local
merchant was insulting to Indians. By that time, he had also been
active for several months in Indians Against Exploitation, a group of
young Navajos in Gallup who had organized to protest against the
Gallup Inter-Tribal Indian Ceremonial on the ground that it was a
white-run business operation that made money for whites by presenting Indian religion in a cheapened form for the entertainment
of tourists. IAE had expanded its criticisms to include the way Gallup treated the Indians who came in to trade and the Indians who
came in to drink, and Larry Casuse had been to City Hall before to
complain or demand or condemn. When the State Commission on
the Bicentennial Celebration met in Gallup in January, Casuse had
been one of the young Indians who appeared to say that money
should be spent not for celebrations but for people in need. When
Pete Derizotis opened the door of the mayor's office on March 1,
the Larry Casuse he recognized had the look of an Indian militant—
blue jeans, long black hair, a red bandanna worn as a headband.

DERIZOTIS: *They say they want to see the mayor. I say they will have
to wait—he's in a meeting at this time. So the mayor hollered, "No, let 'em
come in. Let 'em come in." So I let 'em come in. So Casuse pulled his gun
right away.*

A lot of people who knew Larry Casuse were astounded to hear
that he had pulled a gun on anyone. Young Navajos of the type ac-

tive in IAE have ordinarily gone in for peaceful, even dignified, protest. At the Gallup Ceremonial in August of 1971, when it was clear that the most effective tactic would have been to create enough raucous harassment to frighten away the tourists, the IAE was interested only in a silent, almost funereal march. As far as anyone knew, Larry Casuse had not even been familiar with guns.

There were varying speculations as to what might have caused him suddenly to take up arms. Some sympathetic whites believed that he might have, in the words of one of them, flipped out. Even as a high school student, he was the kind of boy sometimes described as "high-strung," and to some people he had appeared increasingly tense at various public appearances in the previous months. Everyone agreed that he had been particularly upset by an accident in which, while driving toward Gallup at three or four in the morning, he struck and killed a young Navajo woman who had apparently wandered onto the highway. He had been tried twice on a charge of not rendering proper assistance—the prosecution and Casuse differed basically on whether, just before his car became mired on a side road and he pounded on the door of a state policeman's house, he had been searching for help or trying to dispose of the body—and a hung jury on the second trial stood eleven to one for conviction. A date for a third trial had just been set. Casuse's remorse about the accident was such that he could not speak of it without weeping. But he believed that the criminal charge was a matter of the authorities' punishing him for his political beliefs, and those who shared the beliefs tended to agree.

In the view of a lot of his Navajo friends, Casuse decided to do something as drastic as abducting the mayor not out of insanity but merely out of impatience and frustration. A lot of people who knew him at the university describe him as someone who "couldn't sit still." He was apparently becoming more and more impatient with the lack of effect the efforts of the young Indians seemed to have. He was frustrated, his friends say, about his inability to focus attention on conditions in Gallup. In the opinion of one young Navajo who knew him at the university, "He thought he would have to utilize the white man's way of doing things to get anything done—just to shake people up enough to get a few lines in the paper, to grab people in midair and say 'Wait a minute! Listen to me!'"

REPORTER: *How did the activity change places over here to the sporting-goods store?*

DERIZOTIS: *With a gun right to the head, he escorted the mayor all the way down. They broke the glass door, and they entered.*

Casuse said nothing that would have made it clear what he intended to do with the mayor. One of his friends from IAE thinks Casuse obviously intended to hold the mayor hostage as a way of negotiating for an investigation into Gallup's treatment of Indians or a compromise on specific demands. Precisely that type of negotiation was taking place at the time at Wounded Knee, in South Dakota. When students at the Kiva Club are asked what Casuse might have been up to, they tend to base their answer on a remark he apparently made to the mayor at some point during the abduction— that he was going to march the mayor around the state. Navajo college students who are politically active tend to talk more than other young demonstrators do about shame and dignity and ridicule. In planning the protest march at the 1971 Gallup Ceremonial, they decided to have two demonstrators ride on horseback partly on the theory that men riding above the crowd on horses were more difficult to ridicule. When they talk about having Gallup on the run, they sometimes say that Indians are now "snickering at Gallup." "Larry wanted to show the people that the mayor deserved no respect," a Navajo girl at the Kiva Club said later. "Larry wanted to humiliate him, to bring him down to the people's level. For a long time, the Indian people have believed that white men are better than they are. The mayor was an authority figure. I think Larry would

have taken him out and walked him through the streets of Gallup—
to show it was just a man, to show that the Indian people should be
treated with respect."

REPORTER: *Did they indicate what their grief was with the mayor?*
DERIZOTIS: *No, sir, not at all.*

A lot of Gallup residents thought of the mayor, Emmett (Frankie)
Garcia, as what used to be called a real go-getter—an energetic, ambitious, pragmatic young man who was the first person to treat the
mayor's office as a full-time job. He had hired some people from
outside Gallup and had tried to take advantage of any federal money
that was available. He had helped organize an alcoholism project—
working against the inclination of Gallup citizens to believe that
Indian alcoholism is an Indian problem, even if the alcohol is provided in Gallup—and had rounded up financial support from the
city and the county and the state in anticipation of a large federal
grant for a rehabilitation center. He had served all but a few weeks
of his first two-year term, and his reelection seemed almost certain.

To Larry Casuse, Frankie Garcia was the man who presided over
a town that enriched itself on Indians—on their trade, on their ar-
tistic talents, on their ceremonies, on their drinking. Even worse, he
was a part owner of the Navajo Inn, a liquor store a few hundred
feet from the Navajo reservation. The Navajo Inn is a small cinder-
block building surrounded by open space and on some paydays by
so many passed-out Navajos that it takes on the appearance of a
bunker in a recently contested battlefield. Frankie Garcia had said
that, as one-third owner, he had no control over the way the Navajo
Inn was run. He had also argued at times that a liquor store next to
the reservation was less dangerous than one in Gallup, twenty-five
miles away—the difference being how many miles a Navajo had to
drive drunk to get home. It is possible to argue, of course, that the
Navajo Inn, however grotesque and callous and ugly it might be, is
not the real headquarters of the enemy, any more than a Jewish

pawnbroker on 125th Street is the real agent of the miseries afflict-ing black people in Harlem—that blaming the Navajo Inn for the alcoholism problem is no more accurate than blaming tribal prohi-bition or the Navajo bootleggers who support it. But if the Navajo Inn is only a symptom of the condition the Navajos find themselves in, it is a particularly visible and profitable symptom, and the one most despised among Navajos, who have seen many of their people destroy themselves with alcohol. According to Frankie Garcia, the Navajo Inn, a cinder-block hut miles from the nearest large town, has steadily been the single most profitable liquor store in the state of New Mexico.

Larry Casuse and his friends had become increasingly interested in the traditional Navajo way of thought—a way of life based on man's living in harmony with all that surrounds him. Casuse had written poems and fables about the harm brought by change. He had spent some time talking to Navajo medicine men, and had spo-ken to his mother about wanting to go back to the reservation to live simply in the traditional Navajo way. He and his friends seemed particularly taken with the concept of "false people"—people who pretend to understand but actually are so lacking in the compassion and sensitivity inherent in the Navajo way that they have a question-able claim on being human beings. Frankie Garcia, who was chair-man of an alcoholism project while profiting from Indian drinking, was their prime example of a false person. Despite that, the governor of New Mexico had, in January, appointed Frankie Garcia to the University of New Mexico Board of Regents.

REPORTER: *A man has apparently just been shot and thrown out the window. We can't tell at this time if it is the mayor. . . . Another shot has been fired . . . and another shot. . . . Chief Gonzales has a rifle.*

The University of New Mexico student newspaper printed some editorials critical of Garcia's appointment. The student senate, after hearing a speech about the appointment's being a political payoff and watching while a doll representing Garcia was burned, passed a resolution calling for "a more qualified and suitable candidate." But the strongest opposition was from the Kiva Club, and particularly from its president, Larry Casuse. When Garcia's nomination came before the Rules Committee of the New Mexico Senate, Casuse and some other students went to Santa Fe to testify against it. Casuse had gathered documents and photographs and had circulated a petition. "The man is an owner of the Navajo Inn, where numerous alcoholics are born, yet he ironically is chairman of the alcohol-abuse rehabilitation committee," Casuse told the senators. "Does he not abuse alcohol? Does he not abuse it by selling it to intoxicated persons who often end up in jail or in a morgue from overexposure?" The nomination was approved by the committee—"They were just like stone-faced men," one of the students said—and then by the Senate.

When Garcia was about to be sworn in, at a regents meeting held on the UNM campus in Albuquerque, Casuse stood to ask permission to make a statement, and the permission was politely granted. Casuse spoke of the charges he had made against Garcia and of the lack of interest exhibited by the senators. "These are the type of people who run our government, and these aren't The People— these are the false people," he said. "There's no reason for me to scream or shout. There's no reason for me to bring documents. There's no reason, because you people will just turn your head, like you always turn your head. There's no reason for that. So what we're going to do is, we're going to find all the human beings in this country, in this state, and we're going to get the human beings together and we're going to put an end to people like Emmet Garcia, and we're going to start with Emmet Garcia. We don't really care what you people do. Because you people aren't human beings."

Casuse sat down, and there was scattered applause from his supporters. Then the chairman said, "The second item on the agenda is the swearing in."

REPORTER: *City Manager Paul McCollum, can you give us a report on the mayor's condition?*

McCOLLUM: *He is all right. . . . He came out through the window. . . .*

REPORTER: *Do you know at this time what the grievance is?*

McCOLLUM: *I have no idea at this point of time what the grievance might be.*

REPORTER: *Do you know why they released him?*

McCOLLUM: *I think that he must have escaped himself. . . .*

REPORTER: *Shots are continuing to be fired from out of Stearn's Sporting Goods. . . . What appears to be a tear-gas bomb has just been shot into Stearn's Sporting Goods. . . .*

VOICE: *They're going to come out shooting.*

REPORTER: *They're coming out with their hands on their head. One of them thus far has come out. . . . He has been directed by the officers to lie flat. . . . His partner in having taken the mayor hostage remains in Stearn's Sporting Goods store. . . . Police are now pouring into the Stearn's Sporting Goods store. . . . They have now dragged out what appears to be Larry Wayne Casuse. He is covered with blood. . . . I am approaching the body. . . . From a distance of about thirty feet, Larry Wayne Casuse appears to be dead.*

VOICE: *Get a blanket.*

Eventually, someone did get a blanket. But Larry Casuse's body lay uncovered on the sidewalk in front of Stearn's Sporting Goods store for a while—long enough for the local paper to take a picture of it with three police standing over it like hunters who had just bagged their seasonal deer. It is now speculated that the appearance of the picture on the front page of *The Gallup Independent* may have had a lot to do with the outrage expressed even by Navajos who ordinarily have no interest in politics and no sympathy for the activist students of Indians Against Exploitation. For whatever reason, it soon became apparent that the incident had made an extraordinary impact on all sorts of Navajos. A white with wide contacts on the reservation said later, "People I had expected to say 'Well, he asked for it' said the only thing they couldn't understand is why he didn't kill the mayor when he had a chance." The elected chairman of the Navajo Tribal Council, Peter MacDonald, a Nixon Republican who had never been a supporter of the militant young people, at first responded to the incident by expressing his shock and sending his sympathies to Garcia, but by the time Larry Casuse's funeral was held, MacDonald had decided to be among the mourners. When the *Albuquerque Journal* did a long piece on the aftermath of Casuse's death, some of the harshest statements about the city of Gallup gathered by its reporter, Scott Beaven, were from the kind of Indians most despised by the young activists—middle-aged Indians who work for the local government or the Bureau of Indian Affairs. A Gallup protest march Casuse had helped organize on Thanksgiving Day had drawn a hundred and twenty-five young people; a march four weeks after his death attracted a couple of thousand Indians of all ages.

Gallup officials said Larry Casuse had shot himself, although they also said that a bullet wound inflicted by the police would have killed him anyway. Some white sympathizers thought suicide was a possibility—"After all, the whole thing was suicidal," one of them said—but Casuse's Navajo friends said suicide was out of the question, since it was contrary to the Navajo beliefs he had come to hold important. A flyer announcing a march just after his death was headed WAS LARRY CASUSE MURDERED?, and some Indian groups demanded an investigation. But a statement from the Kiva Club—addressed to "All Human Beings"—said, "The real issue is not who-shot-whom, as the national media seem to imply, but rather why Larry Casuse so willingly sacrificed his life in order to communicate with the world his dream of unifying human beings with Mother Earth, the Universe, and Humanity."

REPORTER: *There is speculation that the mayor has been wounded, but he has been taken to his family and is apparently all right.*

The mayor's injuries—a shotgun wound and some cuts incurred when he leaped out of the window—were minor, and it appeared that the incident could only enhance his political career, there being no significant Navajo vote in Gallup. Some citizens were concerned that the shooting might shift the attention of the American Indian Movement from Wounded Knee to Gallup, but Garcia removed the most obvious focus for a demonstration by buying a controlling interest in the Navajo Inn and announcing, after a meeting with local Indian groups, that he would close it for thirty days. He made it clear that during the closing he would either sell the store to the tribe at a reasonable price so that it could be closed permanently or move the license into Gallup.

To the surprise of just about everyone, Frankie Garcia lost the election. The defeat is now usually explained as having been caused by Garcia's apparent reluctance to campaign and by the possibility that Gallup voters had begun to associate Garcia with Indian trouble and figured the trouble might stop if he was no longer there to provoke it. Garcia himself singles out the huge Indian march on the Saturday before the election as the most damaging factor in the campaign. The people in Gallup who were working for an alcoholism-rehabilitation center tend to believe that there is less chance of having one with Garcia no longer present to push the project, although the general cutback in federal funds for such programs made the prospect of an elaborate center highly unlikely anyway. The tribe could still buy the Navajo Inn, but Garcia now sees no reason to accept anything but a good price for it. If a profitable arrangement cannot be made with the tribe, Garcia told a visitor recently, he plans to leave the Navajo Inn right where it is and make as much money as possible from it. "I've gone strictly business now," he said. In that spirit, he has decided to resign from the University of New Mexico Board of Regents.

Harvey St. Jean Had It Made

Miami Beach, Florida

MARCH 1975

Criminal lawyers are not the kind of lawyers who claim to be just as happy if their names never appear in a newspaper. One guide to how well a criminal lawyer is doing, in fact, may be how many times he is mentioned in the newspapers and in what size type—the criminal case that attracts the attention of the press often being one in which the defendant is important enough to be able to pay his attorney. A top criminal lawyer has his biography written serially in the tabloids. In the private office of Harvey St. Jean, by all accounts the top criminal lawyer in Miami Beach, the wall decorations were not just framed diplomas but framed newspaper clippings. His outer office had the Spy caricatures of English judges that most American lawyers must receive from their wives most Christmases, but it also had a series of originals by a local newspaper artist who had drawn the lawyer in the courtroom scenes as a tall, imposing man with gray hair and heavy black eyebrows—Harvey St. Jean. St. Jean had plenty of clients who made the front page of the Miami papers. ("'I'm so happy,' cries Mrs. Shirley Mae Lewis Tuesday after a circuit-court jury acquitted her in the murder of a Miami Beach widow. Donald C. Bliss pleaded guilty Monday to the stabbing of Mrs. Ruth Berkman and accused Mrs. Lewis of handing him the knife.") He also had clients whose fate was of importance to newspapers in Philadelphia and New York. For years, St. Jean was in the papers as the attorney for people who had become familiar enough to be given nicknames, the way halfbacks and middleweights are given nicknames. The Crying Adjmis, for instance, a family of bric-a-brac hustlers accused (and acquitted) of bilking a rich widow out of half a million dollars with the help of a phony French priest who said that only the widow's money could save his orphanage and village from a greedy German named Finklestein. ("I was a softie," the victim acknowledged.) Jack (Murph the Surf) Murphy, who, with a couple of other Miami beachboys, managed to steal the Star of India sapphire and the DeLong Star Ruby from the American Museum of Natural History and pass the ruby along—or so the government alleged—to Richard Duncan Pearson, another client of Harvey St. Jean's. The widow of Arthur (Fat Man) Blatt, who became a widow by putting five bullets into the Fat Man, a jeweler by trade and someone suspected by the police for a while of having the DeLong Ruby in his inventory. And Candy—Candace Mossler, who was accused of having arranged with her nephew Melvin Powers to beat her millionaire husband to death with a large Coke bottle. Candy hired both Percy Foreman and Harvey St. Jean to argue her innocence. The fruits of their triumph included a wire-service picture of Candy kissing St. Jean in appreciation and a huge acquittal headline on the front page of that final law journal for big-time criminal attorneys—the New York *Daily News.*

"Harvey St. Jean had it made," Edna Buchanan and Gene Miller began their front-page story in the *Miami Herald* on December 12. "He had money, a reputation as a crack criminal lawyer, and time to tee off for 18 holes at La Gorce Country Club any afternoon he wanted. Most afternoons he did.

"When he left his apartment at the Jockey Club Wednesday morning . . . he had his golf clubs in the trunk of his Cadillac. Wednesday looked like an easy day. He figured he might pick up a game later with Eddie Arcaro, the jockey. He didn't.

"In the crisp bright light of Miami Beach, someone murdered him. He was found shot to death in his car."

· · ·

Harvey St. Jean started his Miami Beach career digging ditches for the city—a poor boy from Holyoke, Massachusetts, whose résumé could not have gone much beyond some clippings of high school athletic triumphs. It was 1939, with the Depression still on in most of the country. "People came here because things weren't right where they came from," Bernard Wieder, a Miami Beach lawyer who had been St. Jean's friend and fellow ditchdigger in those days, said recently. "This was pioneer country." Some of the pioneers were just drifters; some were ambitious. One of the people who dug ditches with St. Jean and Wieder became president of the bank in whose aqua high-rise, on the Lincoln Road Mall, both of them eventually practiced law. Another was elected mayor of Miami Beach. St. Jean and Wieder both took the examinations to become policemen—a seasonal occupation then—and firemen. Wieder still has an early picture of them as policemen at the Miami Beach version of a community event—a wedding of Bernarr Macfadden, the health faddist. St. Jean saved a picture of himself in police uniform standing behind a posed meeting of Jake LaMotta, Rocky Graziano, and Walter Winchell.

In 1951—when, after years of holding down a regular police job and attending law school at the same time, St. Jean was admitted to the bar—a lot of people considered the practice of criminal law to be a step down from practically anything. The leading criminal lawyer in Miami Beach owed his preeminence to being the favored attorney for members of the S & G Syndicate, which used to control the gambling in South Florida. Many of his colleagues at the criminal bar were considered hacks or shysters. There are now criminal lawyers who spend a lot of their time defending sophisticated businessmen charged with tax evasion, but criminal lawyers are still not quite respectable in the sense that, say, specialists in trusts or corporate mergers are. Their clients are usually not the kind of people with whom it would be appropriate to discuss the case over lunch at a decent club. There is often talk of fees paid in stolen goods or of chumminess with mobsters. "To a professional detective, any criminal attorney has to be a certain part fixer," a professional detective with the Miami Beach force said recently. When Harvey St. Jean was already the leading criminal attorney in Miami and was expanding into some business ventures, those city councilmen who argued, unsuccessfully, against awarding him the contract to run the concessions at the city golf course based their argument on the kind of undesirables he defended and might associate with in business. Like any two groups of people thrown together, criminal lawyers and their clientele sometimes develop complicated links of style, or even of family. One of St. Jean's associates was once married to a woman who had previously been married to one of St. Jean's clients. One of St. Jean's own wives—he had a number of them—was once married to a man identified as a close associate of the mobster Frank Costello. She almost became some criminal lawyer's client herself—so St. Jean said during the divorce case—by pointing a gun at him and pulling the trigger twice on what happened to be empty chambers.

Even people who assume all criminal lawyers to be part fixer refer to Harvey St. Jean as a gentleman. He was a soft-spoken man, closemouthed about important matters but affable about routine ones. People who had known him for years could not recall ever hearing him raise his voice. The judges liked him, and so did the police. As someone who had been a policeman for years himself, he had friends on the force who could steer clients in his direction, and he could translate the stilted jargon of police reports into some vision of what must have really happened. He steadily worked his way up from pickpockets to jewel thieves. St. Jean was never an eloquent or flamboyant man—tables went unpounded and tears went unshed during his summations—but he was shrewd about picking juries and thorough about rules of evidence that often made it possible to exclude from consideration the statement or the jewelry necessary for a prosecution. As the Warren Court decisions increasingly emphasized the rights of the individual, criminal law was increasingly practiced not with eloquent summations but with detailed challenges to the affidavit that led to a search warrant or with hard questions about how the defendant was treated at the station house. Harvey St. Jean became what his partner, Lawrence Hoffman, believes was the finest search-and-seizure lawyer in the country.

As his practice grew and some real-estate investments began to pay off, St. Jean began to lead the South Florida version of life at the top. There may be cities in which the respectability of a self-made criminal lawyer will always have its limits, but in Miami just about everyone seems to have a tenuous hold on respectability anyway. The historic attraction of the area for promoters and grifters and profligates being what it is, Miami remains a hard place to cash a check. The difference between an established family and a new family sometimes seems to be that the established family pulled off some successful land-flipping in the thirties instead of the fifties. The dominant standard of a club like the Jockey Club—often described around town as "the 'in' place" or "a swinging joint" or "the place to be"—is ready money, and motivation by money is assumed. (Some pieces of African sculpture for sale in a showcase are identified as "Rare Collector's Items for Investors in African Art.") The golf club that elected Harvey St. Jean to its board of governors—La Gorce Country Club, in Miami Beach—had, according to an estimate in the *Miami Herald* a few years ago, five hundred millionaires among eleven hundred members, including a Firestone and a Du Pont. It had the final badge of exclusivity in Miami Beach: it excluded Jews, like the one British planters' club in a newly independent African country that can't bring itself to alter its membership rules enough to allow in the new president. But La Gorce was not founded until after the Second World War. And one of its members was accused by the Internal Revenue Service a few years ago of having used it as a base for hustling some five hundred thousand unreported dollars from golf or poker patsies, and a *Herald* story about changes in its board of governors described one of them as "auto dealer, former state senator, and sometime associate of bookmakers."

In the past several years, anyone looking for Harvey St. Jean was likely to find him at La Gorce or the Jockey Club or in his office—

and his office became, increasingly, the least likely of the three. In 1970, St. Jean had an operation for some old knee injuries—the Miami Dolphins' team surgeon was his doctor—and, still in his fifties, he began to tell people he was semiretired. He spent a lot of time on the golf course and on various business ventures. A couple of times a year, he went to the Golden Door spa in California. "He just said he was semiretired as a way to avoid the wise guys who wanted him to do small cases for nothing," Jack Nageley, a Miami Beach criminal lawyer who once worked for St. Jean, has said. "If there was enough money involved, Harvey was there." The money was in the occasional big criminal trial and, more and more, in the divorce work brought in by his fame or by his contacts with rich and important people.

A divorce lawyer who lived at the Jockey Club could feel as secure about his future as a dentist who lived in Hershey, Pennsylvania. The standing joke at the Jockey Club is that the average age of the residents is forty—"that's a sixty-year-old guy and a twenty-year-old broad." The club consists of a couple of high-rises full of condominiums for the live-in members, some tennis courts, a marina in which some of the boats seem large enough to serve as destroyer escorts, a restaurant, and a bar whose patrons are so uniformly the type of people who order drinks by brand ("J&B and a twist, Joe, and an extra-dry Tanqueray martini") that the bartender's reaction to being asked for a Scotch and soda is likely to be a moment of puzzlement, as if he had just been asked for a jug of homemade busthead. The Jockey Club is a place in which the names dropped at the bar are vaguely familiar—familiar because the people were once in films or because their families have even more money than they can spend on boats and alimony payments—and the names displayed on the membership invitations seem designed to trigger the same kind of brand identification as modish brands of gin. Twenty-five years after he stood anonymously behind Walter Winchell, Harvey St. Jean lived, with his wife, in a condominium at a club whose board of governors includes Perry Como and Pierre Du Pont and Fess

Parker. He owned two condominiums at the Jockey Club, in fact, having moved into a larger one after his marriage and held on to his bachelor apartment. He had been talking about trying to consolidate their mortgages. He apparently had a cash-flow problem. But he had sent a check to the condominium sales office at the Cricket Club, which is being built just north of the Jockey Club. The Cricket Club will have a full spa, and many people believe that it will be the new place to live.

Walter Philbin looks and talks enough like a detective to play one in the movies—and has played one, several times. In *Lenny,* the New York detective sergeant who arrested Bruce at a nightclub and then testified, with some embarrassment, in court as to his language and gestures was played by Walter Philbin. In real life, he is a major, the chief of detectives of the Miami Beach Police Department, and in real life he had some dealings with Lenny Bruce. ("I harassed him pretty good.") Philbin joined the Miami Beach force the year after Harvey St. Jean left—another poor boy from Massachusetts. "We more or less grew up together—me on the force, him in the practice of law," Philbin said recently. "I beat him on ten or eleven first-degree-murder cases. I was his nemesis." St. Jean won some, too. "I once collared a guy on a stakeout with two hundred thousand dollars in stolen jewels—*and a gun,*" Philbin says. "Harvey got him off on search-and-seizure." Philbin believes that he and Harvey St. Jean exchanged the respect of competent adversaries, and he recalls thinking about that when he arrived at a public parking lot between the Lincoln Road Mall and the Miami Beach Convention Center late on a Wednesday morning last December and found St. Jean shot to death inside his Cadillac. "When we were taking him out of the car, it was a funny thing to think about, but I thought Harvey would be glad that if anyone had to investigate his murder it would be me—because I think he had respect for me as a homicide investigator," Philbin said. "It was an almost communicative feeling: 'Don't worry about it, Harvey.' And him saying, 'Well, I'm glad you're here, because if anybody can get the son of a bitch, you can.'"

There may be detectives who would regard that as the recollection of a member of the Screen Actors Guild, but any homicide investigator would sympathize with the next thought Philbin recalls having: "Jesus, God! He's got a hundred guys capable of killing him." A disgruntled client? An ex-wife? One of the undesirables that people said St. Jean had as associates in his business ventures? A hit man from the mob? Just a thief who heard that St. Jean often carried a lot of cash with him? Philbin's detectives fairly quickly eliminated the possibility of random robbery and turned up only one undesirable and no strong suspects among St. Jean's business associates. ("I almost wish I could talk to Harvey: 'How could you get involved with this creep?'") The street talk and the prison grapevine produced a theory about St. Jean's murder almost immediately: that he had been killed on the orders of a Cuban cocaine dealer, a former client, who believed St. Jean had a lot of his money and was refusing to return it. The theory was consistent with some of the physical evidence, Philbin thought, such as the fact that St. Jean had been robbed. ("It's a matter of honor with an Italian hit man not to touch anything; Cubans rob the guy as part of the deal—the price plus what he's carrying.") It was the theory in newspaper headlines within a day or two of the shooting, and it remains the dominant theory in the police department today, even though Walter Philbin, for one, is not optimistic about ever finding enough evidence to indict whoever it was who actually pulled the trigger.

Since the St. Jean killing, Philbin has arrived at some strong views on the version of organized crime that has developed among post-Castro Cuban immigrants. He believes that Cuban gangsters often behave the way Italian gangsters did in the twenties, when they had been in the country only fifteen or twenty years themselves—extorting money from their own community's businessmen, for instance, and shooting at each other a lot in arguments over power.

The Cubans differ, he believes, in concentrating on a type of business that some of the old-style immigrant gangsters avoided—drugs. The people in charge of Cuban organized crime learned organization from the American gangsters who were in Cuba at the end of the Batista regime, Philbin thinks, and the eighteen- and twenty-year-olds now used as runners and enforcers learned how to be hoods right in the United States of America. "When the Cubans first came here, we'd always say they were no trouble," Philbin said recently. "Strong family ties. Strong culture. Now, eighteen, nineteen years later, we got nothing but trouble. They've lost their strong family ties, they've lost their strong culture. And the sad thing is that *we've* done it. We've Americanized them. They learned everything on our streets." The organized Cuban operation that uses the street toughs, Philbin thinks, is much more powerful than has been believed. Among the people who may have underestimated the Cubans was Harvey St. Jean.

Why the client in question believed that St. Jean owed him money remains a matter of conjecture, of course. There is a theory, expressed in the newspapers by Dade County state attorney Richard Gerstein, that "some of those people just assume that if they pay large fees they are buying a dismissal or acquittal." There is a theory that St. Jean, a controlled and unemotional man in the courtroom, might have exacerbated such a misunderstanding by carrying on a defense that could have seemed unenergetic to a Latin. It is possible, of course, that the money that changed hands really was for services other than the defense of one case. It is even possible that Harvey St. Jean, a secretive man with a cash-flow problem, really did keep some money he should have returned. "Harvey had almost scrupulously avoided drug cases," Philbin says. "He was doing pretty well without them. But this was so much money he couldn't turn it down." The amount usually mentioned is something over a hundred thousand dollars. "Harvey knew all the angles," Jack Nageley said not long ago. "But his love of money did him in."

. . .

Harvey St. Jean made banner headlines with his funeral. "The friends of Harvey St. Jean, the honest ones, assembled before an open casket Saturday for piped organ music—and the prayers of a priest who never met him," Gene Miller wrote in the *Miami Herald*. "It was simple and quick. Only the last of his seven wives attended. Detectives saw none of his notorious clients. Harvey J. St. Jean, criminal lawyer, is now case number 385393." In a short eulogy, a friend called St. Jean "a sportsman and a sport." His widow, Dorothy St. Jean, got a lot of sympathy letters from important people and ordinary people, and even some people who wrote from prison—the type of client she could remember her husband's considering "a thief, but a nice thief." She also got the cash-flow situation. She is a bright, red-haired woman who, like her husband, came to Miami Beach poor, twenty years ago—a secretary from New Jersey. She worked her way up from cocktail waitress to a job at one of the big hotels organizing conventions and Super Bowl charters. Last fall, she quit her job and devoted her organizing energies to charity work. She was having lunch at La Gorce when she heard of her husband's death. One of the ironies she mentions when she talks about the murder is that she and Harvey St. Jean, two people who had worked their way up, finally had it made. "People came up afterward and said, 'At least, his problems are over now,'" she said recently. "Listen. He didn't have any problems."

Partners

Seabrook, New Hampshire, has the look of those towns that have grown up over the years along Route 1 the way algae sometimes grow along a ship's line that has been underwater too long. It is just across the state line from Massachusetts, near New Hampshire's short stretch of Atlantic shore, and Bostonians of a certain age tend to associate it with quickie-marriage factories—an industrial base that has long since been supplanted by a dog track. In Seabrook, Route 1 is dominated by the type of sign that seems to have been created by mounting the side of an old-fashioned theater marquee on a portable iron frame that can be wheeled to the roadside to attract the attention of a highway driver whose eye may not have wandered far enough to be caught by the signs on the gift shops and farm stands and factory outlets that lie just beyond the blacktop parking lots on either side of the road. All of the iron frames are painted yellow, and a lot of them include a huge yellow arrow curving back to point across the parking lot, and some of the arrows are outlined in multicolored blinking lightbulbs.

The Hawaiian Garden restaurant and lounge, which specializes in "Cantonese-Polynesian Food & Drinks," is right on Route 1, with a parking lot on the side and some motel rooms in a connecting building along the back. Its restaurant serves the sort of Polynesian food that would be familiar to any Samoan or Fijian who happened to have eaten at a Trader Vic's restaurant, as well as four-

teen varieties of chow mein. Its lounge—a more ambitiously decorated room than the restaurant, with a large bandstand and ersatz
tikis and a straw-mat ceiling over the bar—has a repertoire of drinks
that makes it the only place on that stretch of Route 1 for someone
who feels the need of a pick-me-up that comes in a ceramic coco-
nut and is decorated with a tiny paper umbrella. The co-proprietor
of the Hawaiian Garden—the man out in front, not the one in the
kitchen—is a Cantonese immigrant named Wing Chin, who came
with his family to Providence as a teenager in the fifties and, in the
tradition of Chinese American entrepreneurship, spent some time
working as a waiter in other people's restaurants before opening his
own. Last year, after operating the Hawaiian Garden for seven or
eight years, Wing Chin became one of four partners in a corporation formed to establish another Cantonese-Polynesian restaurant
just outside Atlanta, Georgia, in a town called Marietta—a town that
does not have a dog track but does have a large aircraft factory. Each
of the four partners agreed to put up twenty thousand dollars, the
First National Bank of Boston agreed to lend the new corporation
one hundred and sixty-six thousand dollars, the Small Business Administration committed itself to guaranteeing the loan, and a contract was signed for a building in Marietta. Wing Chin remembers
saying to his partners, "I don't think we can miss."

The one silent partner in Chin Enterprises, Inc., was the type of
investor often found in such ventures, a relative of Wing Chin's who
was always referred to by the active partners as Uncle Harry. The
president of the new corporation was Wing Chin, the only partner
who had extensive experience in the restaurant business. The vice
president, a boyhood friend of Chin's named John Oi, had been a
busboy in a Chinese restaurant as a teenager—it was there that he
met Chin, who was working as a waiter—but otherwise his restaurant background was one generation removed. His father, Henry Oi,
was a restaurant proprietor who was also a prominent member of
the Boston Chinatown business community—a man who, starting
as an impoverished immigrant from Canton, had become proprietor

first of a Cantonese-Polynesian restaurant in Boston and then of two more in Connecticut. John Oi, though, was not a restaurant proprietor but a professional soldier—an Army captain who had graduated from West Point and happened to be back in the Boston area during the formation of Chin Enterprises, Inc., only because the Army had sent him to Northeastern University to complete a master's degree in electrical engineering. His wife, Cheryl, who came from a Chinese family in Hawaii, had a doctorate in ethnomusicology and ran an Asian program for one of the Boston television stations. Together, living in an apartment complex in the southwest suburbs, they seemed a long way from the Chinese immigrants working in the steamy kitchens of Chinatown. When a local reporter asked their neighbors for a description of John and Cheryl Oi some time later, what he wrote down was "Very friendly, always seemed busy, highly educated, classy." They apparently looked on the Marietta restaurant as an investment that might eventually turn into a vocation—a place they might go to someday if John decided to leave the service after putting in twenty years. John Oi said nothing about the investment to his father. In a way, John had fulfilled the traditional role of the son of an ambitious immigrant in America. Henry Oi—who, despite imperfect English and no American education, had managed to get into flight school and become an officer in the Second World War—had been given the opportunity to swear in his son as a second lieutenant at John's West Point commencement. But, according to Cheryl Oi, the Marietta restaurant was partly a way for her husband to prove himself to his father as a businessman as well as a soldier—as a successful partner in precisely the same kind of restaurant that Henry Oi operated. "I knew nothing about it," Henry Oi said recently. "If I had, I would have knocked holes in it."

Henry Oi, who had slept on the office floor rather than leave his West Hartford restaurant during its first weeks of operation, might have questioned the wisdom of opening a restaurant so far away. Restaurants may be even more in need of constant supervision than other retail cash businesses, and restaurant proprietors, like commanders of armies in the field, are ordinarily cautious about straying too far from their support operations. As a veteran of the tightly knit ventures of Boston's Chinatown, Henry Oi would also have presumably been put off by the fact that the fourth partner in Chin Enterprises, Inc., was an Occidental—a former New Hampshire state policeman named Armand R. Therrien. A contemporary of Wing Chin's and John Oi's, Therrien was the son of a lumberjack from the center of New Hampshire—a descendant of the poor French Canadians who had come to New England from rural Quebec to work in the forests and the mills, and, for the most part, had remained poor. After a few years in the Air Force, Armand Therrien had worked as a Northeast Airlines ticket agent for five years and then joined the state police, where he showed an aptitude for investigating crimes such as embezzlement. He was eventually made a detective corporal and assigned to an office near Seabrook, a hundred miles from his home. In 1973, he resigned from the state police, moved permanently to Seabrook, and began trying to make a living as an insurance agent. "I wanted to better myself," he said later. He had been divorced the previous year, and he had two households to support. Selling insurance did not turn out to be the route to quick riches, nor did selling real estate. In the synopsis of a résumé Therrien composed at the time, he wrote, "Schooling limited. Capabilities unlimited. Ambition strong. Training varied and diversified. I have enjoyed and done well at all my occupations but to date have not found one that would consume my entire efforts." Therrien had known Wing Chin since the late sixties, when, as a state trooper, he was in the habit of dropping by the Hawaiian Garden—or "the Gardens," as he came to call it. During 1973, he began to work for Chin—first part-time as a sort of security man for the lounge, and then full-time as just about everything except chef and bartender. Therrien lived at the Gardens; his girlfriend was one of the waitresses. He made some junkets to Las Vegas. But he was regular about his checks to his family and regular about Sunday visits to his children. Therrien was not only the secretary-treasurer of Chin Enterprises, Inc., but also the only partner who planned to work as a salaried employee at the Marietta restaurant—as the manager. John Oi and Wing Chin apparently saw Therrien in the role of a sort of white front man in Georgia. The three partners spent a lot of time together in the summer of 1974—planning the Marietta restaurant, hunting, target shooting in a quarry near the Gardens. In January of this year, John and Cheryl Oi took Therrien and his girlfriend to an Italian restaurant in Boston for a farewell dinner before Therrien left to supervise renovation of the building in Georgia. As Cheryl Oi remembers that evening, the only business conversation was some jovial talk about who would buy the first Rolls-Royce after Chin Enterprises, Inc., hit the jackpot.

On February 11, in Westwood, a Boston suburb a few miles from where John and Cheryl Oi lived, Patrolmen William Sheehan and Robert P. O'Donnell were partners for the four-to-midnight shift, riding in police cruiser 92. Bill Sheehan, the senior member of the Westwood Police Department, was known as an amiable and conscientious man who had personally broken in many of the officers on the force. A widower, he often worked nights, and occasionally picked up some extra money doing lawn care during the day. Sheehan's father had been a caretaker on an estate; one of his brothers was a fireman. His daughter was a graduate of Boston College, and his son was a senior at Dartmouth. Sheehan was working that evening— a bitterly cold and occasionally snowy evening—with the most junior member of the force, O'Donnell having been appointed only a month before. A clean-cut, rather laconic man in his late twenties, O'Donnell, like his father before him, had been an ironworker— putting together the girders of Boston high-rises for ten years before turning to an occupation he expected to be both more satisfying and more secure than work in the steadily narrowing construction field. As O'Donnell remembers the events of February 11, he and Bill Sheehan turned onto Canton Street, a wooded but heavily traveled road that feeds onto Route 128, at about seven-thirty and saw a Pontiac Grand Prix parked a few feet from the curb, with its emergency lights flashing. The driver, as seen in silhouette through the fogged window, seemed slumped in his seat. Parking the cruiser and walking back toward the Grand Prix, Sheehan and O'Donnell were met by a man dressed in fatigues, who had come out of the passenger side to say that his friend was ill but no help was needed. The two policemen, suspecting a drunk driver, continued to the Grand Prix and looked in. "Hey, what's all the blood?" O'Donnell said. Someone said, "Hey," there was a blinding flash as O'Donnell turned, and he felt himself falling. There were more shots, and then O'Donnell, feeling a foot next to him, grabbed at it and began struggling with the man in fatigues, only to have him break loose and run. O'Donnell drew his own gun and fired, bringing the man down in the middle of Canton Street. As it turned out, O'Donnell had two minor wounds and serious powder burns of the face. Bill Sheehan lay dying on the street, a bullet from a snub-nosed .38 in his head. The man slumped in the driver's seat had a similar .38 slug in his head and died not long after reaching the hospital. He was identified as Captain John Oi. The man in fatigues was Armand Therrien. His wounds were not critical, and the following morning, in Massachusetts General Hospital, a Westwood police officer was able to inform him that he was being charged with the murder of John Oi. "He was my business partner," Therrien said to the police officer.

"The word 'probably' is not enough," Therrien's defense attorney, a well-known criminal lawyer from Boston named Gerald Alch, said as he explained the concept of "reasonable doubt" during Therrien's trial for the murders of John Oi and William Sheehan. No one had actually seen Oi and Sheehan shot, but the circumstantial evidence seemed overwhelming. The bullets that killed both victims had been fired by the .38 Therrien was carrying. A box of shells and two pairs of handcuffs had been found in Therrien's pocket. A room key, also found in his pocket, had led to the discovery that he had checked in to a nearby motel that afternoon under an assumed name, after a

virtually nonstop drive from Georgia. The telephone in his apartment in Marietta had been left off the hook, and when he telephoned his girlfriend in New Hampshire during the drive north, he
had given her the impression that he was still in Georgia, with no
plans to leave. The police reasoned that Therrien, having parked his
own car in a restaurant lot near John Oi's apartment, was forcing Oi
to drive him toward a deserted spot when Oi, perhaps with thoughts
of escape, suddenly stopped the car on Canton Street—only to be
shot in the back of the head. But why? In the day or two after Oi's
death, the police received a couple of anonymous tips that the crime
had to do with gambling and the mob; the district attorney was
quoted in the local press as saying that the investigation was partly
concerned with the possibility that Therrien was connected with
"the Chinese Mafia." Then police discovered that Chin Enterprises,
Inc., had, as a requirement of its loan, taken out a two-hundred-
thousand-dollar life-insurance policy on each of its officers—policies
that were to be assigned to the bank as soon as the final loan papers
were signed. Oi's death at a time when the policies were payable
directly to Chin Enterprises, Inc., meant that the restaurant would
be capitalized with an additional two hundred thousand dollars. The
corporation would have no need to take a bank loan and operate
under its restrictions—which included a limit of fifteen thousand
dollars a year on salaries that could be drawn by corporate officers.
Neither Oi nor Chin was concerned with salary because Chin had
the Hawaiian Garden and Oi had the Army, the prosecutor, an assistant district attorney named John P. Connor, Jr., told the jury. "But
Therrien cared. Because Therrien wanted to better himself."

Therrien's trial was in the courthouse in Dedham, the seat of
Norfolk County. Bill Sheehan's son and daughter were there, and so
was Henry Oi. Cheryl Oi and Wing Chin were among those called
to testify by the prosecution. Armand Therrien's sisters and his girlfriend and former wife were all among the spectators—all loyal, all
willing to demonstrate by their presence that those closest to Therrien believed he could never have committed the crimes he was

charged with. Except for one moment, when he broke into tears while reading a letter he had sent Henry Oi from jail, Therrien was calm and self-assured on the stand—still enough of a policeman to refer to O'Donnell as "the subject." He offered four or five legitimate reasons to explain his sudden trip north. He said that his girlfriend had been allowed to believe he was still in Georgia because he wanted to surprise her. The gun was with him because he was returning it to its owner in New Hampshire, and the handcuffs and shells happened to be in the pocket of his heavy coat because he had been cleaning out his desk at the Gardens the last time he was in a cold enough place to wear it. He had registered under an assumed name at the motel because he happened to have a female hitchhiker with him at the time. Therrien said he couldn't remember everything that had happened on Canton Street that night because Oi had hit him during an argument that began with Oi's insisting that Wing Chin was heavily in debt from gambling and was planning to cheat his partners in Chin Enterprises, Inc. As Therrien told it, Oi had apparently been shot accidentally during an argument with O'Donnell, who then turned on Sheehan. It was a story that offered some explanation for every piece of incriminating evidence, and Therrien had the restraint not to push it past that.

"You drove thirteen hundred miles to Boston in approximately twenty-four hours to meet your fiancée, and yet you picked up a hitchhiker with the intention of having a liaison with her at a motel?" Connor asked him.

"That is correct, sir," Therrien said.

In his closing statement, Alch made Therrien's story sound at least conceivable. But the story required the jury to assume, among other things, that both Oi and O'Donnell, the West Point captain and the decent-looking policeman, had erupted into irrational violence. The jury had to believe O'Donnell or Therrien, Connor said. "One of them is a hero, one of them is a liar. One of them is a hero, and one of them is a crazed killer." The jury believed O'Donnell. After nine and a half hours of deliberation, Therrien was found guilty of first-degree murder in both the death of William Sheehan and the death of John Oi.

The prosecutors and detectives who had worked on the investigation had the strong belief that they had solved the crime but not the mystery. The prosecution, of course, is not required to prove motive—the insurance policy was offered merely as a possibility—and Connor seemed under no illusion that he had. "We can never get inside that man's mind and discover what the real reason was," he told the jury. Would a man really commit premeditated murder for the rather indirect benefit of acquiring two hundred thousand dollars for a corporation he owned one-quarter of? Would a man murder to remove a ceiling of fifteen thousand dollars on his salary? How much more than fifteen thousand dollars could someone expect to be paid for managing a Cantonese-Polynesian restaurant in Marietta, Georgia? Was there something in the early rumors about gambling and the mob? Was someone else involved? Was Therrien rather than Wing Chin the partner John Oi suspected? What motive would be strong enough to explain murder?

Whether the insurance was the reason for John Oi's death or not, it did make Chin Enterprises, Inc., a rather well-off little corporation. Months before Therrien was brought to trial, the insurance company paid the beneficiary of John Oi's insurance, with no argument. A windfall of two hundred thousand dollars to an eighty-thousand-dollar corporation was, in a sense, the closest Armand Therrien had come to bettering himself in a big way. The corporation has problems, of course. It is the defendant in a civil suit filed by Cheryl Oi. Its vice president is dead. Its secretary-treasurer has just begun serving two consecutive life terms at the Massachusetts Correctional Institution at Walpole.

Melisha Morganna Gibson

Cleveland, Tennessee

JANUARY 1977

Ronnie Maddux met Wanda Gibson eight years ago, when she was a widow in her late twenties with three children and a lot of men visitors. They met in Cleveland, Tennessee, on the southeast side of town—a neighborhood that attracts some poor-white country people, who wander into Cleveland from the hill counties to work in a furniture factory, and some locals like Ronnie Maddux, who never seem to work very long anywhere. "During the first two years, we went together on a regular basis," Maddux said later, in a statement to the Bradley County Sheriff's Department. "I quit going over to see her because of the drunks that hung around over there and because Joe Pete Cochran came over to where Wanda was living on Woolen Street looking for me with a sawed-off shotgun because of a gambling debt. Joe Pete Cochran cheated me out of the title to my car in a dice game, and I had to give him my title, my tags, and my keys. I had another set of keys, so I got Ronnie Goins to get the car and bring it to the corner where I was so I could go home. That was another reason I stayed away from Wanda. We didn't see each other for about eight months. We got back to-gether just before she had Thomas Glenn Maddux, my son. He was born on the tenth day of March, 1970. We were together that time for about a year. Then I got married to Josephine Holder. I lived with her for about three months, then left when I found out she was pregnant when I married her. We got a divorce later. During this time, Wanda got pregnant with Melisha Morganna Gibson by Ronnie Fairbanks. Wanda and I were together again when Melisha was born. I knew when she was born that she belonged to Ronnie Fairbanks." A social worker who had reason to visit the home after the baby was born, in the spring of 1972, has described it as "one drunken party after another." A church worker also visited regularly, bringing clothing for the children and testimonies to the advantages of a Christian life. "Jesus loves everybody," the church worker said recently, "but those people didn't respond real well." The family called the new baby Ganna. When she was eleven months old, Ronnie Maddux and Wanda Gibson were indicted for beating her up. During the court proceedings, Ronnie and Wanda—inspired, some people in Cleveland suspect, less by ardor than by the rule protecting a wife from having to testify against her husband—became man and wife. And that is how Ronnie Maddux became Melisha Morganna Gibson's stepfather.

The doctor who treated Melisha at eleven months—treated her for a black eye and bruises of the back, thighs, chest, and face—was a pediatrician named John Appling, who for ten years had been trying to persuade people in Cleveland that more had to be done to prevent child abuse. At his instigation, the Jaycees had raised enough money to construct a child shelter for temporary care, and a district childcare committee had been established. Before Appling had gone far in his crusade, though, it was clear that many people in town would have been happier if he confined himself to the quiet practice of pediatrics. Cleveland, its boosters often point out to visitors, is not some backward village in the southeast Tennessee hills, but a steadily growing city with the advantages of diversified industry and a location right on the interstate, between Chattanooga and Knoxville. Appling and others have argued that the very jobs Cleveland is so proud of generating are bound to attract the sort of displaced workers who, lacking the support of family and friends they had at home, may turn on their children from the stress of the first layoff. But

Cleveland people tired quickly of being told that they lived in a center of child abuse. Cleveland has always been a place strongly bound to fundamentalist Christianity—a place where Baptists are likely to be found in church on Wednesday evenings as well as on Sunday mornings, a place that serves as international headquarters for two large Pentecostal denominations, a place that has grown from a town into a middle-sized city without allowing bars or even liquor stores. There was some feeling among Cleveland residents that the sort of incidents Appling kept haranguing them about could not happen in Cleveland—a feeling reinforced by the fact that the confidentiality imposed on the court handling child-abuse cases caused most of them to go unreported in the press.

Appling—a man who had treated hundreds of abused children like Melisha Gibson, a man who claimed that six to ten children in Bradley County died every year from child abuse—could not stop the harangue. He can talk about national studies and generally accepted theories on child abuse—about the special risks, for instance, faced by children of teenage mothers and by illegitimate children and by children perceived by the family as being different in some way—but he tends to drift toward specific cases. When he discusses the details of a child-abuse case, he occasionally pauses to take a deep breath, as if willing himself under control. "I've gotten too emotional with it," Appling has said. "I see all these children in the emergency room beat all to hell, and then I see them *back* in the emergency room beat all to hell. The people seem like 'This child here is mine. He's my property. I can maim him. I can kill him. It's none of your business.'" People in the agency officially responsible for processing child-abuse cases in Bradley County—an agency recently renamed Human Services, but still referred to by just about everybody as Welfare—considered Dr. Appling an interfering zealot whose method of protecting children was to keep them away from their parents forever. The policy of the state happened to have the opposite emphasis—reuniting the family whenever possible. Once, a welfare-department county manager reacted to Appling's refusal to discharge a child from the hospital without additional reports on the child's home by threatening to have him arrested for kidnapping.

There was no question of releasing Melisha to the care of Ronnie Maddux and Wanda Gibson, who were then awaiting trial for beating her up. When she was discharged from the hospital, a welfare worker took her to a foster family; when that family moved away three months later, the worker placed Melisha in foster care with Mr. and Mrs. Gilbert Hawkins, who live on thirty acres at the end of a country road seven miles south of Cleveland. Gilbert Hawkins, who works in maintenance at a chemical plant near Cleveland, built his own house a few years ago, with the help of a nephew—a solid brick ranch house that looks as if it has never missed a day's cleaning. The Hawkinses, both of whom grew up in the country within a couple of miles of where they live now, are active members of the Goodwill Baptist Church. Mrs. Hawkins has known Ronnie Maddux's sister for years, but she tends to speak of Ronnie and Wanda Maddux as if they belonged to a different race of beings. "They just don't think like we do," she said not long ago. Mrs. Hawkins sometimes uses "love" as a synonym for "hug," so she can say that when foster babies are in the house, it is not unusual for even her eighteen-year-old son to "pick them up and love them." The Hawkins family loved Melisha in both of the ways they use the word. They called her Missy. She grew into a lovely-looking blond little girl—shy with strangers but apparently talkative at home. She was subject to high fevers but otherwise healthy—an agile child who loved to do acrobatics. She lived as part of the Hawkins family for nearly three years—until it came time, last May, to return her to Ronnie and Wanda Maddux.

The Madduxes had been sentenced to what people in Tennessee call eleven twenty-nine—eleven months and twenty-nine days in the county jail, the maximum sentence for a misdemeanor. After some delay for appeal, they served six months. When they were released, in November of 1974, they settled down to what their social worker saw as a considerably more stable and sober life than they had led before. They eventually rented a tiny house, planted a vegetable garden, and even made a pass at sprucing the place up. They got by mostly on the Social Security payments Wanda Maddux drew as the beneficiary of her first husband. Apparently, Maddux hoped to make a big killing from a lawsuit in which he claimed to have suffered a back injury from falling down some stairs. A woman who lived across the street, Mattie Sue Riggs, said not long ago, "He'd say, 'Now, Mattie, anyone comes around here asking about me lifting anything heavy, don't you go talking to them.' And I said, 'Ronnie, I've not never seen you lift nothing no heavier than a dinner plate.'"

The Madduxes wanted the children back. By last February, the four older children had been returned—at different times, according to the normal welfare-department procedure. The children seemed content and reasonably well cared for, but the social worker, Judy Hampton, was still concerned about returning Melisha—the one child who was known to have been abused. Maddux had denied from the start that he and his wife had beaten Melisha; he even wrote a letter to the local paper denying it publicly. Still, Mrs. Hampton tried to talk Wanda Maddux into putting Melisha up for adoption. She refused. Mrs. Hampton waited until the end of the school year, on the theory that the presence of the older children at home would be a safety factor for Melisha. Then, with the consent of the juvenile court, she took Melisha back to her family.

There was nothing at all unusual about taking an abused child back to the family that had abused her. One alternative—legally terminating parental rights so that the child can be put up for adoption—is difficult practically to the point of impossibility under Tennessee law. Even children who have been beaten up are often eager to return to their own families, and their parents are often eager to have them back—an eagerness that may be affected in some cases by the fact that Aid to Families with Dependent Children payments represent the only form of welfare money available in southeast Tennessee. In the welfare department, there was a natural bureaucratic pressure to close cases and get children out of temporary foster homes. In theory, the inter-agency Child Protection Team that was organized a year ago in Cleveland by David Sweitzer, the regional coordinator from the state's Office of Child Development, was available for consultation about how to approach any child-abuse case, but the welfare department regarded the Child Protection Team mainly as a vehicle for Dr. Appling's interference. Routinely, a welfare worker—often overburdened with cases and paperwork, almost never having had any significant training in child protection—would recommend that a child be sent back home, the recommendation would be approved by the welfare department's chain of command, and the juvenile-court judge would order the child sent home. The judge's assent to the welfare report was considered so automatic in Bradley County that some foster parents who had become concerned about sending children back to homes they considered unsafe approached a local legislator last summer to ask whether it would be possible to have the judge impeached.

The Hawkinses were not among the protesting foster parents, but they were concerned all last summer about Missy. On trips to Cleveland, they found themselves detouring through the Madduxes' neighborhood to catch glimpses of her playing in the front yard. Finally, in the fall, Mrs. Hawkins called Ronnie Maddux's sister to ask if Missy could use a winter coat. The Madduxes relayed an invitation to bring the coat by, and, stretching the rules about visiting former foster children, the Hawkinses accepted. They were greeted cordially. Mrs. Hawkins took Missy's measurements so she could make her some dresses. Mr. Hawkins, who had been uneasy about the visit, could sense nothing amiss. Even Mrs. Hawkins had difficulty putting her finger on any specific indication that Missy was not well cared for—although she said later that when she was about to leave, "Missy looked up with those beautiful brown eyes and said, 'Mommy, can I go back out to your house?'"

On her regular visits, Mrs. Hampton often found Missy being fussed over by her older sisters. The neighbors considered the Maddux family pleasant enough, although Ronnie Maddux seemed strict with the children about such matters as returning promptly from errands. He also had a tendency to let out a prolonged howl occasionally for no apparent reason. "Like none-none talk or people speaking tongues," Mattie Riggs has said. "I'd say, 'My Lord, Ronnie, you crazy?' And he'd say, 'I must be, Mattie.'"

On the night of October 11, about four weeks after the Hawkinses' visit, Ronnie Maddux got angry at Melisha. Apparently, the trouble started when she would not go to sleep, and was aggravated when, in the early hours of the morning, she wet herself. On the morning of the twelfth, Maddux began making Melisha walk back and forth between the kitchen and an organ stool in the bedroom. "I wanted to tire her out so she would sleep," he explained later. "I got some hot sauce and made her take a tablespoon of it. She threw it up on the floor. . . . She began to slow down, so I told her to get on her toes and trot. A while later, I gave her another tablespoon of hot sauce, and she threw up again. . . . I was drinking whiskey. I made her keep walking back and forth all day to try to tire her out so she would sleep that night. . . . She asked me for a drink of water. I got a glass of water and told her if she would take the tablespoon of hot sauce I would give her a drink. She swallowed the hot sauce and I drank the glass of water." Maddux said he continued to make Melisha walk back and forth after supper, hitting her with a stick as she passed him. That night, he got her up and put her in a cold shower, apparently because she had wet her mattress. On the morning of the thirteenth, when he tried to wake her up she didn't respond. He began to rub her with alcohol, trying to bring her around.

That morning, Mrs. Hawkins was hemming some corduroy pants she had made for Missy when the telephone rang. It was her sister-in-law, saying, "There's something wrong down at Missy's house." A moment later, the doorbell rang. "It was two of my welfare workers," Mrs. Hawkins said later. "I knew the minute I saw them. 'Did he beat her up again?' I said. They said, 'Mrs. Hawkins, it's worse than that this time.'" Melisha had never awakened. The next day,

Ronnie and Wanda Maddux were charged with first-degree murder and held without bail.

Investigations were launched. Committees were formed. The state commissioner of human services disciplined three members of the Bradley County office, and almost everybody else in the office joined in a one-day walkout in protest—arguing, rather persuasively, that the workers involved were being scapegoated after handling the case more or less the way it would have been handled by any welfare worker who followed normal state procedures. The commissioner announced a moratorium on returning abused children to their families and speculated on the possibility of easing the procedures available for terminating parental rights. Members of a Teamsters local picketed the Governor's Mansion, urging that Ronnie and Wanda Maddux be given the death penalty if found guilty. Hank Snow, the country-music singer, wrote the governor, "I've heard countless people say that if these radicals were burned in the electric chair or even lynched in the city square, it would start some of these lowdowns to giving some serious thought before committing these gruesome crimes." There was some talk about sterilization as a way to prevent child abusers from producing more children to abuse. Those in the child-protection field who believe that reform should concentrate on prevention of child abuse rather than on punishment of abusers found themselves grateful that the state legislature will not be in session until spring.

In Cleveland, a thousand people attended Melisha's funeral. The Sheriff's Department decided it would be prudent to hold the Madduxes in a jail outside the county—presumably not the state penitentiary, where Melisha's natural father is serving time for armed robbery. Welfare workers complained of harassment and even threats. There are people in Cleveland who believe that the intensity of reaction there can be traced to some acceptance of guilt for not having heeded the warnings of Dr. Appling long ago. Appling and David Sweitzer, who blame Melisha's death partly on rigidity and secrecy in the welfare department, used the public outcry to exert pressure for interagency cooperation and improved training, although in one of his first meetings with the human services commissioner, Appling found himself unable to get away from the subject of three children who had been returned that day to a home he considered potentially unsafe. Appling and Sweitzer finally won agreement that every child-abuse case in the county would be referred to the Child Protection Team—a team that now includes not only a psychiatrist and a pediatrician and a social worker but an attorney to represent the child's interests in court. The public outcry had a different meaning for the forces fighting a referendum in the November election which would have permitted liquor stores in Bradley County: they pointed to Ronnie Maddux's behavior as an example of what drink could lead to, and they defeated the referendum easily. Hank Snow came to Cleveland for a concert to benefit the fund that local people are raising to enlarge the Child Shelter, which has been renamed the Melisha Gibson Child Shelter.

Family Problems

Manchester, New Hampshire

JULY 1978

Hank Piasecny, like a lot of people in Manchester, worked his way up from the mills. The banks of the Merrimack River, which cuts right through Manchester, are still lined with the massive old red-brick buildings that once drew people like Hank Piasecny's parents from Poland and his wife's parents from French Quebec and thousands of other people from Ireland or from the rocky farms of upper New England. The buildings on the banks of the Merrimack were once filled with shoe factories and foundries and the Amoskeag Mills—a textile operation that employed more than twenty thousand people before it went under in the thirties. Hank Piasecny, one of seven children of a shoe-factory worker, started working in a shoe factory himself at fourteen. When he came home from the Second World War, he opened a corner grocery store, and then a filling station that later branched out into hunting and fishing equipment. He was a hard worker, and he was fortunate enough to acquire the New England distributorship for Arkansas Traveler boats at about the time the aluminum-boat market was beginning to expand. By the early sixties, he was the proprietor of a thriving sporting-goods store called Hank's Sport Center. He sponsored a Golden Gloves boxing team that included his own son, Terry, as one of its stars. He had an attractive wife and a teenage daughter who seemed to be talented at anything she turned to. He often joined his customers on deer-hunting trips, and people who discussed his skill as a hunter sometimes said, "Where he goes, the deer follow." In the southern part of New Hampshire, public officials who were also outdoorsmen were likely to be friends of Hank Piasecny. He was an outgoing, rough-talking man—known to have a temper that could transform rough talk suddenly into violence. "He'd give you any damn thing he had," a close friend of Piasecny during that period has said. "But he didn't mind having a fight—I'll tell you."

One person Piasecny didn't mind fighting with was his wife, Doris. Apparently, the Piasecny marriage was violent from the beginning. Doris Piasecny, who worked as a secretary in downtown Manchester, had grown up in a miserable river-bottom neighborhood known as Skeag Village. She had a longing for material objects that strained Piasecny's income and his temper. At one time, the family owned three Cadillacs. Hank Piasecny was ferociously jealous. He drank a lot. His wife took a lot of pills. Terry Piasecny remembers from childhood that when his father's spirits were high—particularly in a hunting camp in the St. John River valley, in Maine—"you could really be on the top of the world with him." More often, his spirits were low. Arguments between him and Doris would build up to the point at which their daughter, Susan, would suddenly burst out of the house to call for help. The Manchester police came out regularly to calm Piasecny down. At least once, he was convicted of assaulting his wife. "I used to hope that one of them would die," Susan Piasecny said later. "So it would all end."

In 1963, after some separations and some false starts toward divorce and some contempt citations against Piasecny for violating a court order barring him from the house, Doris Piasecny was finally granted a divorce. She got the house and most of the possessions. He set up housekeeping in the back of Hank's Sport Center. Terry, who had married young, had been away from home for some time. Susan was in her second year at Colby College. Although Hank Piasecny had seemed unwilling to accept the divorce, he and his wife appeared to get along better divorced than married. She even went out with him occasionally. She also went out with other people. One night, around Christmas of 1963, she invited some people who had been drinking at a bar called the Venice Room back to the house for a nightcap. Among them was a bachelor named John Betley—a prominent Manchester architect who, after leaving his house late that evening to garage his car, had decided to drop in to the Venice Room for a drink. Eventually, the gathering at Doris Piasecny's house began to break up. John Betley and Doris Piasecny were left alone in the house. Not long after that, according to the way the police later pieced together what must have happened, Hank Piasecny emerged from his hiding place, a kitchen knife in his hand, and killed both his wife and John Betley. Doris Piasecny was stabbed eleven times. John Betley was stabbed thirteen times.

In New Hampshire, the legal definition of insanity is rather broad. To accept a plea of not guilty by reason of insanity, a judge or jury need not be persuaded that the defendant was unable to distinguish between right and wrong but merely that his crime was the product of mental illness. A couple of hours after the murders, Hank Piasecny was found in the back of Hank's Sport Center, having smashed his truck into a turnpike guardrail nearby. He was drunk and raving and holding a deer rifle that he managed to fire once before passing out. He was later examined by a prominent Boston psychiatrist hired by the defense. He was examined by psychiatrists acting for the state. It was agreed that Hank Piasecny was legally insane—a paranoid schizophrenic. "Mr. Piasecny has always been a rather seriously disturbed person with masochistic, passive, dependent, narcissistic trends," one of the state's psychiatrists said. "Often he has very effectively repressed realities which were incompatible with his deep need to be recognized as a real man by his wife and a substantial person by the community."

The state accepted Hank Piasecny's plea, and he was committed to the New Hampshire Hospital at Concord—"for life until or unless earlier discharged, released or transferred by due course of law."

The state attorney general's office, which handles all murder prosecutions in New Hampshire, could argue that, the state's own psychiatrists having found Piasecny insane, bringing him to trial instead of accepting the plea would have been fruitless. The suspicion lingered in Manchester, though, that Piasecny had escaped the penitentiary or the electric chair for reasons having nothing to do with psychiatry. Rumors had circulated about the murders from the beginning. Although John Betley and Doris Piasecny were found fully clothed, there were people in Manchester who insisted the bodies were nude and mutilated. It was said that the party at Doris Piasecny's that night had included an important judge, or perhaps more than one judge. It was said that Hank Piasecny's plea of insanity had been accepted because of a cover-up, or because of influence exerted by some of his old hunting buddies. There were a lot of people in Manchester who thought that Hank Piasecny had managed to get away with murder.

After spending a year in a maximum-security section of the hospital, Piasecny settled into a relatively comfortable life in Concord. His brothers and sister, who were trying to maintain his shop for him, visited regularly. Terry brought the grandchildren. Piasecny's children had apparently chosen to believe that he had no idea what he was doing when he stabbed their mother and John Betley; some of his brothers had apparently chosen to believe that he may not have committed the crime at all. The hospital has a pitch-and-putt golf course, and Piasecny spent a lot of time on it. Except for some problems early in his stay with an inmate named John McGrath, who had been committed after killing several members of his own family, Piasecny seemed to have adjusted relatively well to institutional life. Two years after he was committed, his lawyer petitioned for his release, arguing that he was no longer a danger to himself or others.

One of the state-hospital psychiatrists had some reservations about approving the release. His report said, "I cannot in all good conscience in any way state that the patient represents no further

risk to the community whatsoever." In general, though, the psychiatrists agreed that Hank Piasecny, surely insane at the time of the
murders, had recovered to the point of being able to live in his own
community with the aid of some regular psychiatric care. The state
attorney general's office opposed even a gradual release. John Betley's sister wrote the judge in the case a bitter letter, hinting that
Piasecny had been protected from the start and expressing outrage
that the court could sanction the release of "such an evil person."
When the release was indeed sanctioned, the attorney general appealed to the state supreme court—unsuccessfully. On August 6,
1966, two and a half years after he was arrested for killing his wife
and John Betley, Hank Piasecny returned to Manchester, a free man.

The life Piasecny settled into seemed to be calmer than the one he
had left. After a couple of years, an entrance for the interstate sliced
through the property of Hank's Sport Center, and Piasecny did not
attempt to find a new location. He went to work for the boat store
run by Arthur Pellenz, a friendly competitor from earlier times. The
three-Cadillac days were over for Piasecny, but he seemed to get by
with a simpler life. When Terry moved his family to a small house on
a river an hour north of Manchester, Hank Piasecny became a regular Sunday visitor—fly-fishing in the river, taking Terry's eldest son
into the woods for his first buck in the same way he had taken Terry.
Even without three Cadillacs, he was still a man who might show up
at the wake of a prominent citizen, and at Pellenz's boat store he was
still a man who spoke bluntly. But "peaceful" was a word sometimes
used about the life Piasecny led in Manchester—except when it
came to his relationship with his daughter.

It is often said in Manchester that Susan Piasecny was a talented
and remarkably intelligent girl who simply never recovered from the
shock of her mother's murder. In high school, she did appear to be
the sort of daughter who would make any father proud—a fine-
looking girl who seemed to have a natural gift for music and art and
athletics and scholarship. She was an honor student. She was a good

enough athlete to teach skiing and riding and golf. Even before that day in 1963 when the Colby dean met her after class to tell her there was trouble at home, though, there had been episodes that would have surprised anyone in Manchester who took Susan Piasecny to be a model of achievement. When she was fourteen, she arrived home hours late from a babysitting job and reported having been abducted—a story the police eventually decided she might have made up. When she was sixteen, she was taken to a hospital in Nashua, temporarily unable to speak. After her mother's death, she was a patient in a Massachusetts mental hospital for several weeks. She left Colby, and left another college after that. Still, she eventually finished college, got married, and, in the fall of 1967, entered the medical school of the University of Vermont.

After two starts, she withdrew from medical school for good. Her marriage was deteriorating. Depressions had forced her to seek help again at mental hospitals. Shortly after her marriage broke up, she was found unconscious in a small New Hampshire town, apparently having been beaten or tossed from a car. She implied that her husband had hired thugs to beat her up. The Manchester police were not convinced. The incident reminded them of the babysitting abduction. It also reminded them of the reports years before that a local golfer who had become involved with Susan when she was a teenager had been beaten up by friends of Hank Piasecny. In 1970, Susan Piasecny entered the New Hampshire Hospital at Concord, depressed and suicidal. She remained there for three years. Shortly after her release, she married a fellow patient named Edward Hughes. Shortly after that, it was reported that Edward Hughes had walked into the bathroom of their apartment, slit his throat with a Gillette razor blade, and walked back into the living room to die in the presence of his wife.

After her second husband's death, Susan Hughes worked now and then at one nursing home or another, but her life seemed dominated by pills and bad checks and petty brushes with the law and fights with her father. They tried living together for a while—renting the small brick bungalow Terry had left when he moved away—but they finally had to split up. Living in the same house with his daughter, Hank Piasecny apparently started seeing in her the mannerisms that had angered him about his wife. In his anger, he may have sometimes called her Doris instead of Susan. After Susan moved out, there were periods when her father swore he wanted nothing more to do with her. She was regularly in trouble—forging prescriptions for pills or stealing from friends or bouncing checks. The girl who had once seemed capable of doing anything she chose to do was considered by her uncles and her aunts and even her own father a persistent disgrace to the Piasecny name. In June of 1977, Hank Piasecny and his daughter had a violent argument—he may have hit her or shoved her or shaken her—and he said he never wanted to see her or hear from her again.

On the Friday before last Labor Day weekend, Susan Hughes's name appeared in the court column of the *Manchester Union Leader*. The item said, "Sue E. Piasecny, 35, of 367 Hanover St., also known as Susan Hughes, entered no plea to two counts of forgery, both felony complaints." She telephoned the reporter responsible, demanding to know why he had included her maiden name—a mention, she said, that was likely to drive her father to distraction, or violence. That night, she told some friends visiting her apartment that she feared her father might kill her because of his belief that she had dragged the family name through the mud once again. She showed them a knife she intended to use to defend herself. She showed them newspaper clippings about her mother's murder.

Early the next morning—Saturday of Labor Day weekend—the police went to Hank Piasecny's house. Susan Hughes had phoned to say that her father was so distraught she was afraid he might harm himself. They found Piasecny lying facedown in the hallway. Half of his head had been blown off. A shotgun was at his side. The headline in the next day's *Union Leader* said, HENRY (HANK) PIASECNY SHOOTS HIMSELF DEAD. The lead-in headline said, CHARGED IN '63 SLAYINGS. Most people in Manchester figured that the guilt had finally caught up with Hank Piasecny—that he hadn't got away with murder after all. One or two of his brothers were said to believe that Hank Piasecny's daughter had driven him to his death. Susan Hughes herself had another theory: she said her father had been murdered.

She did not stop at merely offering the theory. She called the county attorney. She hounded the police. She suggested some suspects— John McGrath, for instance, the murderer at the state hospital, who had escaped several years before. Once, she pounded on the door of the police chief's office, shouting that her father had been murdered but no one would do anything about it. The police were unimpressed. Susan Hughes, after all, had come in with some wild tales in the past. Finally, three and a half weeks after Hank Piasecny died, his daughter, claiming reasonable grounds to suspect that he had met his death by unlawful means, petitioned the superior court for a warrant to have the body disinterred and an autopsy performed. The petition made a claim that Susan Hughes had often made to the police—that there was a second bullet hole in her father's body. "In the early morning of September 5, 1977," the petition said, "Susan E. Hughes went to the funeral home and examined the body of her father, observing a puncture wound in the left chest which she was able to probe to a depth of 2½ to 3 inches." The petition was granted. The autopsy was performed. A hole was found on the left side of Hank Piasecny's chest. A .22 slug was found in his body.

When photographs taken at the death scene were reexamined, it turned out that the second bullet hole was not the only suspicious detail that had been overlooked. Although Piasecny's head wound would have killed him instantly, the body was at least ten feet away from the pool of blood. The gun was in an awkward position across the back of his right arm; the wound in his head was on the left instead of the right. It may be that the police quickly assumed that what they found was a suicide because that is what they were prepared to find. People in Manchester had been half expecting Hank

Piasecny to commit suicide for years, after all, and those expectations had been brought to the surface by the phone call from Piasecny's daughter. The possibility of reexamining the scene itself no longer existed by the time of the autopsy. The house had been cleaned. The police picked up one lead, though, during conversations at the autopsy: Susan Hughes, it turned out, had told the county attorney and a few other people about the second wound the day after the murder, before her trip to the funeral home. It was true that she had been at the death scene shortly after Piasecny's body was discovered, but the police who were there agreed on one detail: the body was covered, and Susan Hughes had no opportunity to examine it.

A month passed before Susan Hughes admitted having shot her father—shot him first in the chest with a .22 she had stolen from her cousin, and then in the head with his own shotgun. A lot of theories were offered in Manchester as to why, having got away with it, she instigated an investigation that would lead to her arrest. There was a theory that she could collect Hank Piasecny's insurance only if he died by means other than suicide. In fact, Piasecny had very little life insurance, and its beneficiary was Terry. A lot of people thought, of course, that Susan Hughes simply wanted to be punished and had found herself frustrated by the police department's acceptance of a patently sloppy attempt to give the shooting the appearance of a suicide. Some people believed that her real interest was in showing up the police of Manchester—her adversaries for years—or in defiantly dragging the Piasecny name through the mud for the benefit of her uncles and aunts. There were those who thought Susan Hughes might have just wanted attention.

She was examined several times by psychiatrists. A psychiatrist for the state—the same psychiatrist who had been in charge of examining Hank Piasecny for the state in 1964—said she was "suffering from a schizophrenic reaction of the chronic undifferentiated type." It was the same diagnosis he had offered for her father; he testified, in fact, that the trouble might have been inherited. The assistant attorney general in the case, Peter Heed, is normally reluctant to accept pleas of not guilty by reason of insanity. Because of a recent New Hampshire Supreme Court decision, the state can be required to prove beyond a reasonable doubt every two years that an inmate of the state hospital would be a danger to himself or others if released. That burden of proof being almost impossible to meet in the case of anyone who has behaved reasonably well at the hospital, a defendant who is committed for life is more likely to remain committed for two years. Heed did, though, decide to accept a plea of not guilty by reason of insanity from Susan Hughes. It was not the psychiatric reports that persuaded him. In a recent murder case that Heed tried, all four psychiatrists who took the stand had testified that the defendant was insane, and the jury had found him sane—and guilty. Heed says he accepted Susan Hughes's plea because he believes her to be insane, and believes that any juror would find her insane no matter what psychiatrists testified. "She had committed the perfect crime," he said recently. "Her very own action led to her arrest. Susan Hughes was the first person I've dealt with who really comes under what the insanity defense was meant to encompass." Susan Hughes was sent to the New Hampshire Hospital—"for life until or unless earlier discharged, released or transferred by due process of law."

The verdict did not cause the grumbling that had taken place when Hank Piasecny was sent to the state hospital, but there are, of course, people in Manchester who do not believe Susan Hughes is insane. Some of her uncles apparently believe her to be simply evil. Some members of Edward Hughes's family are now wondering out loud whether Hughes committed suicide after all. A former member of the attorney general's office who did not believe Hank Piasecny's plea should have been accepted seems to feel the same way about Susan Hughes's plea. "Of course she wanted to get caught," he said recently. "But that's not insanity—that's a sense of guilt. A lot of murders get solved that way."

. . .

In the two months between her father's death and her confession, Susan Hughes had seemed more and more insane to the people observing her—distraught, obsessive, sometimes hysterical. Once, she went to the police station to show detectives some graffiti she said someone had printed on her car in lipstick—a warning that she would be the next victim. For a while, most of her energies seemed to be taken up with an attempt to persuade an acquaintance to confess to the murder. Now she seems rational and intelligent, sitting in a dayroom at the New Hampshire Hospital—a large room with green linoleum floors and color pictures cut from magazines on the wall and the sounds of afternoon television and desultory Ping-Pong broken now and then by some patient's sudden outburst. Discussing the death of her father with a visitor not long ago, she said she had shot him in self-defense, then shot him again with his own shotgun for seemingly contradictory reasons that didn't seem contradictory in the shock of it all—to put him out of pain if he was still alive, perhaps, or to make certain he wouldn't recover and kill her. "If I had really wanted to make it look like a suicide," she said, "I would have rolled him over and shot him in the chest to obliterate the hole." She said she had insisted on the murder investigation because she believed the family—Terry's family—would prefer to think that Hank Piasecny died a murder victim rather than a suicide. She said she had not believed that the investigation would lead to her arrest. She talked about growing up as the daughter of Hank and Doris Piasecny—about being boarded out during the week as a child while both parents were working, about hearing the arguments start to build and knowing she would have to run for help, about discussions during the last year of Doris Piasecny's life as to whether or not her husband would kill her. "I've talked about all the bad things," she said at the door, as the visitor waited for the attendant to bring the key. "But there was love, too."

Todo Se Paga

Riverside, California

FEBRUARY 1979

The feud between the Ahumadas and the Lozanos, everyone agrees, began late one night in January of 1964, when John Ahumada, Sr., was beaten so badly that slivers of his skull were driven into his brain. It happened in Casa Blanca. Technically, Casa Blanca is a section of Riverside, California, a county seat sixty miles east of Los Angeles; spiritually, Casa Blanca is unto itself. Before the Second World War, when Riverside was still a quiet trading center for citrus growers, Casa Blanca had been isolated from the rest of the town for half a century—a square-mile patch cut out of acre upon acre of orange groves. Mexican farmworkers who settled on the east side of Riverside, close to downtown, gradually learned to deal with Anglos and blacks and the city authorities; Casa Blanca remained something close to a rural Mexican village. In 1949, it had only two paved streets. In the years after the war, the citrus-packing sheds where many Casa Blanca men had worked closed or burned down. A double-lane deposited a strip of automobile dealerships next to one corner of Casa Blanca. Over the objections of many Casa Blanca residents, the local grade school—"the Mexican consulate," one former resident calls it—was closed as part of a citywide integration plan. Eventually, rising real-estate prices and increased industry in Orange County, the sprawl southeast of Los Angeles, began to turn Riverside into a bedroom community for what had itself been a bedroom community—replacing the orange groves near one border of Casa Blanca with a middle-class housing development called Woodhaven. Still, Casa Blanca retained a feeling of being rural. Still, Casa Blanca remained unto itself—a place where uninvited strangers were challenged. Having never expected concern or justice from the outside, Casa Blanca remained a place that took care of its own territory and its own problems and its own feuds.

John Ahumada had been having some drinks with John Hernandez, whose wife was a Lozano. They had apparently been friendly enough in El Flamingo, where the drinking started, but some angry words were exchanged at the Casa Blanca Café, where they found themselves about one-thirty in the morning. Hernandez and Ahumada walked across the street to a parking lot next to the railroad tracks that form one boundary of Casa Blanca. They were joined eventually by two of Hernandez's brothers-in-law who lived nearby, Marcos and Roman Lozano—carrying tire irons, according to one account, or perhaps a part from a commercial ice-cream mixer. John Ahumada ended up in the hospital, on the critical list. Roman and Marcos Lozano ended up in court, where, contrary to the Casa Blanca tradition of not cooperating with outside authorities, John Ahumada testified against them. They were sent to prison for assault with a deadly weapon. Although everyone agrees that the fight across from the Casa Blanca Café was the beginning of the feud, it is not clear which family was left with a wrong to avenge. Was it the Ahumadas, one of whom had been beaten so savagely that his arm was partly paralyzed and his speech remained slurred? Or was it the Lozanos, two of whom served time in state prison because an Ahumada had broken the code that required Casa Blanca people to settle their arguments in Casa Blanca?

For twelve years after Roman and Marcos Lozano were sent to state prison, there were no incidents between the Lozanos and the Ahumadas violent enough to come to the attention of the police. In Casa Blanca, the explanation normally offered for that hiatus is simple: the next generation of Lozanos and Ahumadas, children at the time of the fight across from the bar, needed a dozen years to grow old enough to kill each other. In the meantime, there were some school-yard fistfights. Apparently, Johnny Lozano Hernandez would tell Johnny Ahumada that his father was a snitch, and a fight would start. Words would pass between Richard Lozano and Danny Ahumada, Johnny's younger brother, and another fight would start. "The seeds were there," someone who knew both families said recently. "All they had to do was scrape the earth a little bit."

In those years, the most ferocious battles engaged in by the young men of Casa Blanca pitted them against the young men of some other barrio rather than against each other—Casa Blanca fighting people from the east side who had dared to drive into the neighborhood in force, Casa Blanca fighting a crowd from Corona or Rubidoux because someone had stared too long at a Casa Blanca girl. When Casa Blanca was not fighting another barrio, it was often fighting the police.

There were a few years, beginning in the late sixties, when almost any Mexican barrio in Southern California was dangerous territory for Anglo police. For those years, when confrontation was part of what seemed to be a unified movement for the betterment of La Raza, gang members were transformed into Brown Berets, street toughs began thinking of themselves as Chicano militants, and juvenile offenders learned to refer to the rest of the world as "the Anglo-dominant society" instead of "paddies." In the words of one former Casa Blanca Brown Beret, "We were rebels without a cause who became rebels with a cause."

Even when the movement evaporated, though, hostility toward the police remained in Casa Blanca, fed by the hostility toward outsiders that had existed for decades. Riverside police cruisers were able to drive peacefully through the Mexican or black neighborhoods of the east side, but a policeman driving into Casa Blanca at night could consider himself fortunate to be met by a beer bottle instead of a rifle shot. One night in August of 1975, in a cornfield on the edge of Casa Blanca, sniping and harassment broke into what amounted to open warfare. Five people were wounded. Two young men from Casa Blanca—Danny Ahumada and Larry Romero, a member of a family close to the Ahumadas—were arrested for shooting at a police officer. "Casa Blanca had a reputation for sticking together," a young man who grew up fighting there said not long ago. "Even if we had problems, we'd never think of killing each other."

They started killing each other on Christmas 1976. Richard Lozano and a cousin who was visiting from Arizona, Gilbert Lozano Sanchez, were shot at from a passing car. Lozano was not hit; Sanchez was killed. By the spring of 1978, when James Richardson, a young courthouse reporter for Riverside's *Press-Enterprise,* pieced together court and police records to construct a chronology of the violence that the Lozanos and the Ahumadas had visited upon each other, three people had been killed, two people had been crippled, and any number of people had been sideswiped or shot at. Richard Lozano has been killed since then. Most of the shootings have been carried out with a sudden, dramatic ferocity. Danny Ahumada was grabbed by the hair and shot twice in the head point-blank with a .22-caliber pistol—an attack he somehow survived, although he was even more seriously disabled than his father. Johnny Lozano Hernandez was shot down before a dozen witnesses after a dispute during which, according to Johnny Ahumada, "he began to tell me my brother was a snitch, my brother was a dog." Ruben (Redeye) Romero—who, along with Johnny Ahumada, had been tried but acquitted in Johnny Hernandez's death—was killed at a Casa Blanca filling station by three young gunmen who shot him, knelt at his body, crossed themselves, and shot him again at point-blank range. When Richard Lozano was killed, seven weeks later, his uncle Raul Lozano, who had been tried but not convicted in the shooting of Danny Ahumada, was seen smearing the blood of his fallen nephew on his hand and tasting it, presumably as a symbol of vengeance owed.

.   .   .

The feud between the Lozanos and the Ahumadas lacks symmetry. There are family members who are not involved. John Lozano, the father of the recently murdered Richard, claims that he still has a friendly hello for John Ahumada, Sr., when they meet in Casa Blanca. Even those who are involved seem to go along for weeks, or even months, without retaliation. Most of the encounters that end in death or serious injury seem mere chance—a moment when someone is caught alone or when someone makes an insulting remark. "They're in no hurry," a man familiar with Mexican American neighborhoods in Southern California explained not long ago. "In the barrio, people say, '*Todo se paga.*'" Everything is paid.

In the barrio, the brutal simplicity ordinarily associated with a blood feud—an eye for an eye—is complicated by the element of pride. "You killed my brother, so I will kill your brother" sometimes seems to become "You killed my brother and that makes you think you are stronger than we are and can look down on us, so, to show that's not true, I will kill your brother." When Roman Lozano was asked recently why the feud had started again in 1976, he said, "They knew their dad was a snitch, and they had an uncle who was a homosexual. They had to prove that they were manly." People on both sides have complained of having their houses fired on from passing cars, but they complain even more bitterly of having carloads of their enemies drive by and throw kisses as a gesture of contempt. One of Johnny Ahumada's theories about the origin of the seventies violence is that the Lozanos were jealous because only Danny Ahumada and Larry Romero were singled out after the 1975 cornfield melee for having shot at the police. "They want to prove their heart," Johnny says. "They don't want to lose their pride. That's what makes them revengeful."

There are people in Riverside who believe that the violence between the Ahumadas and the Lozanos no longer has anything to do with the 1964 assault. "It's not like the Hatfields and the McCoys," a man who grew up in Casa Blanca said recently. "The underlying motive is drugs." Marcos and John Lozano have both been convicted on serious heroin charges at one time or another. There are people in Riverside who say that some of the younger Ahumadas—or their allies, the Romeros—may have pushed into Lozano drug-dealing territory while the Lozanos were in prison. There are people in Riverside who say that the argument between the two families is actually an argument between the two Mexican prison gangs that have emerged in California in the past several years—the Mexican Mafia and Nuestra Familia—one of which is supposedly challenging the other over control of drugs in Casa Blanca.

In the barrio, it is common to hear drugs offered as an underlying motive for any excess in violence or wealth. Members of the vice-and-narcotics squad in Riverside tend not to be believers in the drug-war theory. Redeye Romero, who is sometimes described as a "hardcore biker," was, like a lot of hardcore bikers, suspected of being a bagman in the heroin trade, but he was not thought to be in a position to challenge anybody for control of serious drug traffic. The only drug charge ever brought against an Ahumada was made when Danny was shot: the policemen who took charge of his clothing reported finding twelve balloons of heroin in the trousers. An investigator for the Riverside County District Attorney's Office who serves on a state task force dealing with prison gangs says that neither gang had anything to do with the shootings in Casa Blanca or control of the drug traffic there. He says, in fact, that Nuestra Familia conducted its own investigation to make certain that the death of Johnny Lozano Hernandez, apparently a Nuestra Familia member, had been strictly a private affair. "If it's true," a Casa Blanca native said recently of the theory that competing gangs are involved, "it's just one more reason for hating each other."

Mary Ahumada, the wife of the original victim, sometimes speaks of the Ahumadas as respectable citizens who have somehow found themselves locked in a feud with criminals. When she was informed recently that her son Danny might be sent to state prison for having been caught with a stolen pistol while on probation for the drug charge and an old auto-theft conviction, she said, "My boys were never mixed up in that sort of thing." It is true that the Ahumadas have not served time in state prison, although they are familiar with the Riverside County Jail. Mrs. Ahumada is a handsome, loquacious woman who, as Sister Mary, runs a small evangelical congregation that specializes in teenagers who have strayed from the Lord's path. The Lozanos sometimes speak of her as a hypocritical Holy Roller who goads her sons to violence. "People tend to pull you down," she says. "'Why doesn't she save her own sons? Why doesn't she save *their* souls?' Yes, I've had remarks from police officers in the past that have been cruel." (Sister Mary's ministry has not been completely without effect on her sons: Johnny wore a gold cross in his lapel throughout his trial for the murder of Johnny Hernandez.) Although the Ahumadas' ally Redeye Romero was known as a hardcore biker, he was also known as one of the founders of the Brown Berets in Casa Blanca—someone who showed up at meetings now and then as a spokesman for barrio youths. When he was killed, he was referred to in the press as a "street leader," although he was about to go to prison for an armed-robbery conviction. Policemen in Riverside are unimpressed by the prominence of the Ahumadas and the Romeros. In fact, to some policemen, particularly Anglo policemen who are not overly concerned about the effects of heroin on Mexicans in a remote barrio, serious drug dealers have the advantage over street leaders of trying to avoid incidents that only attract the authorities to their place of business—incidents like firing on police cruisers.

Some people in Casa Blanca believe that the Riverside police are not saddened by the sight of Ahumadas and Lozanos killing and maiming each other. The police have, in fact, made a lot of arrests in the shootings, but the closest thing to a conviction has been Raul Lozano pleading nolo contendere to a charge of having been an accessory to the shooting of Danny Ahumada. When Georgie Ahumada, the younger brother of Johnny and Danny, was released without charge after having been picked up for the murder of Richard Lozano, Mary Ahumada said she had told Georgie to trust in God, but most people charged with one of the shootings have trusted in the lack of witnesses willing to testify. After Georgie Ahumada went free, the deputy district attorney who has handled all of the feud shootings said, "This is the usual situation where twenty people see the killing and all of them say, 'I didn't see it.'" Even two of Richard Lozano's uncles who were present when he was killed declined to cooperate with the authorities. Richard's father, John Lozano, does not seem upset that his brothers would not help to bring his son's killer to justice. "They're the type that don't like to testify," he says.

Some people in Casa Blanca who are not related to either family have been unable to stay out of the feud. People who witnessed shootings have had their houses fired upon, making it necessary, in some cases, for their own young men to prove that they cannot be treated as weaklings. One of the young men who is awaiting trial for the murder of Redeye Romero seems to have got involved originally because his mother became friendly with Johnny Lozano Hernandez's mother upon moving into the neighborhood. ("They were the only ones who treated us with respect," he says.) A young man named William DeHaro, who was shot to death last September, may have been killed simply because he remained friendly with the Lozanos after a warning to avoid them. Some people in Casa Blanca—particularly older people—seem to be able to stay out of the feud. "You don't dare choose sides," one of them has said. "You talk to both. You go to the funerals for both."

Many of the Lozanos and Ahumadas and Romeros have moved out of Casa Blanca in the last year or so, partly in an effort to sleep peacefully through the night, but they return constantly. Everyone remains well armed; when the police search the house of someone involved in the feud, they invariably come up with a small arsenal. Complaining recently about some people having shot at his house the previous evening, John Lozano mentioned that he had taken the precaution of borrowing a machine gun. The Ahumadas and the Lozanos both say they would like the feud to end, but no one is optimistic that it will. A new generation is gradually growing old enough to become lethal. "You can see it in the ten-year-olds," Johnny Ahumada said recently. "They look at you, and you can see their hatred." Standing in the hall of the Riverside County Court House not long ago, John Lozano, who had just entered a guilty plea to possession of heroin for sale, was equally pessimistic. "I wish it would end," he said. "I'm facing four years, and I'll be out of the picture—which, in a way, I'm glad."

It's Just Too Late

Knoxville, Tennessee

MARCH 1979

Until she was sixteen, FaNee Cooper was what her parents sometimes called an ideal child. "You'd never have to correct her," FaNee's mother has said. In sixth grade, FaNee won a spelling contest. She played the piano and the flute. She seemed to believe what she heard every Sunday at the Beaver Dam Baptist Church about good and evil and the hereafter. FaNee was not an outgoing child. Even as a baby, she was uncomfortable when she was held and cuddled. She found it easy to tell her parents that she loved them but difficult to confide in them. Particularly compared to her sister, Kristy, a cheerful, open little girl two and a half years younger, she was reserved and introspective. The thoughts she kept to herself, though, were apparently happy thoughts. Her eighth-grade essay on Christmas—written in a remarkably neat hand—talked of the joys of helping put together toys for her little brother, Leo, Jr., and the importance of her parents' reminder that Christmas is the birthday of Jesus.

Her parents were the sort of people who might have been expected to have an ideal child. As a boy, Leo Cooper had been called "one of the greatest high school basketball players ever developed in Knox County." He went on to play basketball at East Tennessee State, and he married the homecoming queen, JoAnn Henson. After college, Cooper became a high school basketball coach and teacher and, eventually, an administrator. By the time FaNee turned thirteen, in 1973, he was in his third year as the principal of Gresham Junior High School, in Fountain City—a small Knox County town that had been swallowed up by Knoxville when the suburbs began to move north. A tall man, with curly black hair going on gray, Leo Cooper has an elaborate way of talking ("Unless I'm very badly mistaken, he has never related to me totally the content of his conversation") and a manner that may come from years of trying to leave errant junior high school students with the impression that a responsible adult is magnanimous, even humble, about invariably being in the right. His wife, a high school art teacher, paints and does batik, and created the name FaNee because she liked the way it looked and sounded—it sounds like "Fawn-*ee*" when the Coopers say it—but the impression she gives is not of artiness but of soft-spoken small-town gentility. When she found, in the course of cleaning up FaNee's room, that her ideal thirteen-year-old had been smoking cigarettes, she was, in her words, crushed. "FaNee was such a perfect child before that," JoAnn Cooper said some time later. "She was angry that we found out. She knew we knew that she had done something we didn't approve of, and then the rebellion started. I was hurt. I was very hurt. I guess it came through as disappointment."

Several months later, FaNee's grandmother died. FaNee had been devoted to her grandmother. She wrote a poem in her memory—an almost joyous poem, filled with Christian faith in the afterlife ("Please don't grieve over my happiness / Rejoice with me in the presence of the Angels of Heaven"). She also took some keepsakes from her grandmother's house, and was apparently mortified when her parents found them and explained that they would have to be returned. By then, the Coopers were aware that FaNee was going to have a difficult time as a teenager. They thought she might be self-conscious about the double affliction of glasses and braces. They thought she might be uncomfortable in the role of the principal's daughter at Gresham. In ninth grade, she entered Halls High School, where JoAnn Cooper was teaching art. FaNee was a loner at first. Then she fell in with what could only be considered a bad crowd.

Halls, a few miles to the north of Fountain City, used to be known as Halls Crossroads. It is what Knoxville people call "over the ridge"—on the side of Black Oak Ridge that has always been thought of as rural. When FaNee entered Halls High, the Coopers were already in the process of building a house on several acres of land they had bought in Halls, in a sparsely settled area along Brown Gap Road. Like two or three other houses along the road, it was to be constructed basically of huge logs taken from old buildings—a house that Leo Cooper describes as being, like the name FaNee, "just a little bit different." Ten years ago, Halls Crossroads was literally a crossroads. Then some of the Knoxville expansion that had swollen Fountain City spilled over the ridge, planting subdivisions here and there on roads that still went for long stretches with nothing but an occasional house with a cow or two next to it. The increase in population did not create a town. Halls has no center. Its commercial area is a series of two or three shopping centers strung together on the Maynardville Highway, the four-lane that leads north into Union County—a place almost synonymous in east Tennessee with mountain poverty. Its restaurant is the Halls Freezo Drive-In. The gathering place for the group FaNee Cooper eventually found herself in was the Maynardville Highway Exxon station.

At Halls High School, the social poles were represented by the Jocks and the Freaks. FaNee found her friends among the Freaks. "I am truly enlighted upon irregular trains of thought aimed at strange depots of mental wards," she wrote when she was fifteen. "Yes! Crazed farms for the mental off—Oh! I walked through the halls screams & loud laughter fill my ears—Orderlys try to reason with me—but I am unreasonable! The joys of being a FREAK in a circus of imagination." The little crowd of eight or ten young people that FaNee joined has been referred to by her mother as "the Union County group." A couple of the girls were from backgrounds similar to FaNee's, but all the boys had the characteristics, if not the precise addresses, that Knoxville people associate with the poor whites of Union County. They were the sort of boys who didn't bother to finish high school, or finished it in a special program for slow learners, or got ejected from it for taking a swing at the principal.

"I guess you can say they more or less dragged us down to their level with the drugs," a girl who was in the group—a girl who can be called Marcia—said recently. "And somehow we settled for it. It seems like we had to get ourselves in the pit before we could look out." People in the group used marijuana and Valium and LSD. They sneered at the Jocks and the "prim and proper little ladies" who went with the Jocks. "We set ourselves aside," Marcia now says. "We put ourselves above everyone. How we did that I don't know." In a Knox County high school, teenagers who want to get themselves in the pit need not mainline heroin. The Jocks they mean to be compared to do not merely show up regularly for classes and practice football and wear clean clothes; they watch their language and preach temperance and go to prayer meetings on Wednesday nights and talk about having a real good Christian witness. Around Knoxville, people who speak of well-behaved high school kids often seem to use words like "perfect," or even "angels." For FaNee's group, the opposite was not difficult to figure out. "We were into wicked things, strange things," Marcia says. "It was like we were on some kind of devil trip." FaNee wrote about demons and vultures and rats. "Slithering serpents eat my sanity and bite my ass," she wrote in an essay called "The Lovely Road of Life," just after she turned sixteen, "while tornadoes derail and ever so swiftly destroy every car in my train of thought." She wrote a lot about death.

FaNee's girlfriends spoke of her as "super-intelligent." Her English teacher found some of her writing profound—and disturbing. She was thought to be not just super-intelligent but super-mysterious, and even, at times, super-weird—an introverted girl who stared straight ahead with deep-brown, nearly black eyes and seemed to have thoughts she couldn't share. Nobody really knew why she had chosen to run with the Freaks—whether it was loneliness or rebellion or simple boredom. Marcia thought it might have had something to do with a feeling that her parents had settled on Kristy as their perfect child. "I guess she figured she couldn't be the best," Marcia said recently. "So she decided she might as well be the worst."

Toward the spring of FaNee's junior year at Halls, her problems seemed to deepen. Despite her intelligence, her grades were sliding. She was what her mother called "a mental dropout." Leo Cooper had to visit Halls twice because of minor suspensions. Once, FaNee had been caught smoking. Once, having ducked out of a required assembly, she was spotted by a favorite teacher, who turned her in. At home, she exchanged little more than short, strained formalities with Kristy, who shared their parents' opinion of FaNee's choice of friends. The Coopers had finished their house—a large house, its size accentuated by the huge old logs and a great stone fireplace and outsize "Paul Bunyan"–style furniture—but FaNee spent most of her time there in her own room, sleeping or listening to rock music through earphones. One night, there was a terrible scene when FaNee returned from a concert in a condition that Leo Cooper knew had to be the result of marijuana. JoAnn Cooper, who ordinarily strikes people as too gentle to raise her voice, found herself losing her temper regularly. Finally, Leo Cooper asked a counselor he knew, Jim Griffin, to stop in at Halls High School and have a talk with FaNee—unofficially.

Griffin—a young man with a warm, informal manner—worked for the Knox County Juvenile Court. He had a reputation for being able to reach teenagers who wouldn't talk to their parents or to school administrators. One Friday in March of 1977, he spent an hour and a half talking to FaNee Cooper. As Griffin recalls the interview, FaNee didn't seem alarmed by his presence. She seemed to him calm and controlled—Griffin thought it was something like talking to another adult—and, unlike most of the teenagers he dealt with, she looked him in the eye the entire time. Griffin, like some of FaNee's friends, found her eyes unsettling—"the coldest, most distant, but, at the same time, the most knowing eyes I'd ever seen." She expressed affection for her parents, but she didn't seem interested in exploring ways of getting along better with them. The impression she gave Griffin was that they were who they were, and she was who she was, and there didn't happen to be any connection. Several times, she made the same response to Griffin's suggestions: "It's too late."

That weekend, neither FaNee nor her parents brought up the subject of Griffin's visit. Leo Cooper has spoken of the weekend as being particularly happy; a friend of FaNee's who stayed over remembers it as particularly strained. FaNee stayed home from school on Monday because of a bad headache—she often had bad headaches—but felt well enough on Monday evening to drive to the library. She was to be home at nine. When she wasn't, Mrs. Cooper began to phone her friends. Finally, around ten, Leo Cooper got into his other car and took a swing around Halls—past the teenage hangouts like the Exxon station and the Pizza Hut and the Smoky Mountain Market. Then he took a second swing. At eleven, FaNee was still not home.

She hadn't gone to the library. She had picked up two girlfriends and driven to the home of a third, where everyone took five Valium tablets. Then the four girls drove over to the Exxon station, where they met four boys from their crowd. After a while, the group bought some beer and some marijuana and reassembled at Charlie Stevens's trailer. Charlie Stevens was five or six years older than everyone else in the group—a skinny, slow-thinking young man with long black hair and a sparse beard. He was married and had a child, but he and his wife had separated; she was back in Union County with the baby. Stevens had remained in their trailer—parked in the yard near his mother's house, in a back-road area of Knox County dominated by decrepit, unpainted sheds and run-down trailers and rusted-out automobiles. Stevens had picked up FaNee at home once or twice—apparently, more as a driver for the group than as a date—and the Coopers, having learned that his unsuitability extended to being married, had asked her not to see him.

In Charlie's trailer, which had no heat or electricity, the group drank beer and passed around joints, keeping warm with blankets. By eleven or so, FaNee was what one of her friends has called "super-messed-up." Her speech was slurred. She was having trouble keeping her balance. She had decided not to go home. She had apparently persuaded herself that her parents intended to send her away to some sort of home for incorrigibles. "It's too late," she said to one of her friends. "It's just too late." It was decided that one of the boys, David Munsey, who was more or less the leader of the group, would drive the Coopers' car to FaNee's house, where FaNee and Charlie Stevens would pick him up in Stevens's car—a worn Pinto with four bald tires, one light, and a dragging muffler. FaNee wrote a note to her parents and then, perhaps because her handwriting was suffering the effects of beer and marijuana and Valium, asked Stevens to rewrite it on a large piece of paper, which would be left on the seat of the Coopers' car. The Stevens version was just about the same as FaNee's, except that Stevens left out a couple of sentences about trying to work things out ("I'm willing to try") and, not having won any spelling championships himself, he misspelled a few words, like "tomorrow." The note said, "Dear Mom and Dad. Sorry I'm late. Very late. I left your car because I thought you might need it tomorrow. I love you all, but this is something I just had to do. The man talked to me privately for one and a half hours and I was really scared, so this is something I just had to do, but don't worry, I'm with a very good friend. Love you all. FaNee. P.S. Please try to understand I love you all very much, really I do. Love me if you have a chance."

At eleven-thirty or so, Leo Cooper was sitting in his living room, looking out the window at his driveway—a long gravel road that runs almost four hundred feet from the house to Brown Gap Road. He saw the car that FaNee had been driving pull into the driveway. "She's home," he called to his wife, who had just left the room. Cooper walked out on the deck over the garage. The car had stopped at the end of the driveway, and the lights had gone out. He got into his other car and drove to the end of the driveway. David Munsey had already joined Charlie Stevens and FaNee, and the Pinto was just leaving, traveling at a normal rate of speed. Leo Cooper pulled out on the road behind them.

Stevens turned left on Crippen Road, a road that has a field on one side and two or three small houses on the other, and there Cooper pulled his car in front of the Pinto and stopped, blocking the way. He got out and walked toward the Pinto. Suddenly, Stevens put the car in reverse, backed into a driveway a hundred yards behind him, and sped off. Cooper jumped in his car and gave chase. Stevens raced back to Brown Gap Road, ran a stop sign there, ran another stop sign at Maynardville Highway, turned north, veered off onto the old Andersonville Pike, a nearly abandoned road that runs parallel to the highway, and then crossed back over the highway to the narrow, dark country roads on the other side. Stevens sometimes drove with his lights out. He took some of the corners by suddenly applying his hand brake to make the car swerve around in a ninety-degree turn. He was in familiar territory—he actually passed his trailer—and Cooper had difficulty keeping up. Past the trailer, Stevens swept down a hill into a sharp left turn that took him onto Foust Hollow Road, a winding, hilly road not much wider than one car.

At a fork, Cooper thought he had lost the Pinto. He started to go right and then saw what seemed to be a spark from Stevens's dragging muffler off to the left, in the darkness. Cooper took the left fork, down Salem Church Road. He went down a hill and then up a long, curving hill to a crest, where he saw the Stevens car ahead. "I saw the car airborne. Up in the air," he later testified. "It was up in the air. And then it completely rolled over one more time. It started to make another flip forward, and just as it started to flip to the other side it flipped back this way, and my daughter's body came out."

Cooper slammed on his brakes and skidded to a stop up against the Pinto. "Book!" Stevens shouted—the group's equivalent of "Scram!" Stevens and Munsey disappeared into the darkness. "It was dark, no one around, and so I started yelling for FaNee," Cooper has testified. "I thought it was an eternity before I could find her body, wedged under the back end of that car. . . . I tried everything I could, and saw that I couldn't get her loose. So I ran to a trailer back up to the top of the hill back up there to try to get that lady to call to get me some help, and then apparently she didn't think that I was serious. . . . I took the jack out of my car and got under, and it was dark, still couldn't see too much what was going on . . . and started prying and got her loose, and I don't know how. And then I dragged her over to the side, and, of course, at the time I felt reasonably assured that she was gone, because her head was completely—on one side just as if you had taken a sledgehammer and just hit it and bashed it in. And I did have the pleasure of one thing. I had the pleasure of listening to her breathe about the last three times she ever breathed in her life."

David Munsey did not return to the wreck that night, but Charlie Stevens did. Leo Cooper was kneeling next to his daughter's body. Cooper insisted that Stevens come close enough to see FaNee. "He was kneeling down next to her," Stevens later testified. "And he said, 'Do you know what you've done? Do you really know what you've done?' Like that. And I just looked at her, and I said, 'Yes,' and just stood there. Because I couldn't say nothing." There was, of course, a legal decision to be made about who was responsible for FaNee Cooper's death. In a deposition, Stevens said he had been fleeing for his life. He testified that when Leo Cooper blocked Crippen Road, FaNee had said that her father had a gun and intended to hurt them. Stevens was bound over and eventually indicted for involuntary manslaughter. Leo Cooper testified that when he approached the Pinto on Crippen Road, FaNee had a strange expression that he had never seen before. "It wasn't like FaNee, and I knew something was wrong," he said. "My concern was to get FaNee out of the car." The district attorney's office asked that Cooper be bound over for reckless driving, but the judge declined to do so. "Any father would have done what he did," the judge said. "I can see no criminal act on the part of Mr. Cooper."

Almost two years passed before Charlie Stevens was brought to trial. Part of the problem was ensuring the presence of David Munsey, who had joined the Navy but seemed inclined to assign his own leaves. In the meantime, the Coopers went to court with a civil suit—they had "uninsured-motorist coverage," which requires their insurance company to cover any defendant who has no insurance of his own—and they won a judgment. There were ways of assigning responsibility, of course, which had nothing to do with the law, civil or criminal. A lot of people in Knoxville thought that Leo Cooper had, in the words of his lawyer, "done what any daddy worth his salt would have done." There were others who believed that FaNee Cooper had lost her life because Leo Cooper had lost his temper. Leo Cooper was not among those who expressed any doubts about his actions. Unlike his wife, whose eyes filled with tears at almost any mention of FaNee, Cooper seemed able, even eager, to go over the details of the accident again and again. With the help of a school-board security man, he conducted his own investigation. He drove over the route dozens of times. "I've thought about it every day, and I guess I will the rest of my life," he said as he and his lawyer and the prosecuting attorney went over the route again the day before Charlie Stevens's trial finally began. "But I can't tell any alternative for a father. I simply wanted her out of that car. I'd have done the same thing again, even at the risk of losing her."

Tennessee law permits the family of a victim to hire a special prosecutor to assist the district attorney. The lawyer who acted for the Coopers in the civil case helped prosecute Charlie Stevens. Both he and the district attorney assured the jurors that the presence of a special prosecutor was not to be construed to mean that the Coopers were vindictive. Outside the courtroom, Leo Cooper said that the verdict was of no importance to him—that he felt sorry, in a way, for Charlie Stevens. But there were people in Knoxville who thought

Cooper had a lot riding on the prosecution of Charlie Stevens. If Stevens was not guilty of FaNee Cooper's death—found so by twelve of his peers—who was?

At the trial, Cooper testified emotionally and remarkably graphically about pulling FaNee out from under the car and watching her die in his arms. Charlie Stevens had shaved his beard and cut his hair, but the effort did not transform him into an impressive witness. His lawyer—trying to argue that it would have been impossible for Stevens to concoct the story about FaNee's having mentioned a gun, as the prosecution strongly implied—said, "His mind is such that if you ask him a question you can hear his mind go around, like an old mill creaking." Stevens did not deny the recklessness of his driving or the sorry condition of his car. It happened to be the only car he had available to flee in, he said, and he had fled in fear for his life.

The prosecution said that Stevens could have let FaNee out of the car when her father stopped them, or could have gone to the commercial strip on the Maynardville Highway for protection. The prosecution said that Leo Cooper had done what he might have been expected to do under the circumstances—alone, late at night, his daughter in danger. The defense said precisely the same about Stevens: he had done what he might have been expected to do when being pursued by a man he had reason to be afraid of. "I don't fault Mr. Cooper for what he did, but I'm sorry he did it," the defense attorney said. "I'm sorry the girl said what she said." The jury deliberated for eighteen minutes. Charlie Stevens was found guilty. The jury recommended a sentence of from two to five years in the state penitentiary. At the announcement, Leo Cooper broke down and cried. JoAnn Cooper's eyes filled with tears; she blinked them back and continued to stare straight ahead.

In a way, the Coopers might still strike a casual visitor as an ideal family—handsome parents, a bright and bubbly teenage daughter, a little boy learning the hook shot from his father, a warm house with some land around it. FaNee's presence is there, of course. A picture of her, with a small bouquet of flowers over it, hangs in the living room. One of her poems is displayed in a frame on a table. Even if Leo Cooper continues to think about that night for the rest of his life, there are questions he can never answer. Was there a way that Leo and JoAnn Cooper could have prevented FaNee from choosing the path she chose? Would she still be alive if Leo Cooper had not jumped into his car and driven to the end of the driveway to investigate? Did she in fact tell Charlie Stevens that her father would hurt them—or even that her father had a gun? Did she want to get away from her family even at the risk of tearing around dark country roads in Charlie Stevens's dismal Pinto? Or did she welcome the risk? The poem of FaNee's that the Coopers have displayed is one she wrote a week before her death:

> I think I'm going to die
> And I really don't know why.
> But look in my eye
> When I tell you good-bye.
> I think I'm going to die.

Called at Rushton

Marilyn McCusker, a woman who had sued to get her job in the Rushton coal mine, was killed one afternoon this fall at the end of the eight-to-four shift. She was working as a roof-bolter helper at the time—placing long bolts in holes that a miner operating a squat little forty-thousand-dollar machine drills straight up every four feet to tighten the roof. The roof had been rebolted in an intersection next to a mined-out area when Mrs. McCusker noticed some movement—what miners mean when they say "the roof's working." The roof-bolter made it out, but Mrs. McCusker was pinned under an eighteen-foot section of roof. She was not crushed. No bones were broken. The death certificate said that she died of shock and asphyxiation. Although the reports being prepared by various agencies on the accident have not been completed, it is believed that one of Mrs. McCusker's knees was bent upward against her windpipe. She had been a miner for almost exactly two years. In 1975, she and three other women had sued the Rushton Mining Company, claiming that they had been denied employment on the basis of their sex. The suit was filed only a few months after Marilyn McCusker, then Marilyn Williams, moved to the central Pennsylvania mining country from Utica, New York. The possibility of applying for work at Rushton had been brought up by a friend named Mary Louise Carson, who was prompted to apply because her sister-in-law was already working as a coal miner in another mine and her husband was not working at all. "If you don't have money, you die in this country," Mary Louise Carson said later. "You can't survive."

People who knew Marilyn Williams at the time say that she probably went with Mary Louise Carson to file a coal-miner application because she was game. "She was the sort of person who'd say, 'Sure—OK' if someone got the idea at the last minute to go to the movies," one of them said recently. As it happens, the movie house in Coalport, where she lived, has been closed for years. Moving to Coalport could qualify as game in itself. It is a small, gray town in a part of central Pennsylvania where the towns tend to be small and gray and to have movie houses that have been closed for years. Just outside Coalport, the view of the surrounding mountains can be spectacular, unless it happens to include one whose top was lopped off by a strip miner who managed to go bankrupt before the time came to reclaim the mined-out land. From the main street of Coalport—a line of dark taverns and fitfully open stores—the mountain that dominates the view is a mountain of spoil left from an abandoned mine called the Sunshine. Apparently, Marilyn Williams moved to Coalport because it happened to be the hometown of a fellow worker at a Masonic nursing home in Utica, where both of them were employed as nurse's aides, and she happened to be at a point in her life when she wanted to live anywhere but Utica, New York. She was thirty, divorced, rather high-strung. She spoke very quickly, and she was quick to smile. She looked, according to one friend, "like someone's third-grade teacher." She brought her son, Michael, then twelve, along with her. A visitor standing on the main street of town can easily assume that the story of postwar Coalport in-migration begins and ends with their arrival.

Mary Louise Carson had heard, apparently incorrectly, that the federal government had told Rushton to begin hiring some women. To a lot of working people in towns like Coalport, male as well as female, it must sometimes seem as if something on the order of federal intervention is necessary to get a job in a deep mine. It is com-

mon for people to put in an application at several mines—mines
that might be forty or fifty miles from where they live—and then
wait to be "called." A conversation in one of the dark taverns of
Coalport or Osceola Mills or Houtzdale sometimes sounds like the
conversation at a conference of Baptist preachers—the man at the
end of the bar talking about the time he was called at Bethlehem,
the bartender speaking of someone who was called at Barnes &
Tucker. The deep mines in central Pennsylvania are unionized, and
the union scale for a coal miner is about nine and a half dollars an
hour. The only other hourly wages in the area that approach nine
and a half dollars are paid in strip mines—where job security is limited not only by the lack of a union but by the tendency of strip-
mine entrepreneurs to take leave of the business without much
warning. For some years, the coal industry has not been thriving, a
condition that just about everyone in central Pennsylvania—labor
and management and chamber of commerce and bystander—tends
to blame on outlandish restrictions by the Environmental Protection
Agency. These days, it is not uncommon for someone to have had
applications on file with four or five mines for years. Alan McCusker,
the young man Marilyn Williams married a year or so after she arrived in Coalport, says that he had an application in at Rushton
himself at the time his future wife applied. Rushton is the deep mine
most convenient to Coalport. It also has the stability that comes
with being what is known as a captive mine—a mine whose entire
production is used by its owner, in this case a utility in the northeastern part of the state called Pennsylvania Power & Light. Alan
McCusker was never called at Rushton. The response to the application of Marilyn Williams and the women who went with her was
more clear-cut: the superintendent of the Rushton mine, Blair
Rickard, told them that there would be women miners in his mine
over his dead body.

Eventually, the mining company settled the suit out of court,
agreeing to hire all four women and to award them back pay. While
the case was in court, there were rumors that the plaintiffs had been

recruited by a lawyer from some women's liberation outfit, but the rumors were untrue. They had found their own lawyer, Mary Ellen Krober, a young woman from Carlisle who was recommended by a local legal-aid attorney. Their interests were not ideological but financial. Nearly all the women who started working at the Rushton mine in 1977 were the breadwinners of their families. Alan McCusker has worked at a number of jobs, but never at one for a number of years. Bernice Dombroski, who had applied at Rushton without knowing about the suit and was called before the litigants were, is married to a man who is partly disabled and who works only seasonally. "If we had to live on what he makes," she said not long ago, "we'd starve to death."

Before the settlement, Marilyn McCusker worked for a while in a local nursing home. Mary Louise Carson worked in a clothing factory. Neither of them made more than the minimum wage. "A lot of people in the sewing factory said I was crazy to apply to the mine," Mrs. Carson told a visitor recently. "But the sewing factory was a sweatshop. I heard of people there having nervous breakdowns. You don't know what a woman has to do." Spending all day at a sewing machine can make a coal miner's job seem almost liberating— particularly when it pays nine and a half dollars an hour. "I like it down there," Mrs. Carson, the only original litigant left among the three women who now work at Rushton, said recently. "It's a different world." It's a dirty world, of course—so dirty that coal miners have to use Ivory dishwashing liquid rather than bath soap when they finish a shift. It is often uncomfortable. It is always dangerous. Within the first few months at Rushton, Marilyn McCusker's nose was broken by a pipe and her arm was wrenched when her shovel got caught in the belt that carries the coal out of the mine. Alan McCusker says that his wife was going to quit coal mining as soon as he completed a house he was building for the family across the road from where they lived, but he also says that her proudest day was the day when, after a year at Rushton, she won her mining papers and was able to trade the yellow hat of a "greenie" for the black hat of a certified miner. "She loved it from the first day," he said recently. "It's dirty and dark and rats running around all over the place. All her life, though, basically she'd never had a good day's pay. She was just doing menial work. When she came back the first day, she was smiling from ear to ear. She just loved it."

Even when the suit was settled, Blair Rickard never pretended to welcome women in his coal mine. Although Rushton picked up a small reputation for innovation a couple of years ago by experimenting with an "autonomous mining" program that gave work crews some say in how the day's work should be approached—the program was eventually voted out by the union—Blair Rickard is an old-fashioned mine superintendent. Except for one six-month period spent wiring buildings, he has been in coal mining since he got out of high school, in 1937. He has worked as a miner "at the face" with a pick and shovel. He has worked as a foreman. He has run his own small mine. He is known as a strong churchgoer who believes that women would have no place in a coal mine even if they could do a man's work. "Honest to God, I love the woman," he said recently. "I respect the woman as a lady. I kind of look up to 'em. I know they have to find their way in society, but there's just oodles of jobs for women—like office jobs. I'm a hundred percent against 'em in a coal mine. They just can't do the work. We're paying them women to get them off our back is all we're doing."

These days, coal is gouged out of the face of a mine with a ferocious device called a continuous-mining machine, rather than with a pick and shovel. The women who work underground claim that the physical labor is no more strenuous than moving aside a couch for a vacuum cleaner or lugging around a husky three-year-old. "It just ain't hard work," according to Mary Ann Baum, a woman who worked at Rushton until recently. Male miners, though, tend to believe that women cannot do the job—cannot handle the sections of tree trunk that are used as props for the roof of the mine, cannot run complicated equipment like the continuous miner, cannot carry their share of rail or heavy pipe. (Blair Rickard acknowledges that there are a few jobs that women could do as well as men if only they were willing to work—including bolter helper, the job Marilyn McCusker was doing when she was killed—but he believes them incapable of running machines, and he doesn't think many of them really are willing to work.) A lot of people in central Pennsylvania, male and female, agree with Rickard that a coal mine is simply no place for a woman. "I wouldn't let my wife down there," a former miner who has sons in the mines said recently. "I'd break her leg first." Some people believe that, apart from the matter of efficiency and propriety, having women in a coal mine is bad luck—or worse luck, really, since working eight hours a day in a place where people are regularly killed or crippled might be considered bad luck to begin with. Miners have generally accepted the fact that equal-employment laws mean the inevitability of women in the mines— many male miners, in fact, have been helpful to the women who do get hired—but nobody pretends that male miners are much more enthusiastic about the presence of women than Rickard is. "Some of the men are OK," Mrs. Carson has said. "But some of 'em goes up your one side and down the other. They don't want us in there."

"As far as Rushton's concerned, the women's always going to have problems," Bernice Dombroski says. She blames the problems not on the men but on Blair Rickard. Women who work at Rushton claim that in matters like shift assignments or certification for mining papers, Rickard favors his friends and relatives over anyone else, and anyone else over a woman. They claim that the United Mine Workers of America local at Rushton is not very useful in protecting their rights—and is too cozy with management in general. ("Rushton's more like a scab hole.") However angry women like Bernice Dombroski and Mary Louise Carson may sound at times, though, they do not think of themselves as militants—and certainly not as feminists. "I believe if a woman does the work she ought to get the pay," Mrs. Carson says. "But I don't believe in women football players or homosexuals or abortion." Although Bernice Dombroski has a sweatshirt that says WHEN GOD CREATED MAN, SHE WAS ONLY JOKING, the sweatshirt is itself meant as a joke. "I don't go along with women's lib or homosexuals or nothing like that," she says. "They're for a lot of things I'm against."

Although Rickard cannot find anything to compliment about Marilyn McCusker's productivity as a coal miner beyond a pleasing personality and a good attendance record, he admits that Bernice Dombroski is one female miner who does her job as well as a man. "I can throw them props as good as any man down there," she said recently. "One of the guys taught me how to sling them over your shoulder." She is a blunt, rough-talking woman who grew up in Coalport, one of sixteen children of a miner at the old Sunshine mine. She is accustomed to taking care of herself. She was Marilyn McCusker's best friend at the mine ("We had a lot in common; we both had hard lives"), and she urged upon her friend the Bernice Dombroski method for getting along with abusive fellow workers—"You give it back, they'll leave you alone." She gets along with her fellow workers pretty well herself—partly, she says, "because I talk like them and I can cuss them out." Her response to hearing that some miners' wives are concerned about their husbands' working in such close quarters with women is likely to be rude remarks about how few of the men she works with would provide significant temptation. Before Mrs. Dombroski started working at Rushton, Blair Rickard lectured his miners about the necessity of modifying their language a bit. "Wouldn't you know it?" he said recently. "It wasn't two weeks before I had her in this office telling her she was embarrassing my men the way she talked." It may have been the first time in the history of the American coal industry that anyone was officially chastised for using strong language in a coal mine.

Alan McCusker stopped work on the new house for a time, but he has now started again. He and his late wife's son, Michael Williams, still live in a small frame house across the road—a house built by McCusker's grandfather, who worked at the Sunshine mine. A couple of weeks after the accident, the mining-company official in charge of workers' compensation phoned to say that he wanted to drop by to explain some differences in the death-benefits claim that arose from McCusker's being a widower rather than a widow. McCusker thought the official meant differences in wording— changing a "his" to a "her" now and then—but it turned out that the difference referred to was a section of the Pennsylvania workers' compensation law that says a widower is entitled to full benefits only if he is incapable of supporting himself and was dependent upon the worker who was killed. McCusker, who is twenty-eight and able-bodied, responded by accusing the company of attempting to treat his wife unequally in death as well as in life. "Marilyn didn't win everything she thought she did," he said. "The legal battle may not be over."

It has been a month since Marilyn McCusker was killed, and the Rushton mine has, of course, long been back in normal operation. The normal operation, though, remains something of a disappointment to Blair Rickard. For some time, the mine has not been meeting his expectations. A bonus plan was put in last spring—a plan that means additional pay for just about everyone in any month when the production of clean coal exceeds about twenty-five hundred tons a day—but the production has met the bonus requirement only once. There have been a lot of equipment breakdowns. There have been the usual problems with absenteeism, particularly on Friday swing shifts. Another miner was killed in July, crushed under a machine he was trying to repair. At times, Rickard connects the problems of the mine with the hiring of women. "It seems to be a jinx," he said recently. "The mine ain't been the same since they came." After Marilyn McCusker's death, Mary Louise Carson says, the mine's front-office secretary asked all the remaining women miners whether or not they intended to quit. "I told her I wasn't planning on it," Mrs. Carson said not long ago. "The men don't quit if one of their buddies gets hurt. If they had the choice—if they could make the money outside—there'd be nobody in that mine."

Resettling the Yangs

Fairfield, Iowa

MARCH 1980

s a refuge, Fairfield, Iowa, has a lot going for it. To Theng Pao Yang and his wife and their four children, who arrived in Fairfield at the beginning of December from Laos by way of a refugee camp in Thailand, it might have looked like any other frigid and startlingly foreign place, but, as the fortunes of Southeast Asian refugees go, the Yang family could have been considered fortunate. The entire state of Iowa seems to have taken upon itself a special responsibility for Southeast Asian refugees. The one state agency among the American organizations resettling refugees from the camps is the Iowa Refugee Service Center. When the nations of the world were trying to decide what to do about the boat people, the governor of Iowa announced that Iowa would take fifteen hundred of them. Iowa's response to reports of widespread starvation among Cambodian refugees in Thailand was to raise more than five hundred thousand dollars in small donations and dispatch what amounted to an Iowa relief column with food and supplies, accompanied by a *Des Moines Register* and *Tribune* reporter to make certain that it reached the people it was intended for. There are, of course, Iowans who believe that the United States should concentrate on the problems of its own citizens instead of worrying so much about displaced Asians—a *Register* poll last year indicated that a shade over half the people in the state were opposed to resettling more boat people in Iowa—but they have not been outspoken about their reservations. The dominant attitude in Iowa toward refugees seems to combine spontaneous generosity and genuine concern and great pride in the leadership Iowa has taken. Asked to account for all of this, Michael Gartner, the editor of both the *Register* and the *Tribune,* tends to smile and say, "Iowa has a better foreign policy than the United States."

Fairfield is a pleasant town of eight thousand people in the southeast corner of the state. It remains financially comfortable through trade with the area's hog-and-grain farmers and the presence of a dozen manufacturing plants and the official business of Jefferson County—conducted out of a magnificent pile of a courthouse that was built in 1891. Fairfield people are accustomed to strangers. In the sixties, the local college, Parsons, was transformed into an education mill that became known nationally as Flunk-Out U. The campus now belongs to Maharishi International University, where students of Transcendental Meditation are said to be instructed in arts that include human levitation—although, as one of the hog-and-grain farmers might say, not so's you'd know it. When the Yangs arrived in Fairfield, there were already three Laotian refugee families in town—ethnic-Lao families from the lowlands—and another arrived a couple of weeks later. The men in the Laotian families were already employed. The older children were in school. Daily English classes had been established for some time in a room at the First Lutheran Church. While the adults learned English, Fairfield volunteers acted as babysitters for their small children.

In Fairfield, it is natural for Christian charity to be channeled through a church. Sponsoring a Southeast Asian refugee family began as a commitment taken on at one church or another, but it quickly turned ecumenical. The sponsorship of the first Laotians to arrive in town—Kesone Sisomphane and his family, who came only last spring—passed from the Episcopal priest to the Lutheran pastor when the Episcopalian moved away. A widower and his children from Vientiane were sponsored by the First United Methodist Church through the Catholic resettlement agency and eventually

decided to attend Sunday services with the Lutherans. Sponsors
shared ideas and problems, and the refugees seemed as compatible as
the sponsors. When congregants of the First Lutheran Church decided to sponsor a refugee family—the family, as it turned out, that
arrived just after the Yangs—the Lutheran pastor, Keith Lingwall,
specifically asked for lowland Lao in order to preserve the homoge-
neity of the group.

The Fairfield church that sponsored the Yang family, First Baptist,
is considerably smaller than the congregations that were already
working together with the Laotians. As an American Baptist rather
than a Southern Baptist congregation, it is not opposed to ecumenism. Its pastor, Lynn Bergfalk—who, like Keith Lingwall, is in his
thirties and bearded and well educated—has served as president of
the Fairfield ministerial alliance. Still, there remain limitations on the
Baptists' ecumenical participation, and there remains in the minds of
other Fairfield Christians some residue of the old notion that Baptists tend to stand a bit apart. Among the refugees in Fairfield, Theng
Pao Yang and his family stood more than a bit apart. Although they
came from Laos, the Yangs were not lowland-Lao speakers but
Hmong—members of a mountain tribe that has had trouble with
the dominant Lao for as long as anybody can remember.

In Laos, the Hmong were always called Meo, which means
"barbarians"—a name they understandably despise. The Hmong
originated in southern China, and over the past century or so many
of them have migrated into the highlands of northern Laos and
Thailand. To readers of *National Geographic* articles, they were mountain tribesmen in intricate ceremonial costumes—deft with the
crossbow, sure-footed on mountain paths, skilled at coaxing a steady
opium crop out of the steep hillsides, persistent in their animism
despite some conversions to Buddhism and Christianity. To military
men in Laos, the Hmong had a considerable reputation as guerrilla
fighters; there were Hmong forces in the Pathet Lao and in the
Royal Laotian Army and particularly in the secret army financed by
the Central Intelligence Agency. In Laos, the Hmong have some-

times been considered naïve hillbillies—people subjected to ridicule or harassment or even extortion.

To refugee workers—such as those in the American Baptist Churches resettlement office, which received the Yangs as part of its refugee allotment from Church World Service—the Hmong are known for being close-knit, even clannish, people who seek each other out through a tribal communication system that sometimes seems to work almost as well in California or Pennsylvania as it did in the mountains of Southeast Asia. The Yangs had requested resettlement in Iowa because of a friend they mentioned as living in the northeast part of the state—in a town that did not, as it happened, have a Baptist church to act as a sponsor for the family. In Fairfield, a hundred and fifty miles to the south, First Baptist, which had sponsored a Burmese technician and his wife who immigrated in 1975, was eager to sponsor a refugee family. Although the Baptist resettlement office was aware that some antipathy exists between Hmong and Lao, the antipathy had never been considered serious enough to require segregation. The presence of any Laotians in Fairfield—their ethnic background was unknown to the resettlement office—had been considered an attraction: it meant that the town was used to refugees and had some facilities in place for them.

No one in Fairfield knew much about the Hmong. The Iowa Refugee Service Center, which does employment and social-service work among refugees as well as resettling, had pamphlets on Hmong culture and a Hmong outreach worker on its staff and knowledge of some Hmong families in Ottumwa, only twenty-five miles from Fairfield, but First Baptist was not in touch with the Iowa Refugee Service Center. There did not seem to be any need for out-of-town assistance. Theng Pao Yang spoke and understood some Lao, so communication was possible through the Laotians who were available every day at English class. A lot of communication was possible through sign language. The church installed the Yangs in a small bungalow that was empty while on the market to be sold. The two older children, an eight-year-old boy named So and a six-year-old girl named Bay, were enrolled at Roosevelt Elementary School and given individual tutoring in English. Theng Pao Yang's wife, Yi Ly, was taken to the doctor for a checkup. The Burmese who had immigrated five years ago began taking the family to the supermarket once a week. After a week or two, the main burden of transporting the family and looking after its daily needs passed from Lynn Bergfalk to a warm and cheerful couple from the congregation—John Heckenberg, a recently retired postal worker, and his wife, Madelon, both of whom had spent the first thirty or so years of their lives on an Iowa farm. John Heckenberg drove the Yangs to English class. Madelon Heckenberg did the Yangs' family laundry in her automatic washer. Even without a common language, Madelon Heckenberg and the Yangs had what she calls "regular laugh sessions."

What Madelon Heckenberg knew about Hmong in general she heard from Kesone Sisomphane, the best English speaker among the Laotian refugees, who told her that they were rather primitive—a remark she took as "sort of a put-down." Other people active in Fairfield refugee work took similar remarks as a natural enough effort on the part of the Lao to distance themselves from people who might make a bad impression on the hosts—or even as a way of pointing out that adjustment might be more difficult for people who had never driven a car or operated a typewriter or spoken any French. To the English teacher, Barbara Hill, it appeared that the other Laotians were trying to help Theng Pao Yang and his family—trying to include them in the joking that sometimes went on in class, trying to commiserate with them when they were sad. Theng Pao was often sad. In English class, he sometimes began sobbing.

One of the Lao explained to Mrs. Hill that Theng Pao was sad about having to leave his parents behind in the refugee camp. It was apparent that the contrast between life in Fairfield and the life the Yangs had left behind was strong enough to be upsetting. The Yangs had been in a refugee camp for five years. The biographical document that had been sent from Thailand on the Yangs summed up the schooling of all members of the family in one word: none. Mrs. Hill, through Kesone Sisomphane, explained to Yi Ly, through Theng Pao, that nursing a child publicly might be considered provocative rather than natural by some American men—an explanation Kesone Sisomphane carried out with dramatic warnings about locking doors and pulling shades. When So and Bay were being registered in school, Theng Pao seemed bewildered, and eventually walked off to squat silently in the hall. Although So, who was more outgoing than Bay, seemed to be responding particularly well to Roosevelt, the two younger children seemed frightened of everybody except their mother—a fact that made for some disturbance in the English class. At first, Mrs. Hill's main concern was for Yi Ly—who appeared troubled, and burdened with her children—but gradually it turned toward Theng Pao.

Although Yi Ly began joining in the classroom joking, Theng Pao often seemed to retreat within himself, chewing nervously on his pencil. He sometimes seemed upset by having the members of his family separated for any reason. He said, through the Lao, that he didn't understand why he couldn't have a telephone. (First Baptist had decided that it would be wasteful to pay for installing a telephone in a house that might be sold at any time—particularly considering the fact that the Yangs could not speak English and might even be alarmed by a wrong number.) An attempt to find Theng Pao a job at a local plant that employed two of the Laotians as sweepers proved unsuccessful. The personnel man found him distracted and asked Mrs. Hill if there was anything wrong with him. Mrs. Hill did not believe that there was anything wrong with Theng Pao—or anything serious enough to bring to the attention of Lynn Bergfalk. Theng Pao was, after all, in a difficult position—suddenly placed in a strange country, where he could communicate with his hosts only through a third language. He presumably did have relatives who had been left behind. He was less equipped to deal with the shock of modern America than the urban Lao were. Mrs. Hill simply thought he would be slower to adapt. Lynn Bergfalk had seen Theng Pao cry a couple of times, but why shouldn't a man in his situation cry? With the Heckenbergs, the Yangs seemed all smiles and genuine affection. "They just smiled," Madelon Heckenberg has said. "It was easy to work with them, because they appreciated what you did for them. That family wanted to please more than anybody I ever heard of."

On a cold Thursday in January, Su Thao, the Hmong outreach worker at the Iowa Refugee Service Center, happened to be calling on a Hmong family in northeast Iowa. He was shown a letter from Theng Pao Yang, who had written that he was homesick and wanted to move in order to be with other Hmong. The next day, Su Thao drove to Fairfield to look in on the Yangs. Theng Pao cried when he saw Su Thao. He told Su Thao that he wanted to move to California, where he had a first cousin. Su Thao tried to comfort Theng Pao. He said there were seven hundred and fifty Hmong in Iowa, some of them as close as Ottumwa. He told him that the people at First Baptist were obviously attentive and caring sponsors. He told him that the Yangs would be wise to remain in Fairfield, where there were people committed to helping them, at least until Theng Pao learned some English. Su Thao did not consider Theng Pao's mood alarming. He had seen a lot of homesick refugees. He had seen a lot of refugees who did not have sponsors as attentive as the people from First Baptist. The family he had been calling on when he heard about the Yangs had been brought to Iowa by a man and wife who then decided to get a divorce. Su Thao left Theng Pao his office telephone number and his home telephone number.

The Tuesday after Su Thao's visit turned out to be a day with a lot of changes in the Yangs' regular schedule. The eight-year-old boy, So, was taken to the dentist to have a tooth pulled. In English class, Mrs. Hill announced that the students would begin coming at two different times so that she could divide up what amounted to the elementary and intermediate speakers. That evening, the Heckenbergs, who had learned of an out-of-town funeral they would have to attend, realized that the laundry they would have ordinarily delivered the next day might be needed before they returned from their trip; John Heckenberg drove over to the Yangs' with it. He found Yi

Ly distraught. Her son, So, was lying on the living-room sofa. The boy's eyes were closed. He was cold to the touch. Theng Pao and Bay seemed to be moaning or grieving in the bedroom. Heckenberg, seeing no light on in nearby houses, drove home, and his wife phoned Lynn Bergfalk, who phoned for an ambulance. Theng Pao and Bay turned out to have been moaning not out of grief but because of serious injury. They were rushed to the Jefferson County Hospital and then taken by air ambulance to a hospital in Iowa City. So was pronounced dead at the scene.

It was not at all clear what had happened. Yi Ly, of course, spoke only Hmong. Finally, she pulled Madelon Heckenberg out of the crowd in the bungalow's tiny living room and led her down into the basement. Some of the Yangs' possessions were on the floor: five dollars in American bills that had been cut up with scissors, a Hmong flute that had been shattered, a knife whose blade had been broken. Over a pipe, there were six cords with nooses tied in them.

Yi Ly told two or three stories—in sign language then, in Hmong later to Su Thao, who had hurried down from Des Moines to interpret—but the one the Department of Criminal Investigation and the county attorney came to believe was that the entire Yang family, upon the decision of Theng Pao and with the acquiescence of Yi Ly, had tried to commit suicide—with the parents hanging the children who were too young to hang themselves. Apparently, Yi Ly had changed her mind at the last minute and had finally managed to cut everyone down—too late for So. If John Heckenberg had not happened to walk in with the laundry, the authorities believed, it might have been too late for Theng Pao and Bay as well.

Theng Pao, rambling and incoherent in his hospital room, had even more stories than Yi Ly. He said that his dead sister had asked him to join her. He said Jesus had given him orders. He said one of the children had broken the case of First Baptist's tape player, and the Yangs were afraid their sponsors would no longer love them. He said that he had read in a book that they would all die anyway. Eventually,

Theng Pao and Yi Ly offered a story that caused consternation among the churchgoing people of Fairfield: they said that Theng Pao had acted because of a threat from the lowland Lao. The threat they related was specific. Theng Pao would be killed. The Lao men would sleep with Yi Ly. The children would be divided up among the Lao families. Yi Ly would be married to the widower from Vientiane whom the Methodists had brought to Fairfield.

To Lynn Bergfalk, it was the first explanation that made sense. "The whole situation, from my perspective, is that the hanging is totally inexplicable unless there was an external factor like a death threat," he told the local paper. "They were a happy family, with no reason to do something like this." To the sponsors of the lowland-Lao families, it was an explanation that made no sense at all. The Lao all denied that anybody had said anything that could even have been misconstrued as a threat. Their sponsors believed them. They pointed out that the Lao had visited the Yangs two or three times, that Theng Pao had used the widower's phone to call his cousin in California, that the Lao families had been present, taking snapshots, when the Yangs were visited by friends from northeast Iowa. The Lao's sponsors were concerned that the Lao were being unfairly maligned and perhaps even endangered: a number of out-of-town Hmong, the noted guerrilla fighters, had begun to show up in Fairfield to see if they could be of assistance. Lynn Bergfalk said it was nonsense for anybody to be concerned about the possibility of retaliation, but for a week or so after the hangings Lao women who were alone while their husbands worked night shifts found themselves with visitors from among the sponsors. Some people in Fairfield thought that what the Baptists had found—during a time when they could be expected to be feeling both grief-stricken and guilty—was not an explanation but a scapegoat. Some Baptists thought that the other sponsors were refusing to consider the possibility that their refugees could lie to them—that Theng Pao and Yi Ly had been telling the truth. As positions hardened, Keith Lingwall, a pastor who is friendly by nature and ecumenical by policy, found himself uncomfortable in the presence of Lynn Bergfalk.

The county attorney of Jefferson County, a young man named Edwin F. Kelly, had a complicated legal situation to deal with. He was satisfied, after a time, that he knew what had happened that night at the Yangs' bungalow, but he was not optimistic about finding out for certain exactly why it happened. He could find no evidence, other than the story told by the Yangs, that a threat had been involved. That still left the question of whether to prosecute Theng Pao and Yi Ly—both of whom had presumably tried to hang their children as well as themselves. Some of the people involved in Iowa refugee work contended that, considering the unchallenged authority of the father in a Hmong household, Yi Ly could hardly have been expected to do other than her husband had instructed her to do. Kelly believed that both Theng Pao and Yi Ly were lacking in what lawyers call *mens rea*—criminal intent. There was another consideration that weighed heavily with Kelly. Whatever crime had been committed had been committed against the children, and Kelly believed that the deportation of the Yang family—an inevitable consequence of a felony conviction—would bring the victims not justice but simply more suffering.

Among the material furnished him by the Iowa Refugee Service Center, Kelly came across a paper by a San Francisco psychologist named J. Donald Cohon which dealt with instances of "trauma syndrome" found in refugees throughout the world. Kelly underlined some of the symptoms of trauma syndrome that were familiar from the investigation of what Theng Pao had been like around the time of the hanging—paranoid tendencies, for instance, and inability to concentrate and loss of appetite and fear that something could happen to members of his family. Kelly's presentation to the grand jury stressed the possibility that Theng Pao had been suffering from trauma syndrome, and that, Theng Pao being Yi Ly's only source of information in Fairfield, his version of reality had become her own. The grand jury returned no indictment. The Yangs were resettled among Hmong in another part of the state, in an arrangement that included some outside supervision of their children. It seemed a humane, Iowa sort of solution—what Keith Lingwall has called "a kind door-closing on a sad and tragic situation." There were presumably people in Fairfield who believed that the Yangs had got off too easy, but, like the people in Iowa with doubts about whether refugees should be there in the first place, they did not make a public issue of it. Everybody seemed satisfied. The way some of the Baptists would describe Kelly's solution, though, was not as "a kind door-closing" but as "a convenient answer that lets everybody off the hook."

"It's easier for everyone else to say 'Let's end this chapter,'" Bergfalk said recently. In the view of some Baptists, the people of Fairfield, comfortable with their humane solution, ended the chapter without investigating thoroughly enough the possibility that Theng Pao Yang was driven to his appalling decision by a threat. Although Lynn Bergfalk has not made any accusations against the Lao families personally, it is apparent to his colleagues in the ministry that he has never accepted Kelly's notion that what Theng Pao did can be explained by a paper written by a psychologist in San Francisco. The reluctance of the Baptists to discount the possibility that the Lao played some role in So Yang's death was bolstered by the Hmong who came to Fairfield just after the incident. To them, the threat Theng Pao described had a dreadful resonance. "It's the sort of thing that would happen at home," Tou-Fu Vang, a Hmong leader, said recently. To Tou-Fu Vang, the fact that the Lao visited the Yang family is not an indication that they were friendly, but an indication that they had designs on Yi Ly. Why else would Lao visit Hmong?

Publicly, there is no argument in Fairfield about the Yangs. Privately, there are hard feelings. A Methodist refers to the Yangs' sponsors as "those Baptist people" in the same tone Lao might use to speak of Hmong. A little girl who goes to the Methodist church is upset because a Baptist friend says, "That old man your church brought caused all the trouble." A clergyman like Keith Lingwall is troubled because he realizes that the door never quite closed. "I need to go visit with Lynn," Lingwall said not long ago. He did, but the visit did not change the views of either of them. "The truth, no matter how unpleasant, has to be faced," Lynn Bergfalk has said. There are expressions of compassion in Fairfield for the anguish the Baptists must have suffered over the death of So Yang, but there is also talk about what the Baptists might have done wrong—the possibility that they "smothered" the Yangs or treated them like pets, the possibility that Theng Pao's self-respect was threatened, the possibility that the Yangs were insulted rather than pleased at, say, having their laundry done for them. There are people in Fairfield who, out of irritation with the Baptists or a paucity of Christian charity or a sincere belief that they are facing an unpleasant truth, say that So Yang would be alive today if the Baptists had been willing to risk having to pay an extra installation charge on a telephone.

Nobody knows, of course, whether a telephone would have made any difference. Nobody knows what caused Theng Pao to decide that he and his family should die. In Fairfield, though, there is no shortage of theories. It may have been, some people say, that Theng Pao, in addition to his other problems, was suffering from an awful failure in communication. What he heard from his hosts, after all, had to be translated from English into Lao, a language that Theng Pao may have understood imperfectly, by someone who only began learning English last spring. Perhaps Kesone Sisomphane's dramatic message about breast-feeding gradually grew in Theng Pao's mind into the impression that his wife was going to be abducted. Perhaps, through the muddle of languages or his own disorientation, what Theng Pao understood from the changes announced in English class that day was that he had somehow been rejected as a student of English. Perhaps the notion that everyone would die anyway had come from a Lao New Testament Bergfalk had given him. It is possible to envision Theng Pao as someone trapped in a horrifying isolation—receiving information only through the short circuits of half-understood languages and his own confusion, communicating only through people he mistrusted. It is possible to envision him entertaining friends or talking to his first cousin in California on the telephone. It may be that Theng Pao Yang, bewildered and unsure of the language, understood a joke, perhaps even a cruel joke, as a threat. It may be that Theng Pao was, in fact, threatened with death by the Lao. It may be that he was suffering from trauma syndrome.

"We were doing everything we knew how," Madelon Heckenberg said recently. "Maybe we just didn't have the know-how." Lynn Bergfalk has given a lot of thought to what the First Baptist Church might have done differently in its sponsorship of the Yangs—whether finding a Hmong interpreter at the beginning would have made any difference, whether searching out the Hmong families in Ottumwa would have made any difference. He has given a lot of thought to whether or not a tendency to believe in the likelihood of some external factor like a threat is simply a way of dealing with feelings of guilt. National agencies involved with the resettlement of the Yangs are considering the possibility that Hmong ought to be settled only in clusters and that sponsors ought to be more carefully briefed on the cultural background of arriving refugees and that refugee agencies ought to figure out how to communicate with each other more effectively. The people in Fairfield who noticed some signs of stress in Theng Pao wonder what might have happened if they had expressed serious concern to his sponsors, who saw only smiles. "We every last one of us feel guilty about this," Barbara Hill said recently. It may be, of course, that there is no reason for anyone to feel guilty. No isolated Hmong has ever before attempted suicide. What would the Baptists have done differently if they had been experts in Hmong culture? Perhaps what happened to the Yangs was caused by something from their past in Asia. Perhaps it came from a combination of the reasons people in Fairfield have offered—or from none of them at all. Barbara Hill sometimes thinks that the Asians she teaches are not as intent as Westerners on finding reasons for everything. "We can't tolerate a void," she said not long ago. "We have to find a cause. It may be that we're trying to find reasons for something Theng Pao never intended there to be a reason for."

Among Friends

Savannah, Georgia

FEBRUARY 1981

P ublicly, George Mercer IV was reported missing on February 7, 1980. His picture ran above a small item in both the *Savannah Morning News* and the *Savannah Evening Press*. The item said he had been missing since January 29. It described him as being twenty-two years old, five feet eight inches tall, about a hundred and fifty-five pounds. It asked anyone having information about him to telephone the Savannah Police Department. The picture showed a young man with the sort of thick mustache and blow-dried hair that make a lot of twenty-two-year-olds seen at racquetball clubs or singles bars or pleasure-boat marinas look pretty much alike to the unpracticed eye. The item in the two papers said little about George Mercer IV beyond giving his physical description, but not many people in Savannah needed to be told who he was. The Mercers have long been a prominent family in Savannah—a city particularly conscious of prominent families. In Atlanta, a successful businessman who wants to upgrade his background beyond simply awarding posthumous commissions to a few Civil War ancestors may allow his neighbors to infer that his family was originally from Savannah, Georgia's first settlement. The Mercers are the sort of family he would be trying to suggest—the sort of family whose discussions of military forebears tend to focus not on the Civil War but on the American Revolution. The Mercers are among the families that people in Savannah sometimes allow themselves to refer to as "the bluebloods"—a phrase that would be difficult to utter without a smile in Atlanta. Bluebloods still have enough power to be taken seriously in Savannah, partly because Savannah has been the sort of place that respects their credentials, partly because Savannah has not been the kind of place that attracts a lot of ambitious newcomers who might shoulder them aside. Until their family company, which manufactured Great Dane truck trailers, was bought up by a con-glomerate several years ago, the Mercers were one of Savannah's major industrial employers. George Mercer III, who did not remain with Great Dane after the purchase, is the chairman of the board of Savannah's Memorial Hospital and a former member of the Chat-ham County Commission. Although no one named Mercer is a force in the business life of Savannah these days, the Mercers remain the Mercers—stalwarts of the Oglethorpe Club, the kind of family that can ordinarily sort out any difficulty with a telephone call. It could be assumed by readers of the *Savannah Morning News* and *Eve-ning Press* that the police would spare no effort in trying to find George Mercer IV. As it happened, there was another agency inter-ested in the search for George Mercer IV—the Federal Bureau of Investigation. The FBI had reason to believe that he had been kid-napped.

On River Street, where bars and restaurants have opened in re-stored warehouses in the past several years, FBI agents were already showing bartenders a photograph of George Mercer IV. The people George Mercer IV went around with often ended up on River Street late in the evening—sometimes early in the evening. "They have a lot of time on their hands," someone who knows them said recently. Some of Mercer's friends were from his childhood—people who had gone to the same private schools and the same debutante parties—and some were just the people a single young man might meet over a pitcher of beer on River Street or at a party after a rugby match or during the quiet exchange of marijuana that young men with time on their hands think of as routine these days. The time they put in on River Street—or in similar bars near Armstrong

State College, on the south side of Savannah—was not a matter of respite from working their way up in their chosen fields. Most of them had not got around to choosing a field. They tended to be young men who had put in a semester of college here and a semester of college there, but not enough semesters to have reached the point of selecting a major. Even those who still had recourse to the family's refrigerator or its speedboats needed spending money, but the jobs they took to get it tended to be temporary or seasonal or part-time. Their ambitions for the future often seemed to settle on schemes for getting rich rather quickly, perhaps through being on the ground floor of some technological breakthrough in communications. For a while, George Mercer IV and a childhood friend talked of opening a videodisc outlet in Atlanta. They also talked about obtaining the Southeast regional franchise for a new electronic method of producing advertising spots.

George Mercer IV had a lot of enthusiasm for the schemes. His friends thought of him as rather gullible. He had been slow in school, with learning problems that included dyslexia. Once, when he was putting in a semester or so at LaGrange College, someone matched up the information that he liked to compose songs on the guitar with the information that his great-uncle was the songwriter Johnny Mercer, and the publicity resulted in the scheduling of a couple of public appearances. At the last minute, though, Mercer withdrew. He had decided he wasn't ready. His father diagnosed the problem as the sort of preperformance nervousness he calls "buck fever." After LaGrange, Mercer tended to play the guitar in public only when there were just four or five people left at the party. He spent some time at Armstrong State and at the night school of the University of Georgia, in Athens. Toward the end of 1979, while back in Savannah living with his parents, he got a job selling vacuum cleaners. It may not have appeared to be an appropriate job for a Mercer, but, as it happened, George Mercer IV seemed to enjoy selling vacuum cleaners. Some of his friends thought that the job had done a lot for George's self-confidence. His father agreed. He was hoping that sooner or later George Mercer IV might move from selling vacuum cleaners to selling Great Dane trailers. Then George Mercer IV disappeared.

Demands for ransom came almost immediately. There were notes. There were telephone calls. The instructions tended to be complicated, even bizarre. George Mercer III was instructed to draw a circle in orange spray paint at a certain intersection to indicate his cooperation. There were instructions to take the ransom—forty-two thousand dollars—in a small motorboat down the Ogeechee River, flying a flag with a yellow triangle sewn onto a field of green. At one point, the ransom was actually left in a wooded area, but nobody picked it up. When the item reporting George Mercer IV missing appeared in the *Savannah Morning News* and *Evening Press*, FBI agents did not even know whether he was dead or alive—but they did have a pretty good hunch about who might have written the extortion notes. When they walked up and down River Street showing George Mercer's picture, they also carried with them a picture of Michael Harper.

Nobody has ever described Michael Harper as slow or gullible. "He could put anything over on anybody he wanted to," someone who knew him told the investigators. A slim, bearded young man about the age of George Mercer IV, Harper had grown up in a suburb of Savannah, the son of a certified public accountant. He didn't have as many semesters of college as Mercer had, but people he came in contact with regularly described him as brilliant and accomplished—a wizard with electronics and math and computers, an expert at scuba diving and flying airplanes, a talker so glib that he had worked as a disc jockey when barely out of high school. They also described him as somewhat mysterious. No one seemed to know precisely where he lived. The jobs he mentioned holding ran from assistant manager of a fast-food chicken outlet to operator of what he described as a hush-hush project at Hunter Army Airfield called Quest Laboratories. The get-rich-quick schemes he discussed with friends were more complicated than opening a videodisc outlet—shadowy mail-order deals, for instance, and a plan to use a

Savannah Police Department badge to hoodwink a couple of dope dealers out of some marijuana. One of Harper's schemes landed him in jail. In 1974, when he was only seventeen, he had been sentenced to fourteen months for trying to extort forty-five hundred dollars from a former neighbor by threatening to kill the man and his entire family. Later, in Augusta, he was convicted of theft by deception and given a probated sentence. Roger McLaughlin, one of the FBI agents assigned to the Mercer kidnapping, had worked on the 1974 extortion case, and he thought he recognized Harper's style. Within a couple of days, the FBI had ascertained that Harper had moved back to Savannah from Augusta and that he knew George Mercer IV. They had met at a rugby match.

One of the people who happened to be sitting at the bar of Spanky's, on River Street, when the FBI showed the bartender pictures of George Mercer IV and Michael Harper was Richard Sommers, an ebullient young man who constitutes the photography staff of a weekly Savannah newspaper called the *Georgia Gazette*. The *Gazette* was founded two and a half years ago by a young man named Albert Scardino and his wife, Marjorie, a lawyer who serves as publisher and occasional typesetter. Albert Scardino, who has a graduate degree in journalism from the University of California, had tried freelance writing for a while, had worked for the Associated Press in West Virginia, and had produced a film on the coastal islands of Georgia that was shown on the Public Broadcasting System. For a while, he had tried to raise money—from George Mercer III, among others—for a series of films on wilderness areas around the world. Aside from the journalistic experience he had picked up, Scardino had another qualification for being the founding editor of a weekly newspaper in Savannah—serious Savannah credentials. His father—a urologist named Peter Scardino, who came to Savannah soon after the Second World War—is not merely a prominent doctor but someone widely respected as a leading force in improving the medical standards of the community. Dr. Scardino is not interested in colonial genealogy—he is quick to say that the only revolution his ancestors might have fought in was the one led by Garibaldi—and he is not the sort of man who would spend much time at any club not organized around the subject of urology. Still, his badges of acceptance in Savannah include membership in the Oglethorpe Club. For years, he and his wife have served on some of the same committees the Mercers serve on and have attended some of the same parties the Mercers attended. One of Albert Scardino's younger brothers grew up with George Mercer IV.

Although a lot of the weekly newspapers that have sprung up in the past decade seem designed specifically for the editors' contemporaries—or for some mythical twenty-nine-year-old purchaser of stereo equipment—the *Georgia Gazette* was founded to appeal to a general readership basically defined by its dissatisfaction with the commonly owned *Savannah Morning News* and *Evening Press*. In Savannah, the *News-Press* is widely described as innocuous or undistinguished; a contemporary of Albert Scardino is more likely to refer to it as "a Mickey Mouse operation." Albert and Marjorie Scardino hoped that after a few years of weekly publication the *Gazette* might gradually increase its frequency until it became a daily alternative to the *News-Press*. From the start, the *Gazette* did not grow at the pace the Scardinos had envisioned. Capital was a problem. They did manage one business coup, though, which promised to buy them some time for building advertising and circulation: in January 1979 the *Gazette* replaced the *Evening Press* as what is known in Georgia as the sheriff's gazette—the newspaper designated to carry the advertisements that lawyers in the county place to satisfy requirements of public notice. The sheriff, one of the three county officials empowered to decide which paper is designated, had persuaded a probate judge to go along with a switch to the *Gazette*—either because the sheriff was impressed by Albert Scardino's arguments about the benefits of encouraging competition or because, as people around the courthouse say, he was irritated at the *Evening Press*. The designation meant thousands of dollars a year in automatic advertising, and the advertising meant a subscription from every lawyer in the county, and the readership of lawyers meant one more sales point to potential advertisers. The *Georgia Gazette* is not the sort of alternative weekly in which official advertisements seem incongruous. It carries conventional business and social news, as well as some pieces that might offend potential advertisers and investors. It has never been known for sensationalism or scatology. Albert Scardino comes to work in a coat and tie. The *Gazette* had obviously taken some care to recognize the value that Savannah places on being respectable—which is why people in Savannah were astounded when Albert Scardino, against the wishes of the Mercer family, published a front-page story on February 11 revealing that George Mercer IV was not merely missing but presumed kidnapped, and that Michael Harper was the chief suspect.

Although the FBI agent at Spanky's had not said why he wanted to know if anybody had seen George Mercer IV or Michael Harper, Richard Sommers could think of only two reasons for the FBI to be involved—a large drug bust or a kidnapping. Sommers had started questioning some of Mercer's friends, and Scardino had bluffed a lot of the rest of the story out of a local police official. Although George Mercer III would not admit that his son had been kidnapped, it was clear that he did not want a story printed. "In the tried-and-true Savannah tradition, he called one of our stockholders," Scardino said later. It was argued, by the stockholder and others, that a story might endanger George Mercer IV if he really had been kidnapped. Albert Scardino was not persuaded. Mercer had been missing for ten days. The FBI was openly looking for him. When Scardino pressed an agent at the Savannah FBI office to say whether a story might be harmful, the agent would only repeat FBI policy about not commenting on a case in progress. Scardino says he could not see the sort of clear and present danger that would have caused him to go along with, say, the embargo on stories about the American embassy employees hiding in the Canadian embassy in Tehran. He telephoned George Mercer III to inform him that the story would be printed and to suggest that the Mercers make some preparation for the press interest that would follow—preparations such as designating a spokesman. The man Albert Scardino was dealing with, after all, was practically a friend of the family. George Mercer III said, as Scardino recalls it, "You'd better quit worrying about a couple of little birds and streams and start worrying about the value of human life."

A lot of people in Savannah thought that Albert Scardino made a mistake in printing the story. They thought that whatever he had learned in journalism school about the people's right to know simply did not apply. Some people thought that Scardino was just trying to make a splash. Some people thought the story might endanger young George Mercer's life. Some people were pretty certain it would endanger Albert Scardino's newspaper. They were amazed that Scardino, whose background had obviously enabled him to understand how the city worked, could have suddenly chosen a course that was so patently self-destructive. The Mercers and those close to them were furious. The Trust Company of Georgia, where people like the Mercers have always done their banking, canceled a large advertising campaign that was about to begin in the *Gazette*. Twenty people wrote angry letters to the editor canceling their subscriptions. Some people pointedly snubbed Albert Scardino on the street. One aunt of George Mercer IV ended an angry telephone conversation with Marjorie Scardino late one night by saying that she hoped the Scardino children would be kidnapped. Albert Scardino heard that a regular subject of conversation at one luncheon table at the Oglethorpe Club was how to put the *Georgia Gazette* out of business.

Some people claimed that the *Gazette* story, aside from any danger it might pose for George Mercer IV, would warn Michael Harper to get out of town, and they may have been right: on the day the story was published, Harper left Savannah. He had the bad luck, though, to hitch a ride with a van that was stopped for speeding. Within a day, he was back in jail—held for a probation violation— and the FBI started amassing enough evidence to charge him with trying to extort forty-two thousand dollars from George Mercer III. Harper admitted nothing. He did say that if the police would let him out of jail he would help look for Mercer—probably in Greenville, South Carolina. Finally, toward the end of April, the police found Mercer themselves—buried in a shallow grave in the woods on the grounds of Armstrong State. He had been shot twice. Michael Harper was charged with murder.

The coroner said that George Mercer IV had probably been killed the first day he was missing. The implication that the *Gazette* story had appeared well after Mercer's death did not do much to reduce animosity toward Albert Scardino. "The real improper thing," Scardino has said, "was not that we endangered his life but that an upstanding, powerful, rich member of the community asked us to do something and we ignored his request." A lot of people in Savannah would probably agree that there was something in the Mercers' anger beyond the genuine concern that any family would have for the safety of a son. Albert Scardino believes that people close to the Mercers were furious not simply because they had been defied but because they had been defied by someone whose family had been accepted into the group of people in Savannah accustomed to sorting out any difficulty with a telephone call. "That was the special betrayal that caused the special animosity," he says. Richard Sommers, who did not grow up with the Mercers and the Scardinos, has a different way of explaining the special animosity. "They didn't consider the crime a crime against society but a crime against them," he said recently. "They wanted it handled their way. We treated it as a crime against society. We made them common."

In July, Albert Scardino learned that at the end of 1980 the legal advertising that had been given to the *Gazette* a year and a half before would revert to the *Evening Press*—cutting the *Gazette*'s annual income by some thirty percent. The official who pushed for the reversion was the same sheriff who had been the *Gazette*'s champion. For a year and a half, of course, the *Evening Press* had been trying to win back the advertising, using every form of pressure at its disposal; the officials in charge of the designation were even lobbied by *News-Press* reporters assigned to cover their activities. Last spring, though, the officials began to receive telephone calls from what one of them has called "surprisingly high places." George Mercer III says he had no part in a campaign to deprive the *Gazette* of legal advertising, but he also acknowledges that he had heard about the telephone calls— made, perhaps, by people he describes as "misguidedly thinking they were representing me." There are, as Mercer suggests, a number of other ways that the reversion can be explained. For a while, Scardino himself had an ornate theory involving the Georgia senatorial election. It may even be, of course, that the sheriff simply changed his mind for sound reasons of public policy—although that interpretation is not bolstered by his refusal to discuss the matter. Albert Scardino now believes that the change was brought about by a combination of factors, but he has become convinced that one of them was a decision made over lunch at the Oglethorpe Club.

This winter, Michael Harper finally went on trial. Just before the trial started, he pleaded guilty to extortion, but he still contended that George Mercer IV had been alive the last time he saw him. According to his defense on the murder charge—revealed by the *Georgia Gazette* just before the trial got under way—everything had flowed from an attempt that he and George Mercer IV made to raise capital for a business they wanted to launch: a custom-stereo-speaker concern called Quest Labs. Harper said that he and Mercer and two other people, whom he refused to name, had tried to raise the capital by buying more than forty thousand dollars' worth of marijuana for resale. They had bought the marijuana on credit, Harper said, but it had been stolen before they could resell it. Under threat of death from the people who wanted their forty-two thousand, the four partners had decided to extort the money from George Mercer's father—with young George himself as a full participant. When the extortion scheme fell apart, Harper said, the four had fled in different directions. Harper calmly, sometimes brilliantly, defended his story on the witness stand. The jury took four hours to convict him of murder. He was sentenced to life imprisonment. Maintaining his innocence to the end, Harper said he could only offer condolences to the Mercer family on George's death. "He was a friend of mine," Harper said.

Not many people in Savannah believed Harper's story. It sounded like a knockoff of the defense in the Bronfman kidnapping. Still, there are a lot of people who don't believe that, as the prosecution maintained, Michael Harper simply kidnapped George Mercer IV and shot him in cold blood to avoid having a prisoner to guard while negotiating the ransom. The *Gazette* coverage has constantly pointed out loose ends in that version of what happened. There are other stories floating around Savannah to explain what might have happened between George Mercer IV, the gullible son of a rich family, and the brilliant but twisted Michael Harper. A lot of them, like a lot of stories that try to explain mysteries these days, have to do with drugs. What makes some people in Savannah feel vulnerable is that George Mercer IV and Michael Harper knew each other at all. George Mercer III still finds it astonishing that the young people Michael Harper came in contact with didn't know or didn't care about his criminal record. Thinking about it recently, a resident of Savannah in his sixties said, "What this business with drugs and the new lifestyle and all that has changed is this: we didn't use to have to worry about our kids' mingling with someone like that."

After a short period of coolness, people close to the Mercers began to treat Dr. Peter Scardino and his wife the way they had treated them before George Mercer IV disappeared. George Mercer III is quick to express his respect for Dr. Scardino. The Scardinos were quick to express their sympathy to the Mercers. Whatever might have been done by relatives of the Mercers, Dr. Scardino has never thought of the Mercers themselves as the sort of people who could tell a mother that they hoped her children would be kidnapped. A few days after the trial, George Mercer III said, "I'm too drained spiritually and mentally and physically to have any animosity toward anybody," but he couldn't speak of Albert Scardino without the animosity's coming to the surface. The family's bitterness toward Scardino had been increased, in fact, by the *Gazette*'s coverage of the trial, which Mercer considered a matter of "gross callousness and insensitivity." Despite prosecution testimony to the contrary, the *Gazette* wrote, investigators had been told that George Mercer IV did some minor dealing in marijuana and perhaps cocaine. Even the *News-Press,* whose coverage of the case had been dominated by politesse (a February feature about George Mercer IV and his friends had been headlined MERCER CALLED "TYPICAL" YOUNG MAN), had been forced to bring up the subject of drugs in covering Michael Harper's defense. A day after the sentencing, the Mercers, who had been dealing with the press through a family spokesman, asked a local television reporter they knew to come to their house with a film crew. Mrs. Mercer read a statement saying that their son had not been involved in drugs and could not have been involved in any schemes with Michael Harper. After she had read the statement, Mrs. Mercer added, "I would like to say that George was not a friend of this man."

The Mystery of Walter Bopp

Tucson, Arizona

MAY 1981

What happened to Walter Bopp is a mystery. In fact, the more that is known about what happened to him, the more mysterious it becomes. The first incident did not seem mysterious at all. In the fall of 1979, Walter Bopp, a vigorous man in his late seventies, was attacked and presumably robbed in downtown Tucson—right in front of the business he and his wife had founded in 1934 as the first health-food store in the city. The incident did not make the newspapers. Tucson is one of those middle-size Sun-belt cities which are becoming accustomed to the routine muggings and burglaries that a few years ago were associated with the huge old industrial cities of the Northeast. It is no longer unusual for residents of Tucson to own a sophisticated burglar-alarm system or a gun or even, as Walter Bopp did, an attack dog. The second incident—a house fire last spring which the fire department blamed on an electrical short circuit—would probably have gone unreported as well except that when firemen reached the cellar they found, to their understandable dismay, a supply of dynamite and blasting caps that, according to a department spokesman, could have caused a large enough explosion to obliterate Bopp's house, all the firemen in it, and a couple of neighboring houses. The mystery of why someone would store dynamite in his basement seemed to be cleared up when Bopp explained that it was from a nonproducing mine he had operated near Arivaca—a tiny gold- and silver-mining town about an hour in the direction of the Mexican border. Last December, though, Bopp was involved in an incident that was not simply mysterious in itself but suffused the previous incidents with mystery. On a Saturday morning, someone phoned Bopp's second store, on East Speedway Boulevard, and informed a clerk that the proprietor had met with an accident and could be found in the back storeroom. Walter Bopp had been bound with tape and badly beaten the night before. He had serious facial bruises, several broken ribs, and a broken pelvis. His attack dog had been killed by having its belly slit open. His pickup truck had been driven to the downtown store and then set on fire. Both stores had been gone through, but no money was missing.

Bopp claimed that all the incidents were related—that the fire had been caused by arson rather than a short circuit, that the mugging a year earlier had been not a simple mugging but an act of terrorism. He even implied that he knew who was to blame—but that was as far as he would go in helping police identify his tormentors. He wouldn't say who and he wouldn't say why. "It's the same people," he was quoted as telling his interrogators. "I don't want to say anything more." Two weeks later, just after Bopp was released from the hospital, it was reported that someone had backed a truck up to his Speedway store and was presumably loading something into it while colleagues stood by with what looked like machine guns or automatic rifles. The police arrived too late, and if Walter Bopp knew who might be removing what from his store he wasn't saying. He still hadn't said in January, when he reentered the hospital and, a day or two later, died of a pulmonary embolism. All of which set a lot of people in Tucson thinking about what in the world might have happened to Walter Bopp.

"I didn't think he had an enemy in the world," one of Walter Bopp's employees had told the *Arizona Daily Star* after the December beating. That is, of course, a remark often made when a respectable citizen meets with what is obviously not random violence. To the casual customer of Bopp Health Food, Walter Bopp probably did appear to be a particularly unlikely candidate for vicious assault—a robust, rosy-cheeked old vegetarian whose knowledge of herbal remedies led some of his customers to refer to him as Dr. Bopp. A Swiss immigrant who retained a slight accent, Bopp was known as a man who worked hard and lived frugally. A lot of people in Tucson had seen him on the back of his pickup truck loading or unloading stock; nobody in Tucson had ever seen him in a necktie. Who would want to terrorize a simple purveyor of wheat germ and herbal tea?

It wasn't long, of course, before it became known that Bopp had interests beyond health food. The *Star* reported in January that he had disagreements with several people about land near Arivaca. It also reported that he had been involved in "supernatural" activities. Then two young reporters for the *Tucson Citizen,* Dan Huff and Shawn Hubler, poked around in Walter Bopp's life and found people who referred to him not as Dr. Bopp but as Dr. Jekyll and Mr. Hyde. Bopp, the *Citizen* reporters discovered, had indeed been capable of great kindness. He had also been, they wrote, a "tight-lipped, sometimes hateful man who believed in witches and who once said that Lyndon Johnson, Lady Bird and Robert McNamara turned into animals and slithered over White House fences at night." It was known in Tucson that Bopp had divorced his wife a few years earlier, after forty-seven years of marriage, but the *Citizen* piece revealed that he was thought to have done so under advice from a psychic. (Most of Bopp's acquaintances—he didn't seem to have any close friends—were unaware that he had remarried until the newspapers carried the name of a second wife as his survivor.) It also revealed that Bopp had strong racist views about Mexicans and blacks. The kindly Dr. Bopp, Huff and Hubler were told, had been a contentious man who never admitted he was wrong and never let loose of a grudge.

Newspaper reports indicating that there were areas in Bopp's life which could indeed have produced an enemy or two did not clear up the mystery, of course; they simply made it more complicated.

Had Walter Bopp been terrorized because of a dispute over a silver claim? Could he have discovered something in Arivaca that someone else wanted to know? Was it possible that he had found himself among the sort of cultists who beat up elderly vegetarians? What were Bopp's tormentors after? Gold? Silver? Information? His store? What could have been secret or private enough to restrain Walter Bopp from helping police find the people who had left him bound and beaten on the floor of his storeroom?

From the start, of course, there were ways of explaining what happened to Walter Bopp that did not require knowledge of his ventures into mining or racial theory or the supernatural. Who leans on respectable businessmen? "They were obviously hit men," a clerk at Bopp's store said after the December beating. Tucson happens to have a substantial and well-publicized colony of the sort of citizens who are photographed by the FBI at funerals, and a lot of speculation naturally centered on the possibility that Bopp had run afoul of the mob. Did Walter Bopp have something the mob wanted? Were mobsters trying to persuade him to do something they wanted? It was also possible, of course, that Walter Bopp had simply wandered into some private dispute over pride or sex or vengeance. People in Tucson developed a stunning variety of theories to account for what happened to him: he was a loan shark, he was a bagman, he was a drug dealer, he was an arms dealer, he was a rich miser. "I know he was sitting on a lot of gold," a bartender at the Poco Loco, a tavern next door to Bopp's Speedway store, said not long ago. "He had been buying gold that'd be worth a million dollars in today's market. I think that's why he was dusted."

Walter Bopp arrived in America in the twenties and, doing farmwork, made his way across the country to California. Just before the crash of 1929, he sent for his childhood sweetheart—a young Englishwoman who had been at a Swiss school in Bopp's village. Apparently, whatever money he had saved was lost in a get-rich-quick real-estate scheme; at the beginning of the Depression he was working as a dishwasher. What brought him to Tucson in the early thirties was a job as a salad chef at the Pioneer Hotel. When Bopp Health Food opened in 1934, in a tiny downtown storefront, Bopp's wife, Mae, used to say that the cash register was worth more than the stock. Bopp let his wife mind the store for a couple of years while he held on to his salad-chef job. Then they both began working—working without taking vacations or weekends, as far as anyone in Tucson remembers—to build what was for a dozen years the only health-food business in Tucson.

Health food was hardly a national fad in the thirties. "It was not just unfashionable," someone who got into the business a decade or so later said recently. "It was practically clandestine." Tucson, though, did have more than its share of potential customers. In those days, doctors used to send patients to the Arizona desert on the theory that the dry air would alleviate suffering from allergies or asthma or arthritis or emphysema—or simply on the theory that it might be a soothing climate for someone whose disease seemed beyond the reach of conventional medicine. Some of the desperately ill looked for remedies in nutrition, and Walter Bopp was their adviser. He also developed a trade supplying grain and cereal in bulk to ranchers. As a businessman, Walter Bopp was old-world—thrifty, hardworking, cautious, impervious to suggestions about merchandising techniques. He didn't hold much with spring sales or regular salary increases. The original store remained the same size, in a part of downtown that gradually became characterized by cheap furniture stores and pawnshops. Bopp didn't open a second store until the sixties—on East Speedway Boulevard, a wide street that for miles seems to be one run-on strip-shopping development. The Speedway store was modern when Bopp built it, but hardly modern compared with the flashy health-food chains that blossomed when the business began to attract people who saw health food as a market rather than a cause. Walter Bopp plugged away—grumbling about the insincere people who had come into the business, moving stock from one store to the other in his pickup truck, working late into the night on his order forms. The block he had chosen on Speedway turned out to be even less uplifting than the old block downtown. After a while, Bopp found himself with the Poco Loco on one side and on the other a place called the Empress Theatre, which offered hardcore films, "adult books and novelties," and a "hot-tub spa." Bopp complained belligerently about tavern and porn-store customers jamming the parking spaces in front of his shop and using the small parking lot he had for his own customers. "An American businessman might have just moved," someone who knew him at that time said recently. "But he was very set in his ways."

Bopp's ways were strange from the start. Mae Bopp—a diminutive, well-spoken woman who seemed almost timid, particularly in his presence—worked constantly in the store, but the Bopps were otherwise not seen together. He seemed to live mainly in the back of the downtown store. He was kind to some employees and cold to others. He fired at least two clerks in the belief that they were witches who were trying to hex him. ("He was good to me until then," one of them has said. "He was a sweet old man.") To a lot of people, he seemed secretive and aloof. His feelings against Jews were even more vitriolic than his feelings against blacks and Mexicans. Some people who knew Bopp for years were unaware of his racial views; some were treated to them in intense, sotto voce lectures in a back corner of the store. "He was very intelligent," one of his former employees said recently. "He knew herbs very well. He was the first one to help you if you went to him with a problem. He had so many good ways—it's too bad he got mixed up in all that weird stuff. He said some weird things about Jewish people. Once, he told me that a customer was a witch and I shouldn't look her in the eye. He'd start talking real mysterious, real low. He told me she would come to my bedroom in the form of a vampire, and I should get a silver cross to ward her off. I don't believe in witches, but, I'll tell you, when he got through with me I wished I had a silver cross."

Among his other views, Bopp had a strong belief that the economic system—or perhaps all of society—would come crashing down

one day, in an even more disastrous way than it had come crashing
down in 1929. At that point, of course, stocks and real estate and
even paper money would not be worth having. The only wealth
would be in gold and silver. There is reason to believe that Walter
Bopp did indeed have some gold or silver stashed somewhere. Gold
and silver would allow him to survive the economic disaster. According to someone who used to work for Bopp, the silver would
have an even more important use: "He figured he could use the silver against Satan. Evil spirits are afraid of silver."

As a young man in Southern California, Bopp had shopped
around in what must have been the Western world's most extensive
display of yogis and mystics and cults, eventually settling on a Hindu
offshoot called the Benares League. His belief in the occult may have
intensified as he grew older. He seemed more certain of the forces
allied against him. He told an acquaintance that he had paid to have
a counter-hex placed on someone who was trying to hex him. The
woman he married a few months before his death is said to be a
soothsayer or a psychic—the same one who advised him during the
dissolution of his previous marriage. A former employee of Bopp's
was told by the police that the closest Bopp would come to identify-
ing his assailants was to say that he had been done in by the Evil
Force. A lot of people who knew Bopp remain convinced that his
death had something to do with his otherworldly beliefs. ("It must
have been that damn cult thing.") But what? A hex does not, in fact,
cause a vicious beating. The secrets of the afterlife are not ordinarily
sought by torturing a man of spiritual powers until he tells. How can
Bopp's silence be explained? Could Walter Bopp—confused, increasingly obsessed with the otherworldly, slipping toward paranoia—
have mistaken a couple of thugs after gold for the Evil Force?

The most romantic notions of what might have happened to Walter
Bopp have to do with mining, which has been part of the folklore
of southern Arizona for much longer than the mob has. A lot of
people in Tucson who may do something else for a living prospect

as a sort of sideline—somewhere between a hobby and a disease—and for at least thirty years Walter Bopp was one of them. Some of them still dream of the big strike—a lode of silver that has somehow been missed by all the holes poked into the desert all of these years, the fabulous lost mines that the Jesuits are said to have left when they were expelled from Arizona in the eighteenth century. Some people in Tucson theorized that Walter Bopp might have hit such a strike, but the mining people around Arivaca find that notion amusing. From what they say, Bopp must have been one of the most consistently unsuccessful miners in the state.

"I don't think he ever shipped a pound of ore out of here," someone familiar with mining in Arivaca said recently. Occasionally, Bopp would show up at the assay office with a test bore that looked mildly promising, but, as far as anyone knows, he never followed it up. Bopp was not simply a weekend prospector with a pan or a pickax. He filed dozens of claims and did dozens of test bores. ("He sank holes all over this country.") Just outside of Arivaca, he kept a couple of miners working for a dozen years to sink two shafts deep into the ground. There are people in Arivaca who believe that Bopp was almost willfully unsuccessful—ignoring promising samples, choosing the least likely place to drill. His method of finding gold or silver was what prospectors call "witchin' it"—trying to divine it, the way a dowser divines water. It is not uncommon for prospectors—even prospectors who don't believe in witches—to try to witch gold or silver, and apparently just about all of them do better at it than Walter Bopp did.

People around Arivaca remember Bopp as a contentious man—quick to assert his rights, quick to take an argument to court. It is possible, of course, that he got into a dispute with someone over a claim or had some mine information someone else wanted or let one of the arguments miners are always having with ranchers in southern Arizona get out of hand. Nobody who knows much about mining thinks that explains what happened to him. They don't think that Bopp got into a dispute of great seriousness, and they don't think what happened to him is characteristic of the way such a dispute would be settled. That doesn't mean that they think there was nothing mysterious about Walter Bopp's mining operations. They wonder where he got all of the money he spent for what miners call "holes in the ground." A lot of them figure he was using someone else's money. Whose? What does that have to do with what happened to Walter Bopp?

The police have been to Arivaca and they have visited one of the people Bopp suspected of witchcraft, but they are apparently not taken with some of the more ornate theories about the fate of Walter Bopp. Detectives, in the accepted manner, appear to have concentrated their attention on those closest to Walter Bopp and on those who might profit from his death and on anyone who both knew him and seems capable of having terrorized him. (One of Bopp's Speedway neighbors, for example, was once charged with extortion and, in plea bargaining, pleaded guilty to aggravated assault.) It has been five months now since Walter Bopp was attacked, and there is some feeling in Tucson that the police have shifted their energies to other matters. The mystery may always be a mystery.

Among people familiar with the case, of course, the speculation continues. Someone has called Dan Huff at the *Citizen* with an involved story based on Bopp's being connected with Swiss banking houses. Someone else reported having seen Bopp at a Klan recruiting meeting. The various aspects of Bopp's life can be put together in any number of combinations: Bopp owed the mob money he had borrowed to pour into holes in the ground around Arivaca; Bopp met some hippie cultists in the desert—where hippies still seem to exist, as if preserved by the dry climate—and made the mistake of telling them that he had a fortune in gold; Bopp's views on race led him into contact with some people whose viciousness went beyond sotto voce lectures; Bopp was using mob money for mining; Bopp was using Swiss banking money for mining; Bopp was using Fascist money for mining.

It is said around Tucson that Bopp's widow intends to reopen the health-food stores, but it is also said that the East Speedway store has been sold to the porno operation next door. Both stores are locked, with ornamental grilles protecting their windows. At the Speedway store, the grille is festooned with signs saying that parking is for customers of Bopp Health Food only. In the window, among the displays of sweet orange-spice tea and the Naturade jojoba hair-treatment formula, is a handwritten note that says, CLOSED DUE TO DEATH IN FAMILY.

A Father-Son Operation

Grundy County, Iowa

SEPTEMBER 1982

The soil in Grundy County is often spoken of as the richest soil in Iowa—which means, Grundy County residents sometimes add, that it must be about the richest soil in the world. "The land is mostly a gentle, undulating prairie with just sufficient slope to thoroughly drain it," somebody wrote of Grundy County farmland in 1860. "There is not the same area in the state with less wasteland. . . . The soil is black mould of the prairie, deep and strong for all kinds of crops." Although the farmers who come in to Grundy Center, the county seat, to do their banking and buy their supplies manage to find plenty about the weather that is worthy of complaint, crop failures in Grundy County are even rarer than armed robberies. "Oh, we get six or seven crop failures a year," a local resident said recently over morning coffee at Manly's drugstore, on the main street of Grundy Center. "But they're all in the bar or the drugstore." Agribusiness spokesmen who routinely talk about the American family farm in the past tense are apparently not familiar with Grundy County. All its farms are family farms. Many of them are owned by the same families that carved them out of the prairie in the last decades of the nineteenth century. In those days, the northern part of the county was virtually all German—it was settled by serious, hardworking farm people from East Friesland, near the Dutch border—and it is virtually all German today. The family names are the same. People in Grundy Center still like to say that you can walk from a point just a couple of miles north of the county courthouse to Parkersburg, fifteen miles away, and almost never be off land that is owned by one member of the Meester clan or another.

In some ways, the lives of the Grundy County Germans have not changed a lot since the days when walking was about the only way to make the trip. It is true, of course, that they now own sixty-thousand-dollar tractors and that they routinely drive twenty-five miles to a shopping mall in Cedar Falls for their groceries and that many of them can easily afford to fly to Germany to visit the villages of their forebears. It is also true, though, that they remain serious, hardworking farm people. Most of them still lead lives that revolve tightly around their families and their land. On Sundays, they go to church—to small country Reformed churches on county blacktops or to conservative versions of Presbyterian or Baptist churches in nearby trading towns like Parkersburg and Aplington. The Sabbath is still taken seriously as a day of rest in northern Grundy County; not many people would mow their lawn or wash their car or repair the roof of their barn on a Sunday afternoon—not within sight of the road, at least. Many people still live in the rambling white farmhouses that their forebears built on the family's original plot of land—what farm people in Iowa still call the home place. The houses stand surrounded by huge groves of shade trees that are visible for miles across an otherwise almost treeless prairie. In all directions, the black Iowa soil is planted in corn and soybeans. In Grundy County, a good farmer can expect a yield of a hundred and fifty bushels of corn an acre, and it is taken for granted that just about all farmers in Grundy County are good farmers. One of the best—one of the best, that is, until his life began to change in ways that his neighbors still can't quite explain—was a man named Lawrence Hartman.

Four or five years ago, when Lawrence Hartman was in his middle fifties, there didn't seem to be much of what life in Grundy County could offer that he didn't have. He owned one of the most prosperous corn-and-bean farms in the county. He ran a large cattle-feeding operation. He had served as a trustee of his township and a trustee of the Presbyterian church and a member of the landfill commission and a member of the election board and a member of the condemnation board. His wife, Esther, was a Meester—a member of the largest and most prominent of northern Grundy County's founding families. His two grown sons, Rodney and Rollyn, worked with him on the Hartman land, as he had worked with his own father. Rodney, who was then about thirty, was a big, beefy, occasionally rambunctious bachelor who was gradually settling back down to life in Grundy County after a couple of years at a business college in Waterloo and a particularly unsettling year as a combat infantryman in Vietnam. Rollyn, eight years younger, was a quieter man, who had only recently left home for the first time: he got married and moved to a farmhouse just down the road from his parents. When Rollyn was asked some time later to describe the sort of farming the Hartmans did, he summed it up in one sentence: "It's a father-son operation."

In farm families, where people who have ties of blood may also be connected as business partners, it is customary to be explicit about the terms of the partnership. When Lawrence Hartman's father retired and moved to town—in 1947, the year Lawrence and Esther Hartman were married—Lawrence began farming the Hartman home place, two hundred and forty acres on a county road known as the Buck Grove Blacktop, in a fifty-fifty partnership. He worked his father's land with his father's equipment for half the profits. Thirty years later, Lawrence Hartman's arrangement with his two sons was as clearly defined. Lawrence and Rollyn Hartman were fifty-fifty partners in a hog operation—the corn for feed provided by the father, the labor by the son. In the main farming operation, Rodney and Rollyn traded their labor—they prepared the ground, their father did the actual planting—for the use of Lawrence Hartman's machinery and his planting expertise on a smaller farm they had bought for themselves with his help. The one person whose labors in the family's enterprises seemed beyond any agreements or categories was Esther Hartman.

Esther Hartman seemed to have inherited undiluted the values brought to Iowa by the God-fearing, thrifty, hardworking settlers from East Friesland. She was strict about going to church and strict about keeping the Sabbath and strict about not having any liquor in her house. Although she was three years older than her husband and had a slight hunch from curvature of the spine, she seemed to have the energy of a strapping farm girl. She kept an immaculate house. She canned vegetables long after most of her neighbors had been won over by the frozen-food cases of the Cedar Falls supermarkets. She baked pies and she baked cakes. In the Hartman household, it was taken for granted that Rodney, who lived nearby, would bring his laundry home to his mother every week. Esther Hartman had always done the laundry and the spring-cleaning for her elder brothers—bachelor twins who together still farmed the Meester home place, a couple of miles away, speaking the Plattdeutsch of their childhood to each other over supper. From the beginning, she had worked alongside her husband on the Hartman farm—not just managing the house but opening gates and helping with the livestock and keeping the books.

After thirty years of hard work by the Hartman family, the books looked remarkably good. The Hartmans had most of their land paid off; their income was more than respectable, even by city standards. As a farmer, Lawrence Hartman was known as a good manager—a man who could get his land plowed and planted with less equipment and less labor than his neighbors required for the same number of acres, a man who could judge the best time to plant and the best time to buy supplies in quantity. He was also shrewd at acquiring property. The Hartman holdings grew steadily. Esther inherited some land from her family, but mostly Lawrence bought land from his neighbors. Several times in the late sixties, he bought nearby farms by first arranging to sell off what is known as the acreage—the

house and the outbuildings and the few acres they stand on—and
then using the money as a down payment. About the most he paid
for land was five or six hundred dollars an acre, and gradually it became clear that Grundy County farmland at that price was a great
bargain. In the middle seventies, the value of farmland in Grundy
County seemed to increase almost daily. The boom was not the result of outside speculation; local farmers were attempting to increase
their holdings. They were trying to expand partly because of two or
three particularly good crops in a row and partly because increasingly efficient and expensive farm machinery made it sensible to
spread a huge investment in tractors and combines over an extra
hundred or two hundred acres of land. There was another factor that
people in Grundy County talk about now and then in the drugstore
over morning coffee or in the tavern over a beer: for one reason or
another, a lot of people had come to the realization at about the
same time that the black soil of Grundy County was limited in supply, and that nobody was ever going to produce any more of it.
Around 1977, prime farmland in Grundy County was changing
hands for thirty-five hundred dollars an acre and going toward four
thousand. Lawrence Hartman—a man whose education amounted
to eight years in a county school, a man who had started with a half
share in a quarter section, a man who had worked with his hands just
about every day of every week except the Sabbath since childhood—
had more than five hundred acres of it.

One evening in 1978, in a bar called the Apartment Lounge in
Cedar Falls, Lawrence Hartman picked up a woman named Katherine Sunderman. The Apartment Lounge is in the College Square
shopping center—a large, modern mall close to the campus of the
University of Northern Iowa. Although the designer of the Apartment Lounge included examples of just about every type of decoration found in any type of American bar, from hanging plants to
brewery art, the design element that seems most appropriate to the
clientele is a series of drawings of Northern Iowa fraternity and so-

rority houses. At the Apartment Lounge, the waitresses are likely to be young women wearing crew-neck sweaters, and the bartender may be a physical-education major in a swim-team T-shirt. In that atmosphere, Katherine Sunderman, who worked as a cocktail waitress herself at one time or another, stood out—a divorcée in her early thirties with a lot of tight blond curls and a habit of calling all women "babe" and all men "tiger." The people who worked at the Apartment Lounge referred to her among themselves as Flo, after the brassy, gum-chewing waitress in a television sitcom. That night in 1978, she and a friend fell into conversation with a couple of men at the next table—Lawrence Hartman and a partner of his in a cattle-feeding operation. Not long after that, Katherine Sunderman and Lawrence Hartman were thought of by the Apartment Lounge staff as a couple—Flo and the quiet farmer.

Why was Lawrence Hartman trying to pick up a brassy blonde over a drink in a Cedar Falls lounge instead of discussing the weather with his neighbors over coffee in Aplington or over a beer in Parkersburg? What had changed a family man and community leader of unassailable reputation? Some people in Grundy County would say simply "Cattle-buying." A corn-and-beans farmer never wanders far; he even comes home in the middle of the day for dinner. Someone who buys cattle—buys them with the thought of feeding them for a year and then selling them—may find himself in a large city with the day's work done and an empty evening on his hands. "It's almost like a traveling salesman," someone in a café in Aplington said recently. "You got to be pretty well-grounded." For thirty years, Lawrence Hartman had, in fact, seemed pretty well-grounded. There was a time when he managed to buy cattle by ordering over the phone from a dealer in Sioux City whom he knew and trusted, or by driving to Sioux City with Esther, so that she could go shopping with the dealer's wife while the deal was being made. By the time he met Katherine Sunderman at the Apartment Lounge, though, he had begun traveling to places like Kansas City to buy cattle, with some cattle-buyers who were known in Grundy County for being interested in big-city entertainment as well as in livestock. "He'd been here thirty-some years farming, and then he got to the city," Rodney Hartman said not long ago. In the city, according to an Aplington man who dealt with Lawrence Hartman for a number of years, "he had some money and he probably found it could buy him some goodies he hadn't been aware of." Lawrence Hartman began to pay less attention to the farm than he had in the past. He began talking about the pleasures of drinking screwdrivers at cocktail lounges. Then, Rodney Hartman has said, "*she* came along."

Rodney and Rollyn Hartman found out who she was almost as soon as their mother finally told them that their father had apparently been seeing another woman for some time. They traced a number from a telephone bill to Katherine Sunderman's mobile home, in a trailer park outside a little town between Aplington and Cedar Falls. When Lawrence Hartman arrived home the next morning and spoke harshly to his wife, apparently not realizing that Rodney was in the house, Rodney hit him hard enough to break his jaw. Even now, Rodney finds it astonishing that he hit the man he had been brought up to respect and obey. "I was probably out of line bad," he said. "But I couldn't handle it." It was not the last violence to pass between father and sons. Once, Rollyn Hartman and his father exchanged blows. Once, Lawrence Hartman threatened Rollyn with a shotgun, and Rollyn tried to knock him down the stairs. Once, Rodney and Rollyn forcibly dragged Lawrence Hartman to the Happy Chef restaurant in Cedar Falls so that the sons could confront Katherine Sunderman as a home-wrecker in their father's presence.

Lawrence Hartman had told his sons that his personal life was none of their business, but they considered it literally their business. They were concerned not just about their mother but also about the future of the farm they had worked on all their lives. "My father lost his ability to manage," Rodney has said. Lawrence Hartman was often gone, even at the time of year when hogs had to be taken to market or planting was imminent. "We had to know what was going to be corn and what was going to be beans," Rollyn has said. "If you farm eight or nine hundred acres, you may have one chance at a crop. You'd better be there when the weather's right." At times, Lawrence said he wanted to work out his marital problems. There were sessions with a marriage counselor and with the Hartmans' minister, Charles Orr. At times, Hartman assured his sons that he had given up Katherine Sunderman, only to disappear again over a long weekend. "We tried a lot of things," Rodney Hartman said recently. "But we never did get the job done." For two Christmases in a row, Lawrence Hartman was absent when his family—his wife and his sons and his daughter-in-law and, the second year, his first grandchild—gathered at the Hartman home place. It was an act that seemed to shock them almost more than anything else he had done. What it all meant in Rollyn's view was that Lawrence Hartman was "no longer part of our family." In the spring of 1980, Esther Hartman, who had been raised in a society where the permanence of the marriage contract was unquestioned, finally began divorce proceedings. She got a court injunction that barred her husband from their farmhouse and severely limited the amount of money he could draw from the family account.

Within a couple of months, she had taken him back. "Oh, he begged her," a close friend of Esther Hartman's said. "He didn't want to be alone, he said. He'd miss her pies. He'd miss her mashed potatoes." Hartman said he was through with Katherine Sunderman. He and his wife took a trip together to Arkansas. He no longer found reasons for being away from the farm all the time. Rodney and Rollyn Hartman allowed themselves to believe that some inexplicable chapter in their father's life might have finally ended. By autumn, Esther Hartman seemed more cheerful than she had been in years. She chatted away with friends about plans for a new garden and a new strawberry patch. Then, shortly after 3 A.M. on a stormy Saturday in September, Charles Orr, who is the ambulance driver in Aplington as well as the Hartmans' pastor, was awakened by a telephone call from Lawrence Hartman. "It's Esther," Hartman said. Orr drove the ambulance to the Hartman farmhouse. Esther Hartman was dead.

She had bruises on her face and hands. All but one of her ribs had been broken, crushing her lungs and cutting off her ability to breathe. Lawrence Hartman said he had been out during the evening—at Katherine Sunderman's new apartment, not far from the Happy Chef, in Cedar Falls, as it turned out—and after his return had found his wife at the bottom of the basement steps, presumably the victim of a fall while carrying laundry on the stairs. Hartman seemed in sort of a daze. "Esther was good to me," he told Rick Penning, who was then a deputy and is now the sheriff of Grundy County. "She always baked me stuff—pies and stuff." His sons—and particularly Rodney—were in a state that seemed in danger of erupting into violence. As the farmhouse began to fill up that night with the sheriff's deputies and doctors and friends, some of the law-enforcement people spent part of their time making certain that Lawrence Hartman was not alone with his sons. "I finally asked the boys if they would go up to Rollyn's home and wait until we called them," William Marten, who was then the sheriff, has said. "Because I felt the situation was becoming out of hand." Before the boys left, though, Rollyn had made their feelings clear to his father. "Someday," he told Lawrence Hartman, "you'll burn in hell."

Around Christmastime of 1980, Lawrence Hartman was indicted for the murder of his wife—the first murder case in Grundy County in thirty years. A few months later, Rodney and Rollyn brought a wrongful-death suit against their father in civil court—a suit that was really about who would own Esther Hartman's share of the farm she had worked on for so long. To defend him against the murder charge, Hartman hired one of the best-known criminal lawyers in the state. (People in Grundy County, speculating about the fee that such a big-city lawyer might command, said, "There goes one farm right there.") It was nearly a year before Hartman was actually tried for murder. The defense argued, without much opposition, that Hartman could not get an impartial jury in Grundy County, and the trial was set for the seat of Black Hawk County—Waterloo, the city right next to Cedar Falls. A lot of people from Grundy County made the drive daily. At times, there were crowds too large to be accommodated in the courtroom. The atmosphere among the spectators was caught by a photograph in *The Des Moines Register*—a row of eight women, middle-aged or older, staring at the proceedings with expressions that carried no hint of forgiveness.

The prosecutor, a young Grundy Center attorney named Richard Pilcher, presented evidence to show that in the summer of 1980, Lawrence Hartman had gone back to Katherine Sunderman after all. He had given her a diamond ring. He had leased a car for her. He had promised her that once the fall harvest was in, he would have his final divorce settlement and would then be able to marry her. They had talked about a honeymoon in Hawaii. Evidence was entered that Hartman had once injured his wife by kicking her and that she had expressed fear that he would attack her again. Pilcher claimed that Hartman had wanted "the best of both worlds"—the pies and cakes and solidity of the home that Esther provided as well as a new and drastically different life with a blonde who had a habit of calling men "tiger." According to the prosecution's case, when Hartman finally had to make a choice—when he was getting pressure from Katherine Sunderman to marry her and getting pressure to straighten out from his wife and his sons and pressure from the court injunction—he saw no way to have both his farm and his new life except to kill Esther. Rodney and Rollyn both testified against their father.

"The truth of the matter is, Rollyn," the defense lawyer said on cross-examination, "you'd like to see him, in your words, 'burn in hell.'"

"Well, if that's justice," Rollyn said.

Hartman did not deny his relationship with Katherine Sunderman—that he had slept with her the night of Esther Hartman's death, that he had lied to his family about her, that he was living with her as he stood trial for his wife's murder, that he planned to marry her. Although he expressed his love for his wife ("Esther was a good person; nothing wrong with Esther"), he said that his marriage had dried up after the boys moved out. He had told Katherine Sunderman that he felt like a slave at times, and that Esther sometimes seemed to care more for her brothers than she did for him. Throughout the trial, it was said that Lawrence and Esther Hartman had become incompatible. The word used to describe the relationship between Lawrence Hartman and Katherine Sunderman was "bouncy"—in Katherine Sunderman's testimony, "very bouncy." There wasn't much brought out about Hartman's behavior that might have softened the stares of the women who drove to the courthouse from Grundy County every day. The defense attorney took care to remind the jury that "Lawrence Hartman isn't on trial here for having an affair."

To refute the testimony of pathologists called by the prosecution, the defense presented some pathologists who said that Esther Hartman's injuries could have resulted from a fall and an effort at cardiopulmonary resuscitation by her husband. Even so, there were a lot of problems with the defendant's explanation of what had happened that night. He had to explain what he was doing in the basement, and why Esther was walking back down the basement stairs with clean laundry of Rodney's that had been seen in the kitchen that afternoon, and why a couple of presumably disinterested neighbors testified that they had seen him in Aplington or Parkersburg when his alibi called for him to be in Cedar Falls. Katherine Sunderman's testimony supported Hartman's story—if that can be said of testimony that she knew he was still in her bed at two in the morning because she had set the alarm clock for two in order to take a twelve-hour cold pill—but she acknowledged making a statement that seemed rather damaging. When an investigator informed her that Esther Hartman was dead, Katherine Sunderman acknowledged, her response had been to blurt out, "Oh, God! Was she beaten?"

Pilcher asked the jury to find Hartman guilty of first-degree murder—murder committed with premeditation as well as intent. It may be that the prosecution itself had poked too many holes in Hartman's story to make premeditation plausible. If Hartman had planned the whole thing, the jurors may have surmised, wouldn't he have done a better job of tying up loose ends than that? They apparently believed, though, that Lawrence Hartman had killed his wife—killed her in a drunken rage, maybe, or killed her because he had started hitting her and couldn't stop. After eight and a half hours of deliberation, Hartman was found guilty of second-degree murder. The judge sentenced him to twenty-five years in prison.

Because the case was appealed to the Iowa Supreme Court, Lawrence Hartman was able to remain free on a hundred-thousand-dollar bond. A couple of months after the trial was over, he and Katherine Sunderman were married. They continue to live in the apartment that Hartman visited the night his wife died. They are not seen around northern Grundy County. For the most part, what Hartman's former neighbors know about him and his new wife is what they read in the papers. A recent item, reprinted in the Grundy County weekly from the Waterloo paper, reported that Katherine Sunderman Hartman had been picked up by the Iowa State Patrol for driving while intoxicated, and that Lawrence Hartman, who was in the car with her, was booked at the same time for public intoxication.

There are, of course, still a lot of different theories in Grundy County to account for how Lawrence Hartman was transformed from a pillar of the German farming community into a man who carried on with another woman and lost the respect of his sons and was eventually convicted of murdering his own wife. Some people think that Hartman simply fell into bad company—high-steppers who exposed an unworldly farmer to temptations he couldn't resist. Some people think he just happened to be smitten—bewitched, maybe—by Katherine Sunderman. ("The defendant becomes obsessed with this other woman," Pilcher said in his closing statement. "He becomes totally dominated by this woman, and she gains con-

trol of his every action. She caused substantial changes in the defendant, in his personality and in his character. His association with her
ruins his relationship with his wife and his two sons, Rodney and
Rollyn.") In the Shamrock Café in Aplington not long ago, one man
offered the possibility that Lawrence Hartman's change had been
almost biological. "I heard that some men have a change of life, just
like women," he said. "Their whole personality changes." The man
across the booth shook his head, held up his hand, and rubbed his
thumb and forefinger together. "Money," he said. "There are very
few people who can stand being rich."

Rodney Hartman seems to share that interpretation, more or
less. When asked what happened to his father, he says, "Inflation." He
means inflation in land values. "All of a sudden, people were coming
up to him and saying, 'Lawrence, you're rich,'" Rodney said recently.
Even now, there are people in Grundy County who don't believe
that Lawrence Hartman killed his wife, but his sons are not among
them. They resent the fact that he is free—living with the woman
they shouted at as a home-wrecker—even after a jury found him
guilty of killing their mother. Rodney and Rollyn planted the Hartman acres in corn and beans this spring without the help of their
father. Under an out-of-court settlement of the civil suit, the sons
farm the Hartman land with the agreement that they pay their father a lump sum of more than two hundred thousand dollars, plus
thirty thousand dollars a year for the next twenty years. Given the
added burden, the younger Hartmans don't sound completely confident of being able to make a go of it, but they are obviously committed to trying. For some time after his mother's death, Rollyn
couldn't bring himself to enter the farmhouse, but now he has plans
to move there with his wife and child. It is, after all, the Hartman
home place.

I've Got Problems

Cairo, Nebraska

MARCH 1985

The first phone call made to Arthur Kirk once a Nebraska State Patrol SWAT team was in place around the Kirk farmhouse was from Jim Titsworth, a reporter for *The Grand Island Independent.* Titsworth had interviewed Kirk that afternoon in the driveway of Kirk's farm, near Cairo—a fading little farm town in flat corn-and-wheat country fifteen miles northwest of Grand Island. At the time, Kirk seemed calm—he had just driven into the farmstead with a truckload of newly cut beans—but he was still angry about his confrontation earlier in the afternoon with some Hall County deputy sheriffs who had come out to serve legal papers for a Grand Island bank. The deputies had no right to come on his land, Kirk told Titsworth—he had what he called "a federal post" on it, excluding government officials as well as ordinary trespassers—and they had no business carrying out "the bankers' dirty duties." He didn't deny that he had pointed a pistol at the head of one deputy; in fact, he pulled a long-barreled .41 Magnum out of his coveralls to show it to Titsworth. About an hour after the interview, Art Kirk called the offices of the *Independent,* but Titsworth was out. Kirk left his name and a short message: "I've got problems."

He had serious problems. Jim Titsworth was returning the call that evening from a command post at the headquarters of Troop C, the Nebraska State Patrol's Grand Island detachment. The Hall County Sheriff's Department had obtained a warrant for Art Kirk's arrest and had asked Troop C's SWAT team for help in bringing him in. Titsworth was using the call from Troop C headquarters partly to nail down some facts for his story—he wanted to know how many acres Kirk had been farming before his operation began to shrink; he wanted to make certain that he had the correct first name of Kirk's wife—but he had also been asked by the state police to do whatever he could to feel out Art Kirk's state of mind. Kirk answered Titsworth's questions—he had once farmed about two thousand acres; his wife's correct first name was Deloris—but he seemed more interested in talking about the problems brought on by his confrontation with the deputies. He said that the deputies had brandished guns themselves. He said that a sheriff's department car had followed him when he went out afterward to cut beans on some rental land several miles away. He said that an unmarked Cessna had been making passes over his house. He had seen roadblocks being put in place on country roads near his farmhouse. His wife had apparently been detained on her way to the farm from Grand Island. Kirk said that his phone had an odd sound in it; he was convinced that it had been tapped for some time. In answer to Titsworth's questions about financial problems—the setbacks that had eventually brought the court papers from the bank—Kirk talked mainly in general terms. "You always thought, you know, that things would improve," he said. "But they have gotten worse." He was quite specific, though, on who was leading the forces against him.

"Mossad," he said to Titsworth. "You ever heard of that?"

"What's that?" Titsworth asked.

"Mossad."

"No, sir, I'm not familiar—"

"M-o-s-s-a-d. Look that up. That's what I'm fighting. That's who I'm dealing with. There isn't much hope. They are the most ruthless people. You think the NKVD and the Gestapo were ruthless—you look up the Mossad and see what they've been involved in."

"I've never heard of that name," Titsworth said.

"I know who I'm fighting."

Titsworth tried a couple of times to suggest that Kirk's problems with the sheriff could be settled without violence. "You know, what you ought to do is you ought to try and call somebody and get this thing over before—just to be sure no one gets hurt," he said shortly after the phone conversation began.

Art Kirk laughed. "They'll be somebody get hurt," he said. "About all I got hopes of doing is taking as many of them with me as I can."

"Another one sneaking down to the north, just like the last one," Kirk said. He was on the phone with Jan Steeple, a deputy sheriff he happened to be acquainted with, and as he spoke he peered out the window toward movements in the farmyard. It was their second conversation of the day. After the confrontation with the deputies, Steeple had phoned from the sheriff's office and discussed the possibility of coming out to talk to Kirk about his problems. But Kirk, a man who was known to have a lot of guns, had insisted that Steeple leave his gun in the mailbox at the side of the road, and the visit had been ruled out as too dangerous. Talking to Steeple again, Kirk berated him for not showing up. He complained that his wife was being prevented from returning home. He complained that his telephone had been tapped. He complained about having had a motorcycle stolen from his barn some weeks before. Steeple tried again to persuade Kirk to come out of the house unarmed.

"I'm coming to no goddam place," Kirk said. "If you want to talk to me, you know where I'm at, and I'll be here."

A state patrol sergeant who had some training in negotiating armed standoffs took over from Steeple. He spoke calmly, in a tone of generalized sympathy. ("I understand what you're saying, Art, and you have some reasons to be upset.") He avoided comment on the specifics of Kirk's complaints. But Kirk seemed to grow angrier as the conversation went on. His voice became high-pitched. Some of his grievances were expressed in a sustained, obscene shout. Eventually, he talked about how the attack on his house might begin—tear gas, or a flamethrower that could burn him to a crisp, or a volley of gunfire.

"Art, nobody wants to shoot you," the sergeant said.

"Well, then, damn it, come up here and talk to me," Kirk said. "I don't want to shoot you, either, but, damn you, you respect my rights."

Kirk said that the deputies he had driven from his property were cowards. He railed against "filthy, lying members of the bar—outlaw bastards." Speaking of a lawsuit he had filed without assistance from members of the bar, Kirk said, "I filed a suit against the goddam bank that's been misusing me for years and years and years, unbeknowned to me, until I started reading the laws myself. . . . I found out them dirty rotten son of a bitches have done everything despicable that they can think of to me. Everything you can think. It's unimaginable. It's covered by the U.S. Constitution and U.S. titles passed by Congress, the highest lawmaking body in the land, and they tell me that my suit is meritless. I'm going to tell you something: if the Constitution and the laws Congress passes are meritless, them son of a bitches are completely discredited."

Sometimes Kirk seemed to ramble. He said that he was a son of Abraham whose birthright had been claimed by Lucifer and that the bankers had been Luciferized. He made an extended play on words comparing the service of court papers to a bull's servicing a cow. Most of the time, though, he focused on the shoot-out that he seemed certain was about to take place. He said he was unafraid—a man who had never let anyone walk over him and wasn't going to start now. "You ain't going to walk over me until I'm cold," he said. "And if you want to make me cold I'm not afraid of it. I've led a damn good life, and I'm not ashamed of nothing I ever done." He said he had fired guns all his life ("Nobody's going to take my guns. Is that kinda clear?") and could even have brought down the Cessna. "I don't intend to kill anybody," he said. "But if you force me, if you shoot at me, damn you, there will be hell to pay. I intend to make the toll as great as I can. That's the only thing you leave me now, and that's what I'll do."

At other times, Art Kirk seemed to be asking why he could not simply be left alone. "Why all this goddam monkey business?" he asked. "Why don't you let me try and make a living?"

"Art," the sergeant said, "I didn't have anything to do with what's—"

"Goddam fuckin' Jews!" Kirk shouted. "They destroyed everything I ever worked for! I've worked my ass off for forty-nine goddam years, and I've got nothing to show for it! By God, I ain't putting up with their bullshit now. I'm tired, and I've had it, and I'm not the only goddam one—I'll tell you that."

"Yeah, but, Art—"

"Farmers fought the Revolutionary War and we'll fight this son of a bitch. We were hoping to do it in court, but if you're going to make it impossible, then, damn you, we'll take you on your own terms."

Deloris Kirk came on the phone for a while, from the command post. She kept reminding her husband that they had discussed what to do in such a situation, but she seemed to have trouble holding his attention. Steeple got back on the line, and again he pleaded for Kirk to come out unarmed.

"Well, hey, Jan," Kirk said to Steeple. "If you're just trying to divert me, I'm going out and clean the bushes out."

"Art, you don't want to do anything silly," Steeple said.

By that time, Deloris Kirk was off the phone. From a snatch of conversation she had overheard on a police radio, she believed that the SWAT team was moving in. She insisted on talking to Chuck Fairbanks, the sheriff of Hall County, who was at an operational headquarters that the police had set up in a state road-repair depot in Cairo, and a phone connection was put through.

"Call all of those people away from my farmhouse," Mrs. Kirk said.

"We can't do that right now," the sheriff replied.

"Why not?"

"Because he threatened deputy sheriffs, that's why," Fairbanks said. "The judge issued a warrant for his arrest."

Sheriff Fairbanks and Mrs. Kirk seemed to be at a standoff.

Mrs. Kirk wouldn't respond to the sheriff's request that she telephone her husband and ask him to come out peacefully. The sheriff continued to say that he could not agree to allow her to go into the farmhouse. They were still talking when Art Kirk burst out of the back door of his house. He was wearing the green coveralls he normally wore around the farm. Strapped to his arms or jammed in his pockets, he had a gas mask and a hundred and sixty rounds of ammunition and a long-barreled .357 Magnum pistol. He was wearing a motorcycle helmet. He was carrying an automatic rifle.

"The trooper who was stationed on the southeast perimeter of the house in a shelter belt area advises that he saw the subject come out of the east door, carrying what appeared to be an AR-15 or M-16 by the sight on its barrel," a report prepared by the county attorney a week later said. "This trooper yelled as loudly as he could in the direction of Kirk, 'Freeze—police.' He then saw a movement in his direction, saw muzzle flashes and heard automatic rifle fire. He returned the fire toward the muzzle flashes and lost sight of the subject." Another SWAT team member had also fired at the flashes. For some minutes, there was silence. Then the SWAT team asked some deputies to shine headlights on the area where the shots had come from. Arthur Kirk lay on the ground near a wire dog kennel, not far from his back door. He had been hit by two bullets. "The cause of death," an autopsy report said several weeks later, "is attributed to exsanguinating hemorrhage secondary to a gunshot wound of the anterior right shoulder and of the upper left thigh." In other words, Art Kirk had bled to death.

Arthur Kirk was born and raised where he died—on the two hundred and forty acres near Cairo that was his family's home place. His mother had been raised on the same farm. Her forebears were among the Germans who had arrived in the late nineteenth century in such numbers that they dominated Grand Island and the rich Platte Valley farmland nearby. Art Kirk's parents were not prosperous. In the years after the Second World War, they were still farming with mules. For a while, Art and his younger brother slept in a brooder house so that there would be enough room for their parents and sisters in the tiny two-room farmhouse. Eventually, the Kirks managed to build an adequate farmhouse, with indoor plumbing. Partly with the money the Kirk children made detasseling corn, a small tractor was bought to replace the mules. By that time, Art was old enough to help adapt the mule-drawn equipment to the tractor. He liked working with machinery. He liked working with farm animals. He was interested in trying various combinations of chemicals and fertilizers to increase crop yields. Art Kirk might have simply remained on the home place to farm except that he and his father did not see eye to eye when it came to farming. The elder Kirk was apparently not interested in trying his son's ideas on crop rotation or irrigation or equipment maintenance. In 1953, Art Kirk got a job with the gas company and moved into Grand Island.

In a small farm-state city the size of Grand Island, a large part of the population consists of people who grew up on the farm and moved into town—people whose connection to farming is made up of childhood memories reinforced every so often by a visit to the home place for a family meal or for a harvest that requires some extra hands. Art Kirk appeared to be one of those people. He and his wife, who had also grown up on a south-central Nebraska farm, began to raise a family in Grand Island. Kirk worked in the gas company's meter-repair shop for about ten years and then switched to the service truck, calling on people who needed a pilot light adjusted or a gas dryer repaired. Altogether, he worked for the gas company for nearly twenty years, but nobody who knew him had any doubt that he still had his heart set on being a farmer.

In 1971, Kirk persuaded Dan Stauffer, who sells farm real estate in Grand Island, to rent him a hundred and sixty acres of farmland that Stauffer owns on the road between Grand Island and Cairo. A common way to rent farmland is for the owner to take a share of the crops as rent, and Stauffer was impressed by what Kirk managed to produce. "He had the crudest damn equipment you ever saw in your life," Stauffer said later. "But the crops he raised were clean, and he had a good yield. He worked like mad all the time, and so did his wife." A few years later, Kirk began acquiring his father's farm on a land contract—an arrangement more or less like a home mortgage. When the elder Kirk died, in 1979, Art and Dee Kirk and their children moved from a house on Stauffer's land to the Kirk home place. By then, Kirk was also renting twelve hundred acres from the federal government—land at the Cornhusker Army Ammunition Plant. A frugal, meticulous farmer with set ideas about how things had to be done, Kirk attacked farming mainly with a nearly limitless capacity for hard work. For relaxation, he hunted and fished. When he wasn't in the fields, he was likely to be in the woods with a shotgun, and neighbors thought of him as someone who didn't spend much time socializing. Aside from using guns for hunting, he collected guns— not an unusual pastime in rural Nebraska. He liked to own guns whose design he admired. He liked to reload his own shells. He liked to rebore guns. According to someone who shared his interest in firearms, Kirk's greatest joy in life was "to take a gun and get it perfectly sighted so that the variance was less than half an inch in a five-shot group at two hundred yards." As he settled down on his home place, where he had once plowed behind a mule, Art Kirk seemed to be fulfilling his dream, whatever the cost in toil. He was a farmer with a full operation—corn and soybeans and milo and some feeder cattle and hogs and horses—and he had nearly two thousand acres under cultivation.

Around that time, the notion that dreams had come true was common among American farmers. There had been a number of good crop years in a row. More important, farmland seemed destined to grow in value indefinitely. There was a lot of talk about how

America would be feeding the world for the foreseeable future—talk meaning that farmers might be selling ever larger harvests at steadily increasing prices. The experts said that effective, ambitious farmers should expand, in order to spread out the cost of expensive farm equipment and to acquire land before its price got even higher. The farmland of America was a finite commodity that could never be replaced, it was said, and you couldn't go wrong owning it. Credit was easy. Even if a loan on land did not, as bankers say, "pencil out"—that is, even if the interest on the purchase price and the other costs of production seemed to be greater than the price of the crops the land could be expected to produce—the bank often went along. The loan was secure, after all, because the farmer's holdings had become worth so much money. Turning down the loan would just mean that the farmer would take his business to the bank down the street. The steady increase in land values, a Nebraska banker has said, "seemed to prove the pencil wrong." But the pencil was right all along.

Grain prices didn't go up, but interest rates did—so at one point farmers were paying interest as high as twenty-two percent on their loans. The value of farmland began to decline even faster than it had increased. In four years, the value of Nebraska farmland dropped by a third. Farmers who had been millionaires on paper a few years before began having trouble keeping up with their interest payments. As some farm-oriented banks got into financial difficulty, bank examiners started insisting that loans show some real prospect of being repaid by cash flow rather than simply secured by net worth. A lot of farmers—particularly farmers who had expanded their holdings during the boom—had to declare bankruptcy.

The experts said that some farmers—especially those sometimes called the Young Tigers, who bought up farmland almost as fast as the previous purchase could be appraised as collateral—had simply overextended themselves. The experts said that some farmers had been shown to be poor managers. That's not the way farmers saw it. Farmers, of course, are accustomed to being buffeted by elements beyond their control—the weather, for instance, or some flip-flop in world grain prices. This time, though, there was something particularly maddening about the combination of a boom—a boom celebrated by farm experts and bankers and government agricultural specialists as proof that expansion was the wave of the future—and a bust that cost some supposedly successful farmers the land that their more modest forebears had managed to hang on to for generations. This time, also, it was more intense. By some estimates, the farm foreclosures of the mid-eighties in the Midwest will be recorded as the greatest dislocation of Americans since the Depression. Some farmers blamed the bankers. In Minnesota, a farmer and his son shot and killed two bankers they had lured to their farm. Some farmers blamed the government or the grain embargo imposed in 1980, and organized tractor caravans to protest to the authorities. A lot of farmers didn't know whom to blame. They carried around a bitter, unfocused anger that sometimes erupted into blockades at farm sales or shoving matches at courthouses. It became common for someone serving papers on a farmer to do so with a weapon handy.

In the tumult—the foreclosures, the public meetings, the demonstrations—Midwestern farmers have been exposed to the message of some organizations that seem quite certain about whom to blame for the plight of American agriculture, or for just about any other problem in American society. The organization that has received the most public attention is the Posse Comitatus, a loosely knit crowd of prairie vigilantes who spend a lot of time stockpiling food and undergoing paramilitary training for the day when they will have to protect themselves against urban hordes desperate for the food supply. According to Posse doctrine, the Federal Reserve System and the income tax are both illegal, and there is no legitimate law-enforcement authority beyond the sheriff and the local posse that may be formed among the citizenry, with or without the sheriff's permission. Adherents sometimes shoot at law-enforcement officials they don't consider legitimate; the Posse owes part of its notoriety to an incident in February of 1983 in which one of its members, a North Dakota farmer named Gordon Kahl, shot and killed two federal marshals who were trying to arrest him for a parole violation.

The other right-wing fringe organizations preaching to American farmers vary from the Posse Comitatus and from one another in the details of precisely how the conspiracy works. Even people who adhere to the same theories vary in the intensity of their adherence—so some people may simply attack the Federal Reserve System as illegitimate, while others refuse to transact commerce except by silver or barter. Still, there is enough overlapping in theory and in membership to form a loose body of fringe-right beliefs. Lawyers are generally seen as the enemy, and court decisions are therefore dismissed as predictably unfair. There is a lot of talk about the Constitution. There is a strong element of anti-Semitism, some of it leaning on the information in hate tracts so old that the place of business of some international Jewish bankers is given as Berlin or Hamburg. There's a tendency to sympathize with the teachings of "identity churches"—churches teaching that Anglo-Saxons are the true descendants of Abraham and that Jews are the people of the Devil. There is often a belief that the loans that banks have made to farmers are illegal and can be dissolved by one sort or another of do-it-yourself legal action—do-it-yourself legal action being the only sort of legal action available to people who believe that lawyers are among the conspirators lined up against them. There is a strong belief that a farmer has the right to keep anybody, and particularly representatives of the government, off his land—by force, if necessary. Some of the no-trespassing signs distributed by the fringe right begin "LEGAL NOTICE—To Federal Officers of the IRS, HEW, HUD, Environmental Health and other *Unconstitutional* agencies; and to all local members of planning & zoning boards. NO TRESPASSING." That sort of warning is sometimes referred to among the fringe right as a "federal post."

. . .

Art Kirk was not one of those farmers who overextended themselves through land purchases. The only land he actually owned was
the home place; he had inherited a one-third interest in it and was
buying the rest gradually, with payments to his brother and a sister.
Still, he borrowed a lot of money from the bank. There was once a
time when farmers borrowed operating money in the spring and
paid off the loan after the fall harvest, but that time is long gone.
Farmers now tend to have what amount to semipermanent bank
loans. A farmer borrows money for planting expenses in the spring.
He borrows money for a combine and other equipment. He may
come in throughout the year to sign small notes—four thousand
dollars for a used pickup, say, or twenty-five hundred dollars for
sharpening blades and "general farm expenses"—as if he had a sort
of drawing account. When he sells his crops, which are normally part
of the collateral for his loan, he brings in the money, it's applied to
paying off the interest and reducing the principal, the loan is refi-
nanced, and the process starts all over again. In the early eighties,
Kirk's loans began to show what bankers call deterioration; he wasn't
producing enough income to take care of all the interest, so each
year his principal got larger and the interest on it even harder to pay
off. By the spring of 1984, his debt at Norwest Bank of Grand Island
was approaching three hundred thousand dollars.

How did Art Kirk get that far behind? There had been some bad
crop years, of course. He was paying high interest on operating loans.
Although Kirk was the sort of farmer who would haggle over the
price of a spare part and adapt scrounged secondhand machinery to
his needs, there are some who say that he never really mastered the
business aspects of modern farming—that he was trying to make up
with labor in the field what he lacked in finesse with the calculator.
According to someone who knew him well, "He didn't understand
bankers or lawyers. He thought they were all bad and greedy. He
thought they were out to get his money. A farmer *needs* a banker. He
needs a lawyer. He *needs* a good accountant." There are some who say

that Kirk was distracted by family problems. The Kirks were having so much difficulty trying to control their teenage son that at one point Dee Kirk tried to persuade the Hall County Sheriff's Department to put the boy in jail. Some years before, one of Art Kirk's sisters had committed suicide by shooting herself in the head with a .357 Magnum; in 1982, one of the Kirks' daughters—a married daughter who had been having emotional difficulties—came to her parents' home, picked up Art Kirk's .357 Magnum, held it to her head, and killed herself.

As Kirk's loan deteriorated, so did his patience. "He became more and more bitter with the establishment," someone who saw him during that period has said. "I think he was beginning to realize that he was getting in deeper and deeper and there was no way to get out." Testifying in an investigation of Kirk's death, Richard Falldorf, who handled Kirk's loan at Norwest Bank, put it this way: "It was just difficult to get Art to answer rational-type questions with rational-type answers." In February of 1984, the lease came up on the twelve hundred acres of ordnance-plant land that Kirk had been farming—the federal government leases out the land for three or five years through sealed bids—and he had to decide whether to bid on a new lease. The bank would agree to back him only on a rental figure that penciled out. Kirk made the bid, but he didn't get the land, so he was faced with the task of making a dent in his enormous loan with the income on the home place and the hundred and sixty acres he was renting from Stauffer. Kirk had always been known as a man with a quick temper, and his temper had grown worse. It was said that he usually kept a gun in his coveralls, even while he was plowing. It was said that when some local kids got too close to his land one day he fired shots over their heads.

In May of 1984, Kirk drove in to Grand Island to attend a meeting of an organization called Nebraskans for Constitutional Government, which has been described by its Grand Island representative, a man named Robert Mettenbrink, Sr., as a group that meets to study the Constitution. At times, the lesson has been led by a speaker from the Posse Comitatus. That night in May, the visiting speaker was Rick Elliott, of Fort Lupton, Colorado, the founder of an organization called the National Agricultural Press Association, or NAPA. Although Elliott had talked from time to time about a plan for NAPA to provide farm reports, the only apparent connection NAPA had with the press was that anyone who joined got a NAPA press sticker for his pickup truck and that Elliott was putting out a newspaper called the *Primrose & Cattlemen's Gazette*—an odd and erratically published mélange of conventional ranch news (HEREFORD BREED DEMONSTRATE STRENGTH AND QUALITY AT COLORADO STATE FAIR) and some of Elliott's other interests (HOW THE JEWISH QUESTION TOUCHES THE FARM). Elliott had been traveling around the Midwest— particularly southern Minnesota and Iowa—telling farmers that there was a legal and nonviolent way to solve their financial problems. He said that all loans made since 1974 were illegal under federal truth-in-lending legislation. He said that by joining NAPA and following its guidance, farmers could, without hiring lawyers, file lawsuits that would result in their bank loans' being declared null and void. He said that NAPA could find low-interest loans for farmers. He said all this in vigorous, dramatic speeches that were laced with patriotic references and historical anecdotes and citations of federal codes. The Kirks joined NAPA, and when Robert Mettenbrink opened a Nebraska chapter in Grand Island, Deloris Kirk worked for a while in its office. According to Mrs. Kirk, her husband had returned home from that first meeting and said, "Mama, I'm sure at last we found the answer to our troubles."

That view would not have been shared by Norwest Bank. In June, the bank found out that Kirk had sold seventy thousand dollars' worth of stored corn and thirty thousand dollars' worth of cattle—property that, by the terms of his note, belonged partly to Norwest—but hadn't brought in the receipts. The bankers had a talk with Kirk, but he still didn't produce any money. What he did instead was to file a case in the federal district court in Lincoln asking that the Norwest loan be declared null and that the bank be ordered to pay him several million dollars in damages for a number of reasons, among them that the bank's conduct "has led to Plaintiff being accused of stealing his own property which Plaintiffs have proof of ownership by bills of sale and checks which is surely the most wanton form of conduct on the part of Defendants that would make a skunk belch from odor while leaving Plaintiff with horrendous damages." Kirk didn't use a lawyer; Robert Mettenbrink notarized the papers.

The chief judge of the federal district court in Nebraska, Warren K. Urbom, was not impressed by Kirk's legal reasoning. Except for one claim that didn't include enough information to permit a judgment, the case was dismissed without a hearing in October. Of the citations of law that Kirk had made, Judge Urbom wrote, "Many of these provisions have absolutely nothing to do with the facts alleged." In fact, the homemade cases inspired by NAPA had been dismissed wholesale by federal judges in the Midwest, and at least one judge had spoken of the possibility of assessing future plaintiffs court costs for taking up the court's time with frivolous litigation. "These cases display a disturbing pattern of identical styles, identical statutory and case-law citations, and even identical typographical errors," Judge Urbom had written in a decision in August of 1984. "Given the meritlessness of the claims, I have to suspect that these complaints are being filed for purposes other than good-faith assertion of legal claims. Whether the plaintiffs have the purpose of harassment or are deceived by some third party into believing there may be merit in their claims, I do not know." The Kirks had a newspaper clipping quoting Judge Urbom's August decision. They also had a smudged photocopy of a clipping from the *Rochester* (Minnesota) *Post-Bulletin* that went further than Judge Urbom had in criticizing what he referred to as the third party. "Rick Elliott, who is helping farmers prepare lawsuits against their lenders and says he can get low-interest loans for farmers, has a criminal record that stretches from 1949 to 1972," the *Post-Bulletin* reporter, Bruce Maxwell, wrote. Maxwell listed convictions for perjury and bad checks and selling stocks without a license. He also reported that the NAPA programs Elliott operated were being investigated by attorney-general offices in several states.

Once Judge Urbom had dismissed Kirk's suit, Norwest's lawyers entered a claim to the property that was security for Kirk's loan—his farm equipment and whatever crops had not been sold and the unaccounted-for hundred thousand dollars. Papers were drawn up notifying him of the date on which the state court would hear the bank's claim and ordering him not to dispose of any more secured property before that date. As was required by Nebraska law, Norwest turned the papers over to the civil section of the sheriff's department for service. The Norwest people also informed the sheriff's department that during their last conversation on Kirk's farm he had been wearing a .45. They may have mentioned that he was suspected of being a member of the Posse Comitatus. The sheriff's department, which had served papers on Art Kirk before, already knew him to be a man with a lot of guns and a quick temper. It was decided to send three deputies, and to send them armed.

When the events of that day are discussed in Grand Island, a lot of people are described as having done what they did because they couldn't be put in the position of doing otherwise. The bank, it is said, couldn't be put in the position of ignoring a debt of three hundred thousand dollars and a debtor who had sold a hundred thousand dollars' worth of secured assets. The bank had a responsibility to its depositors and to its investors. It was required to answer to bank examiners. The sheriff and the county attorney, it is said, couldn't be put in the position of permitting a citizen to avoid service of court papers by threatening deputies with a gun. Since the threatened deputy had responded by telling Kirk that he was under arrest, to which Kirk's response had reportedly been to mention the possibility of shooting the deputy's head off, it was decided that a warrant could be obtained charging Kirk with resisting arrest with a dangerous or deadly weapon. To judge from Art Kirk's conversation on the telephone that evening, he may have believed that he could not be put in the position of permitting armed deputies on land that had been federally posted. Once the warrant had been obtained, the county could not be put in the position of having its law-enforcement officials driven off the Kirk farm again—and that meant alerting the Troop C SWAT team.

"I am just afraid we're going to need some help,'cause I'm afraid the guy's going to do some shooting," the chief deputy sheriff said that afternoon in a telephone call to the state police captain in charge of Troop C.

"Well, you understand if the SWAT team goes out there and there's any shots fired, they'll take him down—they won't worry about the consequences," the captain said.

"Well," the deputy sheriff said, "I don't know that the guy leaves us any choice, does he?"

In deciding to call in the SWAT team, Sheriff Fairbanks was, of course, conscious of the murders that had taken place when law-enforcement officials tried to arrest Gordon Kahl in North Dakota. A couple of months after the North Dakota shootings, Fairbanks had helped organize a Nebraska Sheriffs Association briefing in Grand Island on the Posse Comitatus and other fringe groups—a briefing at which the sheriffs were told that a number of Nebraska farmers and ranchers had been engaging in combat maneuvers.

Late in the afternoon, the SWAT team was officially called in. Negotiators were named. An operational headquarters was set up in Cairo, and a command post was established at Troop C. Arrangements were made for an ambulance to be on hand in Cairo. "At approximately 8:00 pm, the command post was advised that the SWAT team was deployed in the vicinity of the Kirk farm," the county attorney, Stephen Von Riesen, said in his report. "The negotiators interviewed Mr. Titsworth, and it was agreed that he should be the first person to call the Kirk residence."

· · ·

Among Nebraska farmers, one response to the news of Arthur Kirk's death was outrage. From some initial news reports that didn't go into what Kirk believed politically, or precisely why the SWAT team had surrounded his house, Art Kirk seemed to be a harassed farmer trying to defend his family's land against foreclosure—a tragic real-life version of the plucky farm folks that people like Jessica Lange and Sam Shepard and Sally Field had been playing in Hollywood movies. When Kirk, a man who hadn't done much socializing, was buried, several hundred people turned up for the funeral service. One local business took an advertisement in the *Independent* announcing that it would be closed for two hours so employees could attend "the funeral of Arthur Kirk, who was shot to death by State Police while trying to defend his family farm." Farmers held protest meetings. The headquarters of the Norwest Bank, in Minneapolis, sent a security team to the Grand Island branch. Kirk's pastor wanted to know why a churchman hadn't been called in. Kirk's wife wanted to know why she hadn't been allowed to go to her husband. A lot of people wanted to know why it was imperative for Arthur Kirk, a man who held no hostages and didn't seem to pose an immediate threat to the community, to be confronted with such force of arms. At least two state senators called for an inquiry into the circumstances of Kirk's death, and the governor eventually asked a retired district judge, Samuel Van Pelt, to conduct an investigation. The *Independent* got a lot of letters to the editor, most of them expressing sympathy with Art Kirk and condemnation of the law-enforcement authorities. "A large Chicago bank goes on the rocks," one letter began. "What happens? Several banks from around the world donate and the federal government comes with I forget how many billion dollars. . . . A farmer goes broke, they can't get to him to sell him out, so they kill him."

The Hall County authorities and the state police defended themselves vigorously. They pointed out that a number of widely held assumptions about the incident were not true. The SWAT team

was there to arrest Kirk on a felony charge, for instance, not to fore-
close on his farm. The bank had made no claim to Kirk's land. The
superintendent of the state patrol said that SWAT teams were a device for controlling violence rather than raising the level of violence;
the SWAT teams were organized in 1975, he said, and until Art Kirk
started shooting his automatic rifle that night, they had never been
involved in an exchange of gunfire. The burden of the case made by
the authorities was that Art Kirk had been a dangerous man, more
like Gordon Kahl than like Sam Shepard. The morning after the
Independent carried the story of Kirk's death, its lead headline was
LINK BETWEEN KIRK AND VIGILANTE GROUP PROBED. The state patrol
released transcripts of Kirk's telephone conversations on the night of
the shooting—transcripts full of vituperation and threats and ob-
scenity and bigotry. At a news conference, police displayed twenty-
seven weapons that had been seized from Kirk's farmhouse after his
death. Stephen Von Riesen, the county attorney, revealed that papers
seized from the house at the same time included Posse Comitatus
propaganda. They also included material from organizations such as
the Committee to Restore the Constitution and the National Commodity and Barter Association and the Anti-Lawyer Party and the
Christian Nationalist Crusade, whose booklet *Jews and Their Lies,* by
Martin Luther, carried an epigraph of singular ecumenism: "Attention Reader: This book is not published for sectarian purposes. The
publishers, as indicated above, are also publishing the edicts of more
than 20 popes who dealt with the Jewish problem. Their edicts are
as strong as anything contained in this work by Dr. Martin Luther."

Stephen Von Riesen maintained that those who wanted to assign
blame for Art Kirk's death should have been looking not toward
law-enforcement officials but toward the organizations that sell desperate farmers pipe dreams about how to escape their problems. "It's
always easier to blame some amorphous conspiracy," Von Riesen said
not long after Kirk's death. "Farmers have reached the point where
the normal ways of handling problems aren't working. They're faced
with losing their farms, and they're susceptible to radical, spurious

approaches to the problem. Arthur Kirk was a victim of these groups that told him that there is a free lunch. There isn't any free lunch. If you borrow money, you have to pay it back."

Deloris Kirk continued to blame the police and to support NAPA. In fact, she seemed to draw closer and closer to the organization after her husband's death. Requests for interviews were referred to Robert Mettenbrink. When Mrs. Kirk held a press conference in Grand Island just after her husband's death, Mettenbrink introduced her, and Rick Elliott was also on hand. Mrs. Kirk was asked at the press conference how people could help, and she suggested that everybody read five works "that they're trying to destroy"—the U.S. Constitution, the Nebraska Constitution, the Bible, and two booklets associated with the fringe right. She appeared at NAPA rallies to say that her husband had been a happy man from the moment he heard Rick Elliott speak. It was a testimonial that lost some of its impact a few weeks after the shooting, when the *Independent* ran its first large story on Elliott's run-ins with the law. He had just been charged by the attorney general's office in Colorado with nineteen felony-theft counts having to do with NAPA and the *Primrose & Cattlemen's Gazette*.

When Deloris Kirk was asked at her press conference if she considered her husband a martyr, she said, "No, I think he was a victim." It was easy to see Art Kirk as a victim, although there was a lot of disagreement about whose victim he was. Some people agreed with Stephen Von Riesen that Kirk was the victim of those who led him to believe he could get his loan declared null with a do-it-yourself lawsuit and could keep the sheriff off his land with a legally worthless piece of paper. A lot of people saw Kirk as the victim of the pressures that farmers have had to face—a desperate man driven so far from rationality that he could believe that the Mossad, the Israeli intelligence agency, was pulling the strings in Hall County, Nebraska. Some people thought that there was plenty of blame to go around. The *Independent's* editorial on the shooting said, "There are people who are profiting from the plight of farmers, some indirectly and even innocently because they are themselves deluded, and some more maliciously defrauding them," but it also said that the fact that Kirk owed the bank far more than he could ever hope to repay from the income on his land "says something to lenders and borrowers alike." Some Nebraskans who despised the message that groups like NAPA and the Posse Comitatus bring to farmers also thought that what Arthur Kirk chose to read in his own house was nobody's business and no justification for the state's show of force at the Kirk farmhouse that night.

In his report to the governor, Judge Van Pelt said that someone analyzing the circumstances of Arthur Kirk's death could identify several junctures at which a different decision might have avoided catastrophe. If the bank hadn't pressed its legal case or if the sheriff's department had sent out one unarmed deputy instead of three armed ones or if Deloris Kirk and some friends who went to counsel with Art Kirk after the incident with the deputies had stayed around or if Jan Steeple had gone to the Kirk farm to talk things over or if an arrest had been attempted while Kirk was cutting beans instead of while he was barricaded inside his house or if the SWAT team deployment had been delayed until Kirk had a chance to cool off, the judge said, Art Kirk might have survived. Still, Van Pelt found that at each juncture the decision reached had been understandable, given the knowledge and resources available at the time. In other words, a lot of people had acted as they might have been expected to act, and in the end Art Kirk lay bleeding to death in his farmyard. It was not an analysis that offered much comfort to the Nebraska farmers who had been so upset by the shooting in the first place. A lot of them have a lot of Art Kirk's problems.

Right-of-Way

Washington, Virginia

MAY 1985

"The ironic thing is that both of these people came here to find peace," the man said. When he said it, he swept his arm out to indicate a scene of palpable peacefulness—a narrow street with almost no traffic on it, a line of buildings that looked as if they might have originated in the early nineteenth century, some lovely mountains in the distance. He was standing not far from the courthouse in the seat of Rappahannock County, Virginia—a town that is named Washington and is sometimes called Little Washington, to distinguish it from the larger, much less peaceful seat of government in the District of Columbia, an hour and a quarter to the east. The residents of Rappahannock County aren't fond of having their county seat called Little Washington, but the town does have the feeling of a place built on the smaller scale of more settled times. The old brick courthouse is flanked by two diminutive brick buildings that look like toy courthouses themselves. The brochure available to visitors says, "Today the population of Washington, Virginia, barely exceeds that at its 18th Century beginning." In recent years, Washington has acquired a community theater and a restaurant widely known for elegant turns on American cuisine, but there is still not enough bustle to require a public telephone booth.

The theater and the restaurant are, of course, the sorts of institutions brought to rural Virginia by newcomers—along with craft shops and careful restorations and elaborate zoning ordinances. It is only in recent years that Rappahannock County has been thought of as the sort of place that might offer shiitake mushrooms on vermicelli or a remarkable level of peacefulness. In the thirties, when Shenandoah National Park and the Skyline Drive were established in the Blue Ridge Mountains, along the western border of Rappahannock County, a lot of people were resettled from the mountain hollows into what was then a farm county known mainly for apples and cattle. Some of those who were resettled did not immediately abandon their customary ways of resolving disputes or celebrating good fortune or displaying their resentment at having been forcibly removed from their land. Even before the resettlement, there were parts of the county where sheriff's deputies went with trepidation. Rappahannock County, which had always had some large farmland holdings, didn't carry the reputation for random violence that was associated with a couple of the mountain counties nearby, but on a Saturday night in an area like Jenkins Hollow, the peace was breached rather regularly.

"There probably aren't more than one or two Jenkinses left in Jenkins Hollow," a Rappahannock lawyer who sounded as if he rather missed the old sort of Saturday night has said. "I suppose it's mostly retired people from D.C. The houses are very well kept." Of the six thousand or so residents of Rappahannock County, a couple of thousand are people who have moved in within the past fifteen or twenty years. As it happened, Rappahannock County represented a haven to a lot of different sorts of people. For a time, there was an influx of hippies, many of whom drifted on and some of whom evolved into respectable shopkeepers or building contractors or schoolteachers. A lot of people who worked for the government in Washington, D.C.—civil servants or military people at their final posting—bought houses in Rappahannock that began as weekend retreats and became retirement homes. Some people who were trying to escape the steady suburbanization of the northern Virginia counties—people who were more comfortable in small towns, people who wanted a place where it was possible to hunt rabbits or raise

a few crops—moved from Fairfax County to Prince William County
to Rappahannock County. For some rather prominent people in
Washington, D.C., Rappahannock County seemed to have the
beauty of the Virginia foxhunting country just to the east of it—in
fact, it has always had a hunt—but not the social pressure associated
with places where the horsey types have collected in great numbers.
A lot of people who settled in Rappahannock County found it to
be what they sometimes call "a good mix." It's a place where some
families have presided over large holdings long enough to hear
themselves discussed as feudal and where some families continue to
live in the government-built bungalows still known as resettlement
houses. It's a place that has tasteful antique shops as well as, on the
road to Shenandoah National Park, a line of stands selling apples and
cider and Hong Kong statuary. It's a place where life seems simple
but where the guest columnist in the county weekly is Eugene
McCarthy.

Although the man standing near the courthouse in Washington,
Virginia, might have found it ironic that two of the people who had
come to Rappahannock County to find peace had found turmoil
instead, he would have seen no irony in the fact that the cause of the
turmoil was—at the beginning, at least—an argument over property.
The newcomers to Rappahannock County brought with them an
urban precision about property—about precisely where the boundary was and precisely who had the right to cross it. They talked a lot
about property values. Partly because of their presence, of course,
there was more property value to talk about. People in Rappahannock County had always had the occasional title disagreement or
boundary dispute, but the new people seemed to bring a new re-
lentlessness to such disagreements. When the disagreement between
Patricia Saltonstall and Diane Kidwell began, they were arguing, re-
lentlessly, about a right-of-way.

"I fell in love with it when I saw the hills open up," Patricia Saltonstall says of her first impression of Rappahannock County. That was

in 1970, and, like a lot of people who had found the sixties almost too eventful, she was in the market for a peaceful place. She had the sort of credentials that presumably could have been useful in keeping a certain amount of turmoil at bay. Her parents' marriage was a union of two prominent New England families, the Saltonstalls and the Laphams. She had gone to Smith and then married a Yale man whose family owned a factory in Pittsburgh. But by 1970, when she was in her early forties, she had also seen her share of contention. Her first marriage had ended in divorce, and so had her second. Reclaiming her formidable maiden name, she had moved with her three sons to Washington, D.C., and established herself as a society writer for *The Washington Star*. In the mid-sixties, she became caught up in the civil rights struggle; she worked for a while for the federal Community Relations Service and then began to devote just about full time to the District of Columbia school-desegregation case. At the 1968 Democratic National Convention, in Chicago, she and a number of companions—most of them convention delegates who had impressive credentials of their own—were arrested for disorderly conduct, and she responded to the experience by threatening to sue the city to stop the practice of strip-searching female prisoners. In 1970, she was working in Washington for Senator Harold Hughes, of Iowa, mostly on matters concerning the problem of alcoholism, and looking for some land to escape to on weekends and summer holidays. She had the sort of taste and accent that might have been expected from a former society writer with a formidable name, but she also seemed like someone who had been affected by her connection with the civil rights movement and the struggles entailed in raising a family on her own—a direct, rather intense woman with a no-nonsense manner and a lot of pride in her own independence.

The land she found in Rappahannock County was a two-hundred-and-seventy-acre farm not far from the village of Flint Hill, in an area along State Route 729 which includes some relatively simple houses on ten or fifteen acres of land and some imposing places displaying signs such as CLIFTON, ESTABLISHED 1675. The farm was what she has sometimes called landlocked—it could be connected to the state road only by a private road slicing through neighboring properties—but that brought the price down and added to the privacy. It was lovely, rolling land, leading back to include an overgrown mountain—Hickerson Mountain—that could be seen from miles away. She bought the place and named it Points of View. There was an abandoned tenant's house, which she began to renovate—rather gradually, since she had not yet come into her inheritance. She wanted a barn—a barn that, like the house, was tucked into the curves of the fields in a way that made it blend with the landscape rather than something that seemed to have been dropped naked on the top of a hill. An architect from Georgetown built her an ingenious, multiuse version of a faded wood barn, which eventually won an architectural award and was pictured in *The Washington Post*. In 1973, a two-hundred-acre farm a few miles down 729 was divided into eight lots that became known as the Lindgren-Whaley tract, and she acquired three lots that joined her land on the other side of Hickerson Mountain. Although her holdings on that side of the mountain were also blocked from 729, they could be reached without hacking up and down Hickerson: the Lindgren-Whaley deed provided that the owners of all lots had the use for all purposes of a fifty-foot right-of-way that ran back from 729 through a ten-acre parcel known as Lot A.

. For several years, Patricia Saltonstall thought that in Rappahannock County she had found the peace she had sought. Then she started having problems with her neighbors. It may be that the problems started when she changed from a weekender into a permanent resident who was intent on making Points of View an effective agricultural operation—in the late seventies, when, after having come into her inheritance, she decided to make a serious commitment to the farm. In her view, that caused some irritation among the nearby farmers, because it deprived one of them of some grazing land he had been renting cheap and it challenged some of their old Virginia notions about the place of a woman. Whatever notions Pat Salton-stall's neighbors might have had about women, they had different notions from hers about how to approach farming. What they tended to think of as the occasional and inevitable straying of cattle, for instance, she considered "systematic stealing of grazing land"—stealing that was made all the more irritating by the accused neighbor's expressing amiable surprise ("My land! What *am* I going to do with them critters?") and vowing to get at that broken fence just as soon as he could. Some of the neighbors thought that Pat Saltonstall, in her businesslike approach to farming, was inflexible and maybe even self-righteous. "Pat was her own worst enemy," a friend of hers has said. "With her money, she should have just fixed the fence instead of worrying so much about what was right or wrong."

In the view of some people in the area, the real trouble started when Patricia Saltonstall hired Rance Spellman. She had met him during the renovation of her farmhouse; he operated heavy equipment. Spellman came from a family that also had been seeking some space in rural Virginia. His father, who was born and raised and married in Ohio, had gone to Alexandria, Virginia, after the Second World War to work as a heavy-equipment operator, and eventually moved his family out to what the Spellmans had built as a weekend cabin in Culpeper County, only ten or fifteen miles from Points of View. In the meantime, he had managed to create a small heavy-equipment contracting company of his own, despite an inclination to be a lot more comfortable on top of a bulldozer than in front of a ledger book. Rance Spellman worked for that company and took it over after the sudden death of his father. The first time Pat Saltonstall saw him, he was on top of a bulldozer—a bulldozer whose blade had just hit the root of a treasured old ash tree in her front yard. She remembers his courtesy, and the almost delicate way he handled the huge machine, and his blue eyes.

Spellman was interested in what might be done with the top of Hickerson Mountain. "He said he'd like to do the mountain—clear it, stabilize the soil, fence it," Pat Saltonstall has said. "He was just

inspired by it." She hired him to do the mountain. It was soon obvious to her that he was a prodigious worker—a burly young man, six
feet two inches tall, who was meticulous about his equipment and
precise in his estimates and annoyed whenever darkness finally
forced him to quit for the day. It was also obvious, she later said, that
with Rance Spellman's help "I could *do* this farm, and it would be
fun." In early 1980, she hired him, on a contract basis, to be her farm
manager. Eventually, they also had what Pat Saltonstall usually refers
to as "a personal relationship." A small solar house had been built for
the Points of View farm manager, but Spellman moved into the re-
stored farmhouse with Pat Saltonstall.

It was a relationship they didn't advertise—aware, as Pat Saltonstall says, that in the view of her neighbors, "it was not the sort of
thing you did with the help." Rance Spellman was in his early thirties, nearly twenty years younger than Pat Saltonstall, and his education was in earthmoving and stone masonry and horse training
rather than in the sort of subjects taught at Smith. "There was a gap
in age and a gap in cultural background," she has said. "But we had
a lot in common. He could stand alone, the way I do." She saw him
as a sort of blond Marlboro man—an independent outdoorsman in
jeans and boots who patrolled the property and, like the cowboys of
old, always carried a gun. She admired his competence and his almost religious devotion to hard work. He joked about her being his
employer, a relationship he expressed in the diminutive: his private
name for her was Bossie. Together, they built up a herd of registered
Angus cattle. Spellman cleared more fields and built more fences.
On the other side of the mountain, they had some lumber cut and
hauled out through the right-of-way road to the mill.

After a time, Pat Saltonstall became aware that where she saw a
protector—a handsome and basically rather shy protector—some
other people saw a bully. She considered that largely a matter of
jealousy caused by Spellman's looks and his "tremendous presence."
In her view, "There's a kind of handicap that big men have: sometimes other men feel threatened." In fact, some people in Rappahan-

nock County had found Spellman to be unvaryingly soft-spoken and polite; some knew him for obviously genuine and unselfish acts of kindness toward children or animals. But others saw him as a menacing swaggerer. Nobody had ever seen him actually use his size or his guns to attack anyone, but a number of people seemed afraid that he might. According to his brother, Boyd Spellman, their father, whom Rance had revered, had sometimes seemed too easygoing to be in business, and Rance had been intent on becoming the sort of person nobody took advantage of. Along the way, he had some experiences of the kind that can drain off cheerfulness—two failed marriages, for instance, and the early death of his father, and a stint in Vietnam at a time when most people his age seemed to be going about their business at home. For whatever reasons, Spellman had been in some unpleasant confrontations now and then as a heavy-equipment operator, and as the farm manager of Points of View he seemed to be in more. It got so that the owner of straying cattle had to contend not with a stiff note from Pat Saltonstall, but with the possibility that Rance Spellman would impound the cattle and demand board and feed money before giving them back. "They'd done every kind of thing to everybody there," William Buntin, who was the sheriff of Rappahannock County at the time, has said. "They had problems with every neighbor that joins them."

Of course, Patricia Saltonstall might have been right in assuming that some of the ill feeling was brought on by jealousy or prejudice—envy of her money and his appearance and what they had accomplished at Points of View, hatred of the relationship that was suspected between the boss and the farm manager. In the view of a friend of theirs, "They were building a showplace, and I think that people who had always got along with patches resented it." Some of the neighboring farmers said that people who were seriously interested in farming, as opposed to showing off, would not have given priority to putting a pasture on top of a mountain. It did seem, though, that as farm operators, Pat Saltonstall and Rance Spellman complemented each other perfectly—his skills and heavy machinery and stunning capacity for work, her resources and organizational ability and encouragement. But to some people in the county, their alliance was also what made them particularly threatening. If Rance Spellman was a bully, he was all the more so with Patricia Saltonstall's money and influence behind him. If Patricia Saltonstall was a willful rich lady, she was all the more so with a huge, intimidating cowboy to back her up.

Roger and Diane Kidwell were among those people who kept moving west from the D.C. sprawl to find a little country. They had both been raised in Fairfax County, in the days when it seemed more small-town than suburban; after they were married and began to raise a family, they moved in two or three steps from Alexandria to Amissville, not far from where the Spellman family had gone to find some space. Diane Kidwell was a secretary, and until 1975 she worked at a conference center called the Airlie Foundation, in Warrenton, Virginia, twenty miles to the east. Roger Kidwell also worked there briefly, at the front desk. For the Kidwells, as it turned out, escaping the suburbs did not mean escaping turmoil. In the late seventies, Murdock Head, the executive director of Airlie, was indicted for payment of an illegal gratuity. He was accused of having smoothed the way for the foundation's contract applications by slipping cash payoffs to Representative Daniel Flood, of Pennsylvania, through Flood's aide, Stephen Elko, who had become a witness for the government. The payoffs were alleged to have taken place during the time Diane Kidwell worked in Head's office, first as a secretary and for a time as his administrative assistant. After two trials, Head was convicted and sent to jail. Among those who were or had been connected with the foundation, Mrs. Kidwell, who had been laid off by Airlie before the investigation began, was the only person who appeared as a friendly witness for the prosecution to corroborate Elko's story—an act that caused great rancor among her former colleagues. The payoff scandal was not the only source of turmoil in the Kidwells' lives. Apparently, their marriage had been stormy. In 1970, they were legally separated for a while; Diane Kidwell and the children moved into one of the Airlie buildings. Having sold their house in Amissville while they were separated, the Kidwells moved into a rental house after their reconciliation. Roger Kidwell had started selling insurance, and eventually his wife worked with him, in an office in Warrenton. They had their hearts set on building a house of their own—a house on the top of a hill. In the early seventies, they came across Lot A of the Lindgren-Whaley tract. It seemed perfect, Diane Kidwell said later, except for the right-of-way.

The Kidwells built their house on a hill overlooking Route 729. It's a tidy-looking house that wouldn't have seemed out of place in one of the subdivisions they left as they moved west—two stories, with yellow siding and a carport and a basketball goal and an apartment in the basement for Roger Kidwell's parents. The right-of-way, which existed only in the form of a narrow dirt road coming back toward the mountain from 729, was not a source of disturbance. There was only one house on the lots served by the road—a small weekend cottage that generated little traffic. Eventually, the Kidwells bought a second lot, a twenty-five-acre parcel just across the right-of-way. They had no problems with the Lindgren-Whaley tract's largest landowner, Patricia Saltonstall, even after she hired Rance Spellman as farm manager. Until the dispute about the right-of-way began, in fact, the Kidwells were not even aware of who Rance Spellman was. Roger and Diane Kidwell, both of whom commuted every day to Warrenton, were not among those who spent a lot of time at the lunch counter or filling station in Flint Hill chewing over questions such as whether beef prices would ever go up or what the relationship between Patricia Saltonstall and Rance Spellman really was. The Kidwells were not well-known in the area except as a family that raised what seemed to be particularly ferocious dogs. (Sheriff Buntin has said that when he canvassed the county for his final election campaign, the Kidwell house was the only place where he decided against getting out of the car.) What little contact there had been between the Kidwells and Pat Saltonstall was cordial.

Diane Kidwell's brother had been given permission to fish in a pond at Points of View. Like Pat Saltonstall, the Kidwells believed strongly in the importance of maintaining one's property ("We've always been interested in our property, and in keeping our property values") and in the necessity of keeping hunters and other trespassers off the mountain. Although Diane Kidwell and Patricia Saltonstall may not have had the same taste in architecture or the same circle of friends, they had what Pat Saltonstall calls "a fairly normal neighborly acquaintanceship."

The trouble started in the spring of 1982. The subject of the right-of-way came up when Diane Kidwell wrote to Patricia Saltonstall asking if she would contribute to the cost of putting down some new gravel. After that, a lot of issues were raised. Eventually, lawyers for the two parties were exchanging letters, none of them conciliatory. Paragraphs in the county deed book and statutes in the Virginia code were cited. Questions were raised about a gate that had been placed across the right-of-way back near the mountain. Patricia Saltonstall had, in violation of the deed, put it up without the permission of the other lot owners—she said it was to discourage lumber thieves—and the Kidwells had removed it without the permission of Patricia Saltonstall. There was the question of the Kidwells' having installed a cattle guard on the road. There was the question of whether the Points of View lumbering crews had left the Kidwells' gates open. There was the question of whether the Kidwells had been trespassing on the mountain. There was the question of whether Rance Spellman's excavation work on the mountain had interfered with the Kidwells' water supply. At the center of the dispute, though, was Pat Saltonstall's announced intention to exercise her right to make use of a full fifty feet of right-of-way, so that there could be "more frequent and regular use of the road." Since road improvements would begin shortly, she informed the Kidwells, they should remove any shrubbery or trees or posts that they had within the fifty-foot strip stipulated in the deed. The Kidwells didn't want to remove their shrubbery and trees and posts;

they didn't want more frequent and regular use of the road. Pat Saltonstall had said that the widening was necessary for keeping a close watch on valuable herds of Angus grazing on the mountain and for putting into effect "other plans I have for one of the lots." The Kidwells thought it was unnecessary except as a matter of spite. Their lawyer said that anyone who attempted to clear the right-of-way without a court order would be held liable for any property damage. Presumably, the lawyer, a young man named David Konick, intended to file for an injunction; but no injunction had been filed by November 8, when Patricia Saltonstall's lawyer, unable to reach Konick, left a message on his answering machine saying that work might begin as early as the next afternoon. It was actually early the next morning when Rance Spellman climbed onto a bulldozer, drove over the mountain he had cleared, and came out on the right-of-way to begin his work.

Sheriff Buntin and a state policeman arrived at the Kidwells' together that morning. Diane Kidwell had phoned Buntin's office to demand that Spellman be stopped, but the sheriff, who had neither the authority nor the inclination to referee a right-of-way dispute, had not hurried out. Diane Kidwell's brother had phoned the state police and warned them that an armed confrontation might take place. When the two lawmen arrived, Rance Spellman was sitting in the driver's seat of the bulldozer, which was parked only twenty yards or so from where the Kidwells' driveway meets the right-of-way. From the appearance of the land around him, he had already done considerable work. He was dressed in his usual outfit of blue jeans and boots and a couple of work shirts and a down vest. He was slumped over. The state trooper climbed up on the bulldozer to have a closer look. Rance Spellman had a small amount of blood coming from his mouth and nose. A volley of shotgun pellets had torn through his down vest. He was dead.

The story that the authorities eventually put together was this: Rance Spellman had begun his work near the Kidwells' driveway—

tearing up trees, pushing over gateposts. When Diane Kidwell's brother tried to reason with him, he just smiled—sneered, really—and kept working. After a while, Mrs. Kidwell took a shotgun from the house and, holding it in a way that concealed it from Spellman's view, walked to the family's pickup. She pulled the pickup into the right-of-way, close to the beginning of her driveway, and sat in the front seat with the shotgun next to her. Her brother pleaded with her to come back to the house and wait for the state police, but she said she had decided to take her stand. Her husband watched from the back door; one of her sons watched from a field above the house. For twenty minutes or so, Diane Kidwell watched the bulldozer, which took several swipes perilously close to the pickup. After one of them, she pointed the shotgun out the window and fired one blast at Spellman—shouting, "Get off! Get off!" She said that she thought he was reaching for a gun and she had therefore been in fear for her life. Spellman was armed, as usual. He had a carbine on the bulldozer and a pistol in his shoulder holster. But the carbine was still in its scabbard and the pistol was buttoned up under one of his shirts and the vest.

The only witnesses alive to testify to what had happened were Diane Kidwell and people related to her, and they had been sequestered in the house by their lawyer, David Konick, long enough to have compared stories. The authorities, though, tended to think that the shooting had taken place pretty much the way the Kidwells said it had. The witnesses had reported, after all, that Diane Kidwell had put herself in the path of the bulldozer, which never left the fifty-foot right-of-way. They had reported that Spellman had been shot with a concealed weapon when his own gun was nowhere in sight. They had reported Diane Kidwell's shouting not "Help!" or "Don't shoot!" but "Get off!" If the Kidwells had been trying to concoct a story that would justify the killing of Rance Spellman, it was thought, they would have managed to come up with a better one. The grand jury heard testimony, and four weeks after the shooting Diane Kidwell was indicted for murder.

Rance Spellman's funeral was at Points of View farm. There was an unconventional service, full of symbolism. Spellman's horse stood nearby, with a pair of boots reversed in its stirrups, in the traditional symbol of a fallen cavalryman. Then a cortège of four-wheel-drive vehicles moved slowly up the mountain, where Spellman was buried on the mountaintop he had cleared. Spellman's friends and family were there to mourn him, but it was already apparent that his death had not erased the difference between the view of Rance Spellman held by Patricia Saltonstall and the view of him held by a lot of other people in Rappahannock County. A lot of people were saying, "He had it coming." A lot of other people were saying of Diane Kidwell, "If she hadn't done it, somebody else would have."

In a claim of self-defense, the reputation of the deceased is admissible evidence. Lawyers for the accused can try to demonstrate that their client had been particularly fearful because of having been threatened by someone known for "turbulence, violence, and pugnacity." The trial lawyers Diane Kidwell had hired to defend her— her chief counsel was John Dowd, a former federal prosecutor who had led the investigation of Murdock Head—could be expected to do just that. Protection of home and property is not a ground for a claim of self-defense, but none of the attorneys involved doubted that it was relevant to the way jurors were likely to view the issues. As it happened, an early news story had reported incorrectly that Spellman began his work despite a court hearing's having been scheduled for the very next day, but even jurors who were not under that misapprehension could be expected to have a certain sympathy for a woman watching a huge, sneering man on a twenty-ton bulldozer tear up her property in front of her dream house. Also, Diane Kidwell presented a sympathetic figure—a neatly dressed woman with a careful hairdo and thick glasses and a soft voice. News stories tended to identify her as "43-year-old mother of four."

Still, the prosecution thought it had a case that could overcome sympathy for Diane Kidwell. The commonwealth's attorney of

Rappahannock County, Douglas Baumgardner, brought in a special prosecutor, because he himself had to testify in a closed hearing concerning a rather bizarre side issue that was not made public until nearly a year later: David Konick, the young lawyer who had been called by the Kidwells on the morning of the shooting and later dismissed, had admitted that, acting on his own, he had wiped the barrel of the Kidwells' shotgun clean of fingerprints, and he was therefore in danger of being indicted himself. (As it turned out, he was not indicted, but his actions were finally made public at a rather awkward moment—the closing days of what turned out to be an unsuccessful race he ran for commonwealth's attorney.) The special prosecutor—Steven A. Merril, a former assistant prosecutor in Fairfax County—argued that by Diane Kidwell's own admission, she had chosen to confront Spellman, she had hidden a shotgun beside her, she had rejected her brother's plea to return to the house, she had become angrier and angrier as she watched Spellman work, and she had previously seen Spellman reach into his shirt two or three times and come out each time with nothing more dangerous than a cigarette. Whatever the rights and wrongs of the right-of-way argument and whatever the nature of Rance Spellman, Merril said, Diane Kidwell had "absolutely no right to eliminate Rance Spellman from the face of the earth."

The defense lawyers said that Pat Saltonstall's decision to widen the right-of-way to fifty feet was a "spiteful, punitive act," and that Spellman had confirmed that by beginning his work right in front of the Kidwell house, four hundred yards from where the road began. They called as witnesses four or five people who related experiences that led them to consider Spellman violent and turbulent and pugnacious. The owner of some adjoining land, for instance, testified that a front-end loader being used for work on the edge of his property had once been left a few feet onto Points of View land overnight, and that Rance Spellman waited near the machine the next morning with two guns and demanded fifty dollars before he would release it to its operator. There was testimony that just a week or so before the shooting, Roger Kidwell and his son-in-law had run across Spellman while they were out cutting wood, and Spellman had challenged Kidwell to step out in the right-of-way path and settle the dispute with bare hands. Dowd said that Diane Kidwell had concealed her shotgun because she didn't want to provoke "this madman on the bulldozer." She testified that Spellman had threatened to turn over the pickup and that, just before he reached toward his vest, his expression had changed to one of rage. Dowd built an impassioned summation on the theme of why Diane Kidwell had walked from the house to sit in a pickup truck right in front of where Spellman was moving earth around. ("Why does a fireman go into a burning house and pull out a child? Why does a man jump into a cold river and pull a young boy out? Why do men do what they do on the battlefield and save lives, with holes in them? Why? Because they are strong, that's why.") He said that Diane Kidwell had indeed been intent on protecting her home ("Nowhere in the laws or Constitution of this country does it say that a citizen on her own property has to submit to the tyranny of a professional bully on a forty-one-thousand-pound bulldozer"), but had fired because she honestly believed that Rance Spellman was about to pull out a pistol and kill her.

The jury couldn't reach a verdict, but only because of a single holdout. Everyone else wanted to acquit Diane Kidwell. Shortly after the trial ended, three prominent landowners from around Flint Hill went to the commonwealth's attorney and suggested that, considering the size of the majority for acquittal and the continued feeling against Spellman in the county, it would be a waste of money to try Diane Kidwell again. Merril, who had decided to hold a second trial, thought about trying for a change of venue, but he concluded that Rappahannock County jurors were the appropriate people to hear the case. "I felt people who lived there had a stake in it," he has said. "They have to live there, and they have a right to say what they consider criminal activity and what isn't." Merril thinks that he presented a better case the second time around. He tried to narrow the issues, avoiding as much as possible ensnarlment in the right-of-way dispute; he was more aggressive in his cross-examination of the accused. This time, there was no holdout. Diane Kidwell was found not guilty.

The people who watched the trials with some detachment— reporters, courthouse workers, lawyers who dropped in and out of the courtroom—tend to agree that Merril put forward a strong case. Half a dozen of them took a survey among themselves to predict a verdict before the jury came back in the first trial, and the predictions ranged from guilty of manslaughter to guilty of murder. In retrospect, they tend to agree with Merril that a conviction was nearly impossible. "I feel that a typical jury, in addition to analyzing the facts and applying the law, subconsciously takes out a set of scales," a Rappahannock lawyer with considerable trial experience said after the second trial. "It values the liberty of the accused on one side of the scale, and attaches a certain value or weight to the life of the deceased on the other." The decision of twenty-three jurors in the death of Rance Spellman could be taken as an indication that they placed considerable value on the freedom of Diane Kidwell, a demure wife and mother and grandmother who had no previous criminal record and was hardly a threat to the community. The other way to look at it, the lawyer went on, was that Rance Spellman's life was not given great value—that "the community had decided that someone's life is not worth punishing someone for taking."

That's the way Patricia Saltonstall interpreted the jurors' votes. She also saw the case presented by Diane Kidwell's lawyers in court as an attempt to get someone off the hook by dragging the name of someone else through the mud—someone else who was no longer alive to defend himself. Pat Saltonstall took on that defense herself. She saw her mission as "having his name and his life put in perspective." In August of 1983, nine months after Rance Spellman died and two months before Diane Kidwell's second trial, a number of people in Rappahannock County received an invitation from Pat Saltonstall to "come and celebrate the life of Rance Lee Spellman." The celebration, the invitation said, would include country music, a roast-pig picnic, a dedication of the mountaintop cemetery where he was buried, and the announcement of a living memorial—an agricultural prize to be awarded through a nearby community college. Under Rance Spellman's name, the invitation listed some of the things he had been—including farmer, horseman, mason, welder, artificial-insemination technician, surveyor. The guests—a couple hundred of them—arrived at Points of View to find that a tent had been erected for the celebration. It was decorated with thirty-six nearly life-size photographs of Rance Spellman, one for every year of his life. "We wish to remember Rance not for the cruelty of his senseless death by one act of human violence," the invitation said, "but for the glory of one man who left place upon place more beautiful because of his work."

One piece of Spellman's work that Pat Saltonstall intended to finish was the widening of the right-of-way in the Lindgren-Whaley tract. The legal question of whether she had the right to widen the right-of-way to fifty feet—not what her motives were or whether she really needed to but simply whether she had a right to—was not difficult to settle. In December of 1983, two months after Diane Kidwell's acquittal, a circuit-court judge heard one day of testimony on the Kidwells' motion for a permanent injunction barring the road widening, and in January of 1984 he handed down a ruling denying the motion, on the ground that the deed's grant of the fifty-foot right-of-way showed "unambiguous intent." When the warm weather came, in May, a contractor hired by Points of View farm showed up on the right-of-way to begin the grading at precisely the spot where Spellman had left off. Patricia Saltonstall was also there. In a press release, she said that the work was dedicated to Rance Spellman. "Saltonstall called the new construction 'a clear statement about who was right and who was wrong that tragic morning,'" the press release said. "'This project had to be completed, not only because we badly need a good farm road up the north side of the mountain ... but because such a violent act could not be allowed to be the last word on this project.'"

By then, people in Rappahannock County had begun to wonder whether there was ever going to be a last word. Even before the second trial, Patricia Saltonstall had applied for planning permission to build two-family houses on two of her lots in the Lindgren-Whaley tract—she said she would eventually need them for farmworkers—and the Kidwells protested to the zoning authorities that she should not be given a special-use permit to build two-family houses in an area zoned for single-family dwellings only. The zoning argument involved not only the same disputants but some of the same supporting characters. Douglas Baumgardner, who as commonwealth's attorney had presided over Diane Kidwell's indictment, eventually represented Patricia Saltonstall. The zoning administrator of Rappahannock County at the time was David Konick, who had been accused by Roger Kidwell in a letter to the *Rappahannock News* of using the position to carry on a vendetta against the Kidwell family. As the argument about the new houses was carried through the various levels of appeal, it seemed to blend into the murder trials as part of the endless litigation set in motion by Diane Kidwell's letter concerning gravel on the right-of-way.

After the second murder trial, in fact, contention had burst out on several fronts at once. Responding in the *Rappahannock News* to a letter from a county resident that criticized the verdict, Diane Kidwell managed in the course of defending her own conduct to mention that Rance Spellman's estate had been inherited not by an elderly black man who had long worked for the Spellman family, as had been reported, but by Patricia Saltonstall herself. That one was answered by a letter from Patricia Saltonstall expressing outrage ("How, in the name of any kind of fairness and decency, does Kidwell see this as her business?") and then taking issue with Mrs. Kidwell in detail not only about the will but about the facts of the right-of-way dispute. That one was followed by a letter to the paper from Diane

Kidwell pointing out that the burial of Rance Spellman on Hickerson Mountain seemed to be contrary to the burial instructions in his will and contrary to the zoning code, which permitted burial on farmland only in the case of family graveyards.

Perhaps developing her lots in the Lindgren-Whaley tract makes economic sense for Patricia Saltonstall, but the Kidwells see it as a simple act of harassment. ("There's no other reason to build those monstrosities," Diane Kidwell has said.) Perhaps their protest against the houses has been based on the desire to protect their tranquillity and their property values—according to testimony at the zoning hearings, the two houses could generate seventy more automobile trips per day on the right-of-way road—but Patricia Saltonstall sees it as part of a vendetta against her. By now, the disputants can credit each other with only a single motive—the desire to torment. After a couple of letters to the zoning administrator, the Kidwells did not pursue the grave site complaint ("It was a sensitive issue for some people," Roger Kidwell has said), but that does not keep them from believing that Rance Spellman was buried on Hickerson Mountain so that they would be reminded of him every time they glanced up from their carport. In Roger Kidwell's view, "The house was harassment, the grave site was harassment. We know there is no end to this thing." Speaking at the same time of the large memorial advertisements that Patricia Saltonstall has placed in the *Rappahannock News* each year on the anniversary of Rance Spellman's death, Diane Kidwell said, "She might be very genuine in her reasoning for doing that, but it's like she wants to remind me. On the ninth, when I pick up my local paper I see his picture. I see that as harassment. I feel like when I'm sixty-five I'll pick up my local paper and there he'll be."

It has been common for some time to hear people in Rappahannock County say that Patricia Saltonstall and Diane Kidwell are, despite the differences in their backgrounds, very much alike. Both of them tend to complain about having been singled out for unfair treatment. Patricia Saltonstall often talks about the difficulty of having been the only girl at her boarding school who was completely cut off from family during the war—her family was in Hawaii—and of having spent her first years in Rappahannock County making neighborly gestures that were never returned or even acknowledged. Diane Kidwell has implied at times that pressure from a variety of enemies was the only reason she was indicted. Each of them sees herself as a woman capable of standing up to the considerable forces allied against her. One way to view what has happened, Diane Kidwell has said, is as "the story of a wealthy northern woman who came down here to a small Virginia county and wanted to do everything her own way, and the story of the mother and grandmother who stood in front of a forty-thousand-pound bulldozer simply to protect her own property and was forced to shoot somebody to protect her own life." Both women tend to describe their own motives in high moral terms. Asked why she would make an issue over where Spellman was buried, Mrs. Kidwell said that the grave site was contrary to the burial instructions in his will, and "we have a kind of sacred feeling in our family about wills." Patricia Saltonstall has often compared her effort to right what she considers a wrong in Rappahannock County with the efforts of lone black people to right wrongs in the counties of the Deep South. She sometimes says, "I feel like the Rosa Parks of Rappahannock County."

In December of 1985, both the house that Patricia Saltonstall had already built on one of her lots and the house she wanted to build on the adjoining lot were given special-use permits as two-family dwellings by the Rappahannock County Board of Zoning Appeals. The decision did not leave the combatants without a court case. The previous month, just before the statute of limitations for civil litigation was reached, Patricia Saltonstall, in her role as an executor of Rance Spellman's estate, filed a wrongful-death suit against the Kidwells; on her own, she filed a suit claiming three million dollars in damages on the grounds that the Kidwells "have engaged in a persistent course of conduct, commencing before the killing of Rance Spellman and continuing up to the present time, to harass plaintiff, to defame her, to invade her privacy, to interfere with the use of the right-of-way ... and to interfere generally with the use of her property and the operation of her farming business and other farming operations." At around the same time, Diane Kidwell filed a two-hundred-and-twenty-five-thousand-dollar malpractice suit against David Konick, claiming that his suppression of material evidence and subsequent contraventions of the rules of confidentiality had caused doubts to be cast on her innocence. In the reply that Konick filed, he said that Diane Kidwell had "intentionally and maliciously confronted Spellman" in disregard of his advice, and that if he had, in fact, revealed all the confidential information at his disposal, she "would likely have been convicted of a felony in connection with the homicide of Spellman." That statement was, of course, of great interest to Patricia Saltonstall. She saw it as an opening to reinvestigate the circumstances of Rance Spellman's death.

No one knows how far the latest law cases will be carried, but the feeling in Rappahannock County is that the Kidwell and Saltonstall forces will manage to find one battlefield or another. It is assumed that by now Diane Kidwell and Patricia Saltonstall hope to drive each other away. It is also assumed that both of them are people not easily driven off. A lot of Rappahannock residents find that a cause for regret; they were tired of hearing about the dispute a long time ago. Sympathy for both of the participants has pretty much evaporated. There are people who say that Patricia Saltonstall is not trying to rehabilitate Rance Spellman's name but working out her own guilt ("Let's face it: if she had just said, 'Rance, wait until tomorrow,' he'd be alive right now"); there are people who think that Diane Kidwell, in her relentless concern with what impinges on her rights or property, somehow seems to have lost track of the fact that she killed someone. (The headline on one letter to a local paper was SHE COULD HAVE SAID SHE WAS SORRY.) Old-time residents of Rappahannock County are sensitive to the possibility that talk about the murder-trial verdict—particularly in conjunction with another case, in which a man who tracked down his estranged wife's lover and killed him was fined a thousand dollars for manslaughter—will rekindle suspicion among outsiders that Rappahannock might still be one of those counties with backwoods notions about crime and punishment. Some newcomers simply hate the publicity and the turmoil caused by the dispute. Many of them, after all, came to Rappahannock County looking for peace.

Rumors Around Town

Emporia, Kansas

JANUARY 1986

The first headline in *The Junction City Daily Union*—EMPORIA MAN FATALLY SHOT—seemed to describe one of those incidents that can cause a peaceful citizen to shake his head and mumble something about how it's getting so nobody is safe anywhere. The Emporia man was Martin Anderson, a peaceful citizen who had a responsible job and a commission in the Army Reserve and a wife and four little girls. Early on a November evening in 1983, he was murdered by the side of Kansas Highway 177, which cuts south from Manhattan through the rolling cattle-grazing land that people in Kansas call the Flint Hills. According to the newspaper story, the authorities had been told that Anderson was killed during a struggle with an unidentified robber. At the time of the murder, Anderson was on his way back to Emporia from Fort Riley, the infantry base that lies between Junction City and Manhattan. Apparently, the trip had been meant to combine some errands at the fort with an autumn drive through the Flint Hills. His wife was with him, and so were the little girls.

There is a special jolt to the headline EMPORIA MAN FATALLY SHOT. For many Americans, Emporia, Kansas, conjures up the vision of a typical American town in the era when people didn't have to think about violent men bent on robbery—a town where neighbors drank lemonade on the front porch and kidded one another about their performances in the Fourth of July softball game. The vision grew out of the writings of William Allen White, the Sage of Emporia, who, as owner and editor of *The Emporia Gazette,* was widely thought of during the first forty years of this century as the national spokesman for the unadorned values of the American Midwest. The residents of Emporia in those days may have thought of their town as even more tranquil than its national reputation. What White had been looking for when he set out to buy a small-town newspaper, in 1895, was not a typical town but a college town—a place where his editorials could be understood and appreciated by "a considerable dependable minority of intelligent people, intellectually upper-middle class." Emporia, the seat of Lyon County and a division point for the Santa Fe Railway and a trading center for the surrounding farmland, had two colleges—Kansas State Normal School and a small Presbyterian liberal-arts school called the College of Emporia. During the years that people across the country thought of Emporia as a typical Midwestern town, its boosters sometimes spoke of it as the Educational Center of the West, or even the Athens of Kansas.

In some ways, Emporia didn't change much after William Allen White passed from the scene. The White family continued to own the *Gazette.* Even now, Mrs. William L. White—the widow of the Sage's son, who was an author and a foreign correspondent known into his seventies around Emporia as Young Bill—comes in every day. Commercial Street still has the look of the main trading street in a Kansas farm town—two-story buildings separated by a slab of asphalt wide enough to accommodate angle parking on both sides and four lanes of traffic. The College of Emporia folded some years ago, though; its campus is now owned by a religious cult called The Way. Although the Santa Fe's operation has been shrinking in recent years, Emporia has, on the whole, become more of what was called in White's day a lunch-bucket town. The construction of the Wolf Creek nuclear power plant, forty miles to the southeast, brought a few thousand construction workers to the area, and some of them remained after the plant was completed. Although Kansas State Normal expanded as it evolved first into Kansas State Teachers College and then into Emporia Kansas State College and then into Emporia State University, the largest employer in town these days is not a college but a big meatpacking plant, most of whose employees are not the sort of citizens who spend a lot of their time perusing the editorial page. There is less talk than there once was about Emporia's being the Athens of Kansas.

Still, a lot of people in Emporia lead an updated version of the peaceful front-porch life that White portrayed—a life revolving around family and church and school and service club and neighbors. The Andersons seemed to lead that sort of life. When they walked into Faith Lutheran Church every Sunday, the little girls wearing immaculate dresses that Lorna Anderson had made herself, they presented the picture of the wholesome, attractive American family that a lot of people still have in mind when they think of Emporia. Marty Anderson, a medical technologist, ran the laboratory at Newman Memorial County Hospital. He was on the board of directors of the Optimist Club. His wife was working part-time as the secretary of Faith Lutheran. She was a member of a social and service sorority called Beta Sigma Phi, which used its annual Valentine's Day dance as a benefit for the local hospitals. The Andersons were among the young couples who saw one another at Optimist basketball games or church fellowship meetings or Beta Sigma Phi socials—people who tended to recall dates by saying something like "Let's see, that was the year Jenny started nursery school" or "I remember I was pregnant with Bobby."

Faith Lutheran Church is dominated by such families. It's a young church, in a former Assembly of God building on the west side of Emporia—an area filled with split-level houses along blocks so recently developed that most of the trees are still not much higher than the basketball goals. Faith Lutheran was founded in 1982, when the one Missouri Synod Lutheran church in Emporia, Messiah Lutheran, decided that the way to expand was to ask for volunteers to form what was thought of as a "daughter congregation" on the west side. Faith Lutheran grew so quickly that in October of 1982, just

eight months after its founding, it was chartered as a separate congregation. The church—a pale brick building on a corner lot across
the street from a school—turned out to have been well placed,
but the congregation had other advantages besides a fortunate location. The people who had volunteered to move from Messiah tended
to be active young families with a strong interest in a range of church
activities—what was sometimes called at Messiah "the early-service
crowd." Thomas Bird, the minister who had been called from Arkansas to Messiah to lead the new undertaking, turned out to be a
dynamic young pastor who fitted right in with his congregation.
Tom Bird had been a long-distance runner at the University of
Arkansas. He was married to his high school sweetheart, an aston-
ishingly energetic young woman who had a master's degree in
mathematics and managed to combine the responsibilities of a pastor's wife with some teaching at Emporia State. Like a lot of couples
in the congregation, they had three small children and a small split-
level and a swing set in the backyard.

The Missouri Synod is a particularly conservative branch of
American Lutheranism. Tom Bird thought of himself as conservative
in doctrinal and liturgical matters but flexible in dealing with the
concerns of his congregation. Distinguishing Faith Lutheran from
Missouri Synod churches more set in their ways—Messiah, for
instance—he has said that he wanted his church to be more interested in people than in policies. Faith Lutheran lacked the stern,
Germanic atmosphere sometimes associated with Missouri Synod
churches. The attachment of some of the young west-side couples
who soon joined the founders from Messiah was more demographic
than liturgical. A lot of them were attracted by a friendly, almost fa-
milial bond among contemporaries who tended to be interested in
the church volleyball team as well as the Bible classes. The Andersons, who had been active at First Presbyterian, were introduced to
Faith when Lorna Anderson decided that its preschool, the Lord's
Lambs, might be a convenient place for their two youngest children,
twin girls. Eventually, Martin and Lorna Anderson found Faith Lu-

theran a comfortable place for the entire family. Lorna Anderson went to work half days as the church secretary. Marty Anderson put the pastor up for the Optimists.

A memorial service for Marty Anderson was held at Faith Lutheran. Tom Bird, Lorna Anderson's boss and friend as well as her pastor, was by her side. He could have been assumed to have sad cause for empathy. Only four months before, his own wife had died—killed, from what the authorities could ascertain by reconstructing the event, when her car missed a nasty curve next to the Rocky Ford Bridge, southeast of town, and plunged over an embankment into the Cottonwood River. On the day of Martin Anderson's memorial service, the sanctuary of Faith Lutheran Church was full. Tom Bird delivered the eulogy. The Optimists sat in the first few rows.

The day before the memorial service, Susan Ewert, a friend of Lorna Anderson's from the Andersons' days at First Presbyterian, walked into the office of *The Emporia Gazette* first thing in the morning with an angry complaint. She said that the *Gazette* article reporting Martin Anderson's murder—a short Saturday-afternoon item that had been written near deadline on the strength of telephone conversations—implied that Lorna Anderson wasn't telling the truth about what had happened. The *Gazette's* implication, according to Mrs. Ewert, had so disturbed Mrs. Anderson that her pastor, who was trying to console her, had found her nearly suicidal. The managing editor of the *Gazette,* Ray Call, said that the paper would be happy to give Mrs. Anderson the opportunity to tell her story in detail, and when the *Gazette* came out that afternoon, it carried a story headlined MURDERED EMPORIAN'S WIFE RECALLS TERROR ON HIGHWAY.

Lorna Anderson's story was this: She was at the wheel of the family's van as it headed down 177 from Manhattan toward Emporia that evening. Apparently having eaten something in Manhattan that disagreed with her, she felt that she was about to be ill, so she stopped the car. As she got out, she took the keys with her—her husband had always insisted that she remove the keys any time she left the van—and then accidentally dropped them in the field at the side of the road. When her husband came out to help her look for them, he told her to return to the van and shine the headlights in his direction. While she was doing that, she heard someone say, "Where's your wallet?" She turned to see her husband hand his wallet to a masked man, who started shooting. Her husband fell to the ground. Then the man grabbed her, held the gun to her head, and pulled the trigger. The gun failed to fire. He fled into the darkness.

The story presented some problems. Would someone who was about to be ill really pull the keys out of a car parked on a deserted stretch of highway when her husband was sitting right in the front seat? What were the odds of a bandit's being on that stretch of highway when the Andersons' van stopped? The original item in the *Gazette*—an item that followed Lorna Anderson's account with the sentence "Officers are investigating the story"—had, in fact, reflected the skepticism of the Geary County officers who listened to the account the night of the murder. The implication of that skepticism was clear in a headline run by *The Junction City Daily Union* the next day: VICTIM'S WIFE AMONG SUSPECTS IN KILLING. The *Emporia Gazette* was not as blunt, but that didn't mean an absence of suspicion in Emporia. There were a lot of rumors around town.

Emporia, with a population of twenty-five thousand, is about the right size for rumors. In a tiny town, people are likely to know firsthand what is true and what isn't. In a large city, most of the population won't have any connection at all with the people under discussion. In a place the size of Emporia, though, people tend to have an uncle who knows the cousin of someone through the Kiwanis, or a next-door neighbor who has the word through a lawyer who has a kid in the same Boy Scout troop. The Andersons had been in Emporia for only seven years—Marty Anderson was from a small town south of Wichita, and his wife had grown up in Hutchinson—

but a lot of people knew someone who knew them. Just about everybody had something to say about them.

Marty Anderson sounded like a person who had been both easy to like and easy not to like. "He could be very aggravating, and the next minute he could get you laughing," a fellow Optimist has said. The way Anderson tried to get people laughing was usually through needling or practical jokes, and in both forms he occasionally passed over the line from funny to mean. Sometimes the object of the needling was his wife. He was a big man, more than six feet tall, and not the sort of big man who slowed up coming into second base for fear of bowling over a smaller player. At Newman Hospital he sometimes employed an army-sergeant manner that irritated people in other departments, but the technologists who worked for him considered him an essentially fair man who tried to run a meticulous laboratory. Basically, they liked him. Outside the hospital he was known as a man who after quite a bit too much to drink at a party might decide to play a prank that turned out not to have been such a good idea after all. His wife was given to tearful recitals of how miserable life with Martin Anderson could be, and some of the people who tried to be of comfort were told that he beat her.

"Everybody was always comforting Lorna," a female associate of Martin Anderson's has said, putting a little twist on the word "comforting." Lorna Anderson cried easily. Until a couple of years before her husband's death, she had often phoned him at the lab, distraught and tearful, but she was better known for seeking her comfort elsewhere. The Emporians of William Allen White's day could have described her with one sentence: she had a reputation. A trim, dark-haired, pleasant-looking woman of about thirty, she did not have the appearance of the town bombshell. But there were women in Emporia—women who worked at the hospital or were members of Beta Sigma Phi—who said that they avoided parties where the Andersons were likely to be present because they knew that before the evening was out, Lorna Anderson would make a play for their husbands. There were people in Emporia who said that a police investigation that included scrutiny of the Andersons' marriage had the potential of embarrassing any number of prominent business and professional men—men who had met Lorna Anderson when she worked at one of the banks, or men who knew her through her work as local fundraiser for the American Heart Association, or men who had simply run into her late in the evening at a place like the Continental Club of the Ramada Inn. Some people in Emporia—people who, say, worked with someone who knew someone connected with Faith Lutheran Church—were saying that Lorna Anderson's latest catch was Pastor Tom Bird. "Just after we got home from Marty's funeral, the phone rang," a colleague of Martin Anderson's has said. "The person calling said there was a rumor that Lorna and Tom Bird had something to do with Marty's death."

Pastor Bird had been one of the people who were always comforting Lorna. Almost from the time she began working at the church, in early 1983, there were whispers in the congregation about the possibility that the pastor and his secretary had grown too close. After Sandra Bird's death, in July of 1983, Lorna Anderson was just one of a number of women from the congregation who concentrated on providing whatever support they could for the young pastor, but she was the only one whose relationship with Tom Bird continued to cause uneasiness in the congregation. The pastor of Messiah had spoken confidentially to Bird about what people were saying, and so had Faith's lay ministers—the equivalent of church elders in some Lutheran congregations. At one point, the lay ministers, intent on avoiding even the appearance of impropriety by the pastor, considered asking Lorna Anderson to resign. Finally, it was agreed that she would remain church secretary but would limit her presence at the church to the hours that her job called for. Bird had assured the lay ministers that there was, in fact, no impropriety in his relationship with his secretary. She had a troubled marriage and a tendency to "spiral down," he told them, and he was only doing his best to counsel and support her. He continued to stand by her after

Martin Anderson's death and after suspicion was cast on her. He continued to stand by her when, only a couple of weeks after Anderson's death, Daniel Carter, an Emporia man who had been picked up by the Geary County authorities on a tip, said she had given him five thousand dollars to see that her husband was killed. Pastor Bird's support did not waver even when, shortly after Carter's arrest, Lorna Anderson herself was arrested for conspiracy to commit first-degree murder.

Lorna Anderson said she was innocent. Daniel Carter said he was guilty. He agreed to cooperate with the authorities investigating the role of Lorna Anderson and others in the plot.

"Do you recall when it was you first had occasion to meet her?" Steven Opat, the Geary County attorney, asked during one of the times Carter testified in court.

"Yes," Carter said. "I used to cut her hair."

That was at Mr. & Ms., on Commercial Street, in 1981. The relationship was strictly business for about a year, Carter testified, and then there was an affair, which lasted a few months, and then, in August of 1983, Lorna Anderson asked him to find someone to get rid of her husband. By that time, Carter was working on the construction crew at Wolf Creek, where he presumably had a better chance of finding a hit man among his co-workers than he would have had at the hairdresser's. The Geary County authorities didn't claim that Carter had concocted a scheme that actually resulted in the death of Martin Anderson. As they pieced the story together, Carter took five thousand dollars from Lorna Anderson and passed it on to Gregory Curry, his supervisor at Wolf Creek, who passed it on to a third man, in Mississippi, who, perhaps realizing that nobody was in a position to make a stink about having the money returned if services weren't rendered, didn't do anything.

That left the mystery of who killed Martin Anderson, which meant that a number of investigators from the Geary County Sheriff's Department and the Lyon County Sheriff's Office and the

Kansas Bureau of Investigation were still asking questions around Emporia—scaring up a covey of rumors with each interview. When the next arrest came, though, it was not for murder but for another plot, which nobody claimed had gone any further than talk. On March 21, 1984, four and a half months after Martin Anderson's death, the Lyon County attorney, Rodney H. Symmonds, filed charges against Thomas Bird for criminal solicitation to commit first-degree murder. In an affidavit filed at the same time, a KBI agent said that the prosecution was acting largely on information it had received from an Emporia housebuilder named Darrel Carter, Daniel Carter's older brother. Shortly after the arrest of Daniel Carter, the affidavit said, Darrel Carter had gone to the authorities to inform them that in May of 1983, three months before the plot his brother had described, he, too, had been asked to help get rid of Martin Anderson. According to the affidavit, Darrel Carter had gone to Faith Lutheran Church one weekday morning at Lorna Anderson's request, and there had been asked by Tom Bird if he would help in a murder scheme that was already worked out. After Martin Anderson's death, the affidavit said, Darrel Carter had got word that Tom Bird wanted to meet with him again in order to "reaffirm their trust," but this time Carter had shown up wearing a hidden transmitter provided by the Kansas Bureau of Investigation.

"Who would have thought that little old Emporia would have *two* hit men?" a professor at Emporia State University has said. Even to people in Emporia who had spent the months since Martin Anderson's death savoring the ironies or embellishing the rumors, though, the idea of a minister plotting a murder scheme right in his own church was shocking. There was an accompanying shock in what the affidavit said about one of the possible murder plans that Bird was accused of presenting to Darrel Carter: "Bird told Carter he found a place with a bend in a road and a bridge outside of Emporia, which had an approximately fifty-foot drop-off to the river and that a person could just miss the curve, especially if the person were drunk, and go off down the embankment. Bird told Carter they were going to drug Marty, take him out there, and run the car off into the river."

Anyone who might have missed the implication of that could see it spelled out in the *Gazette*'s coverage of Bird's arrest. "On July 17, Sandra Bird, Mr. Bird's wife, was found dead near the wreckage of her car that went off the road at the Rocky Ford Bridge southeast of Emporia," the *Gazette* said. "According to the accident report, Mrs. Bird had been driving northbound on the county road when the car apparently went off the roadway at the approach to the bridge and down a 65-foot embankment.

"An autopsy concluded that Mrs. Bird's death was accidental, caused by severe abdominal and chest injuries.

"Mr. Symmonds declined to comment on whether he considered Mrs. Bird's death to be accidental.

"'Whenever a person dies, it's always subject to further investigation,' he said."

Members of Faith Lutheran offered to post Tom Bird's bond. The church's attitude was summed up by *The Wichita Eagle* with the headline CONGREGATION RALLIES AROUND PASTOR. There were people in the congregation who had been put out at Tom Bird at one time or another—he was known as someone who could be strong-willed about having things done his own way—but in general he was a popular figure. To people who might have expected a Missouri Synod Lutheran pastor to be a severe man on the lookout for sin, Tom Bird had always seemed accessible and informal and concerned. "We're going to stand behind him all the way," one young woman in the congregation told the reporter from Wichita. Faith Lutheran people spoke of Christian love and the American principle that a man is innocent until proved guilty. A lot of them considered the charge against Tom Bird a horrible mistake that would be straightened out at his first hearing. There were some people in the congregation, however, who believed that it would be inappropriate for Bird to continue in his pastoral duties as if nothing had happened, and there were a few who thought he should resign. Bird said that he had no intention of resigning or asking for a leave of absence. In a congregational meeting, a compromise was reached: it was decided that as a way of easing the pressure on Pastor Bird while he dealt with his defense, he could be relieved of preparing and delivering sermons while retaining his other pastoral duties. That arrangement was supposed to last until Bird's preliminary hearing. When the hearing was postponed for some weeks, Bird said that he would prefer to take the pulpit again, and the lay ministers, to the irritation of a few members who were outspokenly opposed to Pastor Bird's continued presence, agreed. On the Sunday that he preached his first sermon after his arrest, the worshippers emerging from the church after the service were greeted not only by their pastor but also by a couple of television crews and some out-of-town reporters.

In Bird's view, the presence of the press that Sunday effectively ended his ministry at Faith Lutheran by making it clear that the church would be no sanctuary from temporal concerns as long as Thomas Bird was its pastor. With or without television cameras at Sunday services, it was a hard time for Faith Lutheran. The atmosphere of relaxed fellowship that had attracted so many young families had turned tense. The effort of most members to withhold judgment meant that no one was quite certain of where anyone else stood. A few families had dropped out of the congregation, and some people came to church less often. "I didn't feel comfortable going to church," a member who was a strong supporter of Pastor Bird's has said. "I felt people judging us as well as judging Tom." Faith members also felt some pressure from outside the church. The questions and remarks they heard from outsiders often seemed to carry the implication that the attitude of the congregation toward its pastor was naïve or silly. In the view of one Faith Lutheran member, "It got to be socially unacceptable to go to our church." In the days after Bird's return to the pulpit, it was clear from the pressure within the church not simply that he would no longer deliver sermons on Sundays but that he would have to resign. He delayed the announcement by several weeks in order to avoid going into his preliminary hearing carrying the burden of having resigned under pressure.

Bird had often expressed gratitude for the congregation's support, but even before his arrest he had written in a church newsletter that his reputation was being "sullied by the local gossips." Some of the people who thought the congregation had not been strong enough in its support believed that in the strained atmosphere that followed his arrest, the pastor had reason to feel "unwelcome and unloved" in his own church. When he finally resigned, two months after his arrest, his farewell speech to the congregation was partly about such subjects as authentic Christian love and the purposes of the church, but it also included some rather bitter remarks about his treatment. "When I remained silent, I was judged to be unfair for not informing people; when I have spoken, I was judged to be defensive," he said. "When I looked depressed, I was judged to be full of self-pity; when I smiled and looked strong, I was judged to be failing to take matters seriously. When I acted timid, I was judged to be weak; when I acted boldly, I was judged to be manipulating. When I was indecisive, I was judged to have lost my leadership capacity; when I acted decisively, I was judged to be using my position to railroad matters. To multiply the anguish of my predicament, I only hear these judgments second or third hand, so that I cannot share directly what is in my heart and my intentions to my accusers within the congregation."

By the time of Tom Bird's resignation, a folklorist at Emporia State who is interested in the sorts of jokes people tell was collecting Tom-and-Lorna jokes. The folklorist, Thomas Isern, believes that the range of humor in the mass media these days has forced folk humor to be scurrilous in order to remain folk humor, and scurrilous jokes flowed easily from a situation that included a couple of stock folklore characters—the preacher and the loose woman. The relationship between Tom Bird and Lorna Anderson was not the only subject of intense speculation in Emporia. A lot of people were talking about whether Sandra Bird's death had really been an accident. A couple of months after Bird's arrest, the *Gazette* reported that Sandra Bird's family, in Arkansas, had asked a Little Rock lawyer to supervise an investigation into the circumstances of her death. Once some doubt about the incident was made public, it became apparent that a number of people had at the time entertained doubts about whether Sandra Bird had simply missed a curve. A lot of people—neighbors, for instance, and people at Emporia State—had driven out to the Rocky Ford Bridge to have a look at the scene. What had given them pause was not any suspicion of Tom Bird but a feeling that the physical evidence didn't make sense. If Sandra Bird liked to take late-night drives by herself to unwind, as her husband had reported, why would she drive on the distinctly unrelaxing gravel road that approached the Rocky Ford Bridge? If the car was going so fast that it missed the curve at the bridge, which is the second half of an S curve, how did it negotiate the first half? If the car was going that fast, how come it wasn't more seriously damaged? It turned out that there were people in Emporia who for months had not actually believed the official version of how Sandra Bird died. They thought that she might have committed suicide or that she might have been abducted in the parking lot at Emporia State, where she sometimes went late at night to use the computers, and murdered by her abductor.

By far the most popular topic for speculation, though, was what people in Emporia began to call simply the list. The prosecution, it was said, had a list of Emporia men who had been involved with Lorna Anderson. In some versions of the story, the *Gazette* had the list. In some versions, it was not a list but a black book. In some versions, the men who were on a list of potential witnesses for Lorna Anderson's trial had been informed of that by the prosecution so that they could break the news to their families themselves. The version of the list story some of the reporters on the *Gazette* liked best turned into one of the jokes that could be collected by Tom Isern:

A prominent businessman calls an acquaintance on the *Gazette* news staff and says nervously, "I have to know—does the *Gazette* have a list?"

"No," the *Gazette* reporter says, in a soothing voice. "But we're compiling one."

Those people in Emporia who were counting on Lorna Anderson's trial to end the suspense were in for a long wait. The case against her got tangled in any number of delays and legal complications. As it turned out, the first person to come to trial for plotting to murder Martin Anderson was Tom Bird. The defense asked for a change of venue, providing the court with the results of a survey indicating that an overwhelming majority of Emporia residents were familiar with the case. The motion was denied. In Kansas, there is a strong tradition against granting changes of venue even when there is wide community awareness of a case, and, as it happened, the survey indicated that a relatively small percentage of those who were familiar with the charges and the rumors had already made up their minds. But among the ones who had, there was a strong indication of how Emporia opinion was running: out of thirty-nine people with firm opinions, thirty-two thought Tom Bird was guilty.

Bird's mother and his father, who is also a Lutheran minister, came up from Arkansas for the trial. So did Sandra Bird's father and mother and stepfather—who, it was noted around town, seemed to keep their distance from their former son-in-law during the proceedings. Reporters and television crews from Wichita and Topeka were in town; despite objections from the defense, a fixed television camera was permitted in the courtroom for the first time in Lyon County. There were members of Faith Lutheran who had come to testify for the defense and members who had come to testify for the prosecution and members who had come merely because, like most residents of Emporia, they were attracted by the prospect of seeing witnesses under oath clear up—or perhaps improve on—the rumors that had been going around town for eight months. The courtroom was jammed every day. "I've never been to anything like this before," one of the spectators told the *Gazette*. "I feel like I know them all; I've heard their names so many times."

The prosecution's case was based on the assumption that Tom Bird and Lorna Anderson had been lovers. According to the prosecutor, they wanted Marty Anderson out of the way, and they weren't interested in a less violent means of accomplishing that—divorce, for instance—because they also wanted the four hundred thousand dollars his death would bring in insurance money. The prosecution's witnesses included the Andersons' insurance agent—he turned out to be the president of the Optimist Club—and a babysitter, who said that she once heard Lorna Anderson say on the telephone, "I cannot wait for Marty to die; I can't wait to count the green stuff." There was testimony from Faith Lutheran people who had been concerned that the pastor and his secretary were growing too close. "I saw a sparkle in their eyes when they talked to each other," said the preschool teacher, a young woman who under cross-examination acknowledged that she herself had wrestled with a crush on the pastor. "I felt electricity in the air." There was testimony from a development director of the Heart Association, who reduced the talk of electricity and eye-sparkling to more direct language; according to her testimony, Lorna Anderson had told her about having an affair with the pastor and had said that she was using Heart Association business as a cover for trysts in out-of-town motels. The Andersons' nine-year-old daughter, Lori, testified that she had seen her mother and Tom Bird hugging; Marty Anderson's brother and a KBI agent both testified that what Lori had said when she was first questioned was that she had seen her mother and Tom Bird kissing.

The prosecution's star witness was, of course, Darrel Carter. He testified that the meeting at the church in the spring of 1983 was not the first time Lorna Anderson had asked for his help in killing her husband. She had first asked him a year or so before that, he said, at a time when the Andersons and the Carters knew each other casually from Beta Sigma Phi functions. "I was really kind of shocked to think that she would ask me that," Carter testified, "'cause Martin

Anderson was a friend of mine." According to Carter's testimony, that friendship hadn't prevented him from having his own fling with Lorna some months later. To back up Carter's story of the meeting at Faith Lutheran, the prosecution called a couple of people he had mentioned the scheme to at the time. "I was doing a little work there one evening in my garage on an old Corvette that I'm restoring," one of them, a neighbor of Carter's, said, in testimony that summoned up the traditional vision of summertime in Emporia. "We visited about several things, which I can't tell you all they were, but the one that sticks in my mind right now is that he told me that someone had contacted him about killing someone."

What the defense asked the jury to do was to view Darrel Carter's testimony not as a story he had finally come forward with after his brother's arrest but as a story he had concocted in order to win some leniency for his brother—who had, in fact, been given probation, while Gregory Curry, his confederate in the scheme, was sentenced to prison. From that angle, the details that Darrel Carter knew could be seen as coming from police reports available to the defense in his brother's case. The similarity of the murder plan to the circumstances of Sandra Bird's death could be explained by the fact that when Carter concocted the story, he knew how Sandra Bird had died. The meeting at Faith Lutheran had indeed taken place, the defense said; its purpose was not to plot murder, though, but to explore the possibility of Faith youth-group members' working at Carter's fireworks stand in order to raise money for a trip to see the Passion play in Eureka Springs, Arkansas. After Marty Anderson's death, Bird had indeed let it be known that he wanted to talk to Carter, the defense said, but that was because Susan Ewert, Lorna Anderson's friend, had told Bird that Carter was spreading rumors about him, and Bird wanted to put a stop to that. "I've heard enough rumors for sure," Bird could be heard saying to Carter on the tape. "Rumors are rampant."

During that conversation with Carter, in a bowling-alley parking lot, Bird made what the prosecution presented as incriminating remarks about the meeting at his church ("I just wanted to touch the bases and make sure that we just talked about possibly my youth group sellin' firecrackers for you"), and about the murder of Martin Anderson ("Well, maybe we ought to be glad that we didn't follow through"), and about how he felt about Anderson's death ("I ain't celebratin', but I ain't mournin', either"). Still, nothing on the tape was absolutely explicit, and Bird took the stand to provide a benign explanation for every remark—mostly based on the contention that what he and Carter hadn't followed through on was a plan to refer Lorna Anderson to an agency that assists battered wives. When the prosecution managed to bring into evidence two notes from Tom Bird that the police said they had found in Lorna Anderson's lingerie drawer, Bird said that they were meant simply to buck up Lorna's spirits and that such sentiments as "I love you so very much and that's forever" were expressions not of romantic attachment but of "authentic Christian love."

In describing his efforts to counsel Lorna Anderson, Bird admitted that, emotionally drained by his wife's death, he might have used bad judgment in providing the gossips with even the appearance of something worth gossiping about. In explaining why he had arranged the parking lot meeting through a go-between, a woman he knew from an inquiry she had made about the Lord's Lambs Preschool, he admitted a pressure tactic that some jurors might have considered un-Christian: he happened to know that the woman and Darrel Carter were having an affair, he testified, and he figured that making Carter aware of that knowledge might send "the message that everybody is capable of being a victim of rumors." But that was about all he admitted. Bird said that people who saw him hugging Lorna Anderson while comforting her might not have understood that standing across the room with consoling words would not have been "full communication." She had a "self-esteem problem" that required a lot of comforting, he said, and he had provided it as her pastor and her employer and her friend, but not as her lover.

"If only he had admitted the affair," a remarkable number of people in Emporia said when talking about Tom Bird's trial for criminal solicitation. The defense had insisted that the case amounted to a simple choice of whether to believe Tom Bird or Darrel Carter. In some ways, it was an unequal contest. Darrel Carter was nobody's idea of a model citizen. He did not claim that his response to having been asked to help murder a friend of his had included outrage or a telephone call to the authorities. He acknowledged—boasted about, the defense might have said—two affairs with married women while he was married himself. Someone who had hired him to build a house took the stand to say that he was "the biggest liar in ten counties." In contrast, several character witnesses testified that Tom Bird was a trustworthy, God-fearing man. "He is very conscious of the Word of God," the chairman of Faith Lutheran's board of lay ministers said, "and he is very deliberate in his close attention and following of the Word of God."

But practically nobody in Emporia believed Tom Bird when he said he had not had an affair with Lorna Anderson. If only he had admitted the affair, people in Emporia said, the jury might have believed the rest of the story—or might at least have been understanding about what passion could have led him to do. The defense that Emporia people thought might have worked for Tom Bird amounted to a sort of Garden of Eden defense—a tragic twist on the jokes about the preacher and the loose woman. To some people in Emporia, it seemed that Tom Bird could have been presented as a vulnerable man who, at a particularly stressful time in his life, had been led by his passion for a temptress to do some things he came to regret, but who would never have conspired to break God's commandment against murder. A lot of people in Emporia, in other words, thought that Tom Bird's only hope was to repent. The people from Faith Lutheran who continued to believe in Pastor Bird right through the trial found that approach enraging. He could not repent, they said, for the simple reason that he had done nothing that required repentance. That, apparently, was not the view of the jury. Bird was found guilty of soliciting murder. He was sentenced to a term of two and a half to seven years in the Kansas State Penitentiary.

"Like most Emporians, we love a bit of juicy gossip now and then," an editorial in the *Gazette* said a month or so after Tom Bird's conviction. "But in recent weeks here, the saturation point for rumors has been reached and innocent people are being hurt." The *Gazette* mentioned some rumors about the possibility that "the defendant in a recent sensational trial had remarried." There were also further rumors about Lorna Anderson, who had moved back to Hutchinson, and about what might be revealed in her trial. Time had swollen accounts of the list. "At first the list was said to contain 20 names," the *Gazette* said. "Now the number has grown to 110 and includes 'bankers, lawyers and other professional men.' This is a case of gross exaggeration." The *Gazette* thought it necessary to inform its readers that a professional man who had recently left town had not, in fact, fled because he was on the list and feared exposure.

The *Gazette* had begun a campaign to have the rumors surrounding Sandra Bird's death tested in a court of law. "Was it only coincidence that Mr. Bird's wife died in the manner and in the place that the minister had suggested for the murder of Mr. Anderson?" its editorial on the verdict in Tom Bird's trial asked. Two *Gazette* reporters, Roberta Birk and Nancy Horst, pounded away at the Sandra Bird case with stories carrying headlines such as CIRCUMSTANCES OF DEATH RAISE SUSPICIONS and TROOPER THOUGHT DEATH NOT ACCIDENT. The *Gazette* made a reward fund available for information on the case and ran a series of stories about contributions to the fund from Sandra Bird's friends and family. In a sheriff's election that November, the *Gazette* editorialized against the incumbent partly on the ground that he had bungled the original investigation of Sandra Bird's death, and he was defeated. Eventually, Sandra Bird's body was exhumed, a second autopsy was performed, and a grand jury began investigating the case. In February of 1985, the grand jury handed up an indictment against Tom Bird for the murder of his wife.

The *Gazette's* campaign angered the people in Emporia who continued to believe in Bird's innocence. In the months since the headline CONGREGATION RALLIES AROUND PASTOR, of course, their ranks had suffered serious attrition. Some supporters had dropped away as they heard more and more about the relationship between Tom Bird and Lorna Anderson. A lot more had defected after the revelations of the trial or after the guilty verdict. But there remained people in the Faith Lutheran congregation who believed that the verdict was just wrong—a result of Darrel Carter's perfidy and the judge's perverse refusal to move the trial out of a community that had convicted Tom Bird before any witnesses took the stand. The Bird supporters who remained could point out inconsistencies in prosecution testimony. But basically they believed Bird was innocent partly because they thought he was incapable of the deeds he was accused of and partly because he said he was innocent. "He told me that he swears before God he's innocent," one of the lay ministers has said. "I have to believe him. I don't think he would say that if he were guilty."

Almost everybody else in Emporia tended to believe that Bird was guilty not only of plotting to kill Martin Anderson but also of murdering his own wife. According to a survey taken for Bird's lawyer to support a motion to move his murder trial out of Emporia, virtually everyone in town was familiar with the case, and more than ninety percent of those who had made up their minds about it believed that he was guilty. The motion was denied. In July of 1985, the familiar cast of characters gathered once again in Lyon County District Court—Tom Bird and his parents, the family of Sandra Bird, the small band of Faith Lutheran members who remained loyal to Bird, County Attorney Rodney H. Symmonds, Darrel Carter, the TV crews from Topeka and Wichita. As the trial got under way, though, what most Emporia residents seemed to be discussing was not any revelation from the witness stand but news from Hutchinson that Lorna Anderson, whose trial was finally scheduled to begin later in the summer, had remarried. The bridegroom was a Hutchinson man named Randy Eldridge, someone she had known for years. In answer to reporters' questions, Eldridge said he believed that his new wife was innocent. She said that he was "a wonderful, Christian person"—someone who, it turned out, was a member of a gospel-singing sextet in his spare time. That fact and the rumors that both Eldridges were quite active in an Assembly of God church in Hutchinson had some people in Emporia concerned. It looked as if Lorna Anderson Eldridge might be planning to come to court as an upstanding Christian wife and mother who couldn't have had anything to do with plotting murder—and presumably the prosecution might attempt to destroy that picture of probity by calling to the stand any number of men from the list.

In Tom Bird's trial for murder, there was even more testimony about his relationship with his secretary than there had been in the previous trial. The prosecution called witnesses, Sandra Bird's mother among them, who testified that the pastor's wife had been so distraught over the relationship that she had been unable to eat. But a lot of the testimony was rather technical—testimony from pathologists and accident-reconstruction specialists—and there were days when finding a seat in the spectators section was no problem. The prosecution called expert witnesses to testify that neither the injuries to Sandra Bird nor the damage to the car was consistent with an accident; the defense called expert witnesses to testify the opposite. By pointing out inconsistencies in Tom Bird's account of that evening and presenting some physical evidence, such as the presence of bloodstains on the bridge, the prosecutor suggested that Bird had beaten his wife, thrown her off the Rocky Ford Bridge, run their car off the embankment, and dragged her body over to it in order to create the appearance of an accident. The defense argued that inconsistencies were to be expected from a man who had been up half the night worrying about where his wife was and had had to start the day by telling his children that their mother was dead. Tom Bird was on trial not for how he ran his personal life, his lawyer said, but for the crime of murder, and "there's no evidence that a crime of any kind was committed." The testimony required twelve days. After that, the jury deliberated for six hours and found Tom Bird guilty of first-degree murder. He was sentenced to life in prison.

"Even a lot of people who thought he was guilty didn't think the trial proved it," a supporter of Bird's said after it was over. It is true, at least, that the prosecutor was not able to provide an eyewitness, as he had done in the criminal-solicitation case. It is also true that he went into the trial holding the advantage of Bird's conviction for plotting Martin Anderson's murder. Among people familiar with the case, it is taken for granted that without the earlier conviction Bird would never have been brought to trial for his wife's murder. Discussing the astonishing chain of events that transformed Tom Bird from a popular young minister to a lifer convicted of killing his wife, a lot of people in Emporia continue to say, "If only he had admitted the affair."

A month after Bird's second conviction, Lorna Anderson Eldridge sat in the same courtroom—neatly dressed, composed, almost cheerful—and said, "I believe it was in June, 1983, Thomas Bird and I met with Darrel Carter at the Faith Lutheran Church. During that meeting we discussed various ways of murdering my husband, Martin Anderson." In a last-minute plea bargain, she had agreed to plead guilty to two counts of criminal solicitation to commit first-degree murder and to tell the authorities anything she knew about a case that had presumably already been decided—the death of Sandra Bird. In her plea, she said that Tom Bird had also been involved later in trying to hire a hit man through Danny Carter, and had, in fact, furnished the five thousand dollars. Lorna Eldridge's lawyer said she wanted to purge her soul. A month later, she was sentenced to a term of five and a half to eighteen years in state prison.

Her plea was a blow to those who had continued to believe in

Tom Bird, but it did not significantly reduce their ranks. At one point, one of them has said, Bird had told his supporters, "There are very few left. They are falling away. And sooner or later you, too, will be gone." As it turned out, the people who had stuck with Tom Bird even through the murder trial did not fall away just because Lorna Anderson stated in open court that what the prosecution said about Tom Bird was true. They figured that she might be lying because she thought a plea bargain was in her best interests, or that she might be lying simply because she liked to lie. They continue to believe that someday something—a large criminal operation like a drug ring, perhaps—will come to light to explain events that the state has explained with accusations against Tom Bird. At times, they sound like early Christians who manage to shake off constant challenges to their faith. "Questions come up," one of them has said. "And I stop and think. But I always work it out." Tom Bird, when asked by a visitor to the Kansas State Penitentiary about the loyalty of his supporters, also explained their support in religious terms—as the action of Christians who understand that we are all sinners and that it is not our role to judge others. "They've grown in their faith," he said.

It is possible that the challenges to their faith in Tom Bird are not at an end. It is not known yet precisely what, if anything, Lorna Anderson Eldridge had to tell the prosecutors about the death of Sandra Bird. So far, nobody has been charged with the murder of Martin Anderson. In Geary County, though, investigators believe that they have made considerable progress. Presumably acting on information provided by Lorna Anderson Eldridge, the Geary County Sheriff's Department drained several farm ponds and eventually found the gun it believes was used in the killing. It is said that the gun belonged to Martin Anderson. Shortly after the sheriff began draining farm ponds, Tom Bird was taken to Junction City from prison to answer questions. Each step in the investigation in Geary County set off ripples of speculation in Lyon County. Will Tom Bird be charged with another murder? Had one of the murder schemes already uncovered by the authorities resulted in Anderson's death after all? Or could it be that little old Emporia had *three* hit men?

To some extent, Lorna Anderson Eldridge's guilty plea meant that William Allen White's hometown could get back to normal. Faith Lutheran Church, which had absorbed a fearful blow, has begun to recover. Nobody claims that it has regained the momentum of its early days, but the new pastor—another athletic and personable man with several children—believes that the church has come through its crisis into a period of consolidation. The Lord's Lambs Preschool is back to its routine. So are the Optimist basketball games and the laboratory at Newman Hospital and the front page of the *Gazette*. Presumably, Mrs. Eldridge's guilty pleas brought a great sense of relief to those residents of Emporia who had reason to look with some trepidation on the prospect of her coming to trial. There was now less danger that what the *Gazette* called "the most sordid case in Emporia's history" would extend to sworn testimony about the sexual escapades of prominent citizens.

One change in Emporia is that two families are no longer there. The adults are dead or imprisoned, the children living in other cities. (The Anderson children have been adopted by Randy Eldridge; the Bird children are living in Arkansas with Tom Bird's parents, who are in the midst of a custody suit brought by the family of Sandra Bird.) Also, there are some people who believe that what happened to the Birds and the Andersons has to have changed what Emporians think of their town and their neighbors. People who have long taken the guilt of Tom Bird and Lorna Anderson for granted are still left with questions about how they could have brought themselves to do such awful deeds. Was Lorna Anderson a temptress who merely used Tom Bird to help get rid of her husband? Or did the death of Sandra Bird—perhaps caused by her husband in some fit of rage—lead inevitably to the death of Martin Anderson? If Tom Bird and Lorna Anderson were bound together, were they bound together by love or by guilty knowledge? Lately, there has been more talk in Emporia about the possibility that what happened can be explained through some sort of mental illness. In a 1984 story about the background of the Birds, Dana Mullin of *The Topeka Capital-Journal* reported that Tom Bird was once hospitalized with severe heatstroke after a six-mile run in Arkansas and that such heat strokes have been known to cause brain damage. Putting that information together with some of the bizarre behavior attributed to Lorna Anderson even before her husband's death, some people in Emporia have theorized that perhaps Tom Bird and his secretary, who seemed so much like their neighbors, had mental difficulties that somehow meshed to result in deeds their neighbors consider unthinkable.

What was sordid about Emporia's most sordid case, of course, was not simply the crimes but the lives they revealed—lives full of hatred and maybe wife-beating and certainly casual, apparently joyless liaisons. (When Daniel Carter testified that his affair with Lorna Anderson had ended because she seemed to want more from him than he was willing to offer, the prosecutor asked what he had been willing to offer. "Nothing," Carter said.) Although the *Gazette* may have criticized rumors about a hundred-and-ten-man list as a "gross exaggeration," the prosecutors have never denied that a list, perhaps of more modest size, existed—assembled, it is assumed, in case the state of the Andersons' marriage became an issue. A jury had concluded that an Emporia minister beat his wife until she was unconscious or dead and threw her body off a bridge. A church secretary acknowledged involvement in plans to get rid of her husband, who was murdered virtually in front of their own children. What now seems remarkable about the outrageous rumors that gripped Emporia for so long is that so many of them turned out to be true.

Outdoor Life

Sisters, Oregon

AUGUST 1986

Central Oregon is an outdoor sort of place. Edwin Dyer, who moved to a Central Oregon town called Sisters in 1969, was an outdoor sort of guy. He had grown up in cities—mainly Portland, and then Eugene, where his father worked as a printer for the University of Oregon—but he always felt attached to the country. When Dyer was in his mid-forties and his children were getting nearly old enough to think about families of their own, he wrote down some of what he remembered from his childhood, and all he had to say about Portland, where he lived all but a few of the first fifteen years of his life, was that he had hated it. His reminiscences about his childhood concentrated on the summers he had spent on his grandparents' farm, near Yamhill, Oregon—an old-fashioned farm where the plowing was done behind a team of draft horses, butter was churned in the parlor in the evenings, baths were taken in a washtub in the kitchen, the beef was butchered right out in the farmyard, and Grandpa's way of announcing a trip to the outhouse was to say, "I'm going to see Mrs. Murphy." What Ed Dyer tended to recall about his boyhood was hunting and fishing and horseback riding and Boy Scout hikes. What he remembered about high school was shop class and the rifle club. After high school and a hitch in the Navy, he got married—he and his wife, Tona, met at a Mormon church function—and got a job with an organization that could offer a career in the outdoors, the U.S. Forest Service. When he moved to Central Oregon, six years after joining the service, it was to work at the Sisters Ranger Station, which is responsible for the trees and wilderness trails and campgrounds and mountain lakes in the northwest quarter of a vast and magnificent patch of the outdoors called the Deschutes National Forest.

Sisters is the first town travelers come to when they drive through the central pass of the Cascade Range from what people in Oregon call the Valley—the Willamette River valley, where most of the state's population is concentrated in a string of cities that includes Portland and Salem and Eugene. When the Dyers moved to Sisters, it was a quiet old logging town of six hundred people, known to a lot of travelers in Oregon as the place they stopped for gasoline and a short chat about the rigors of mountain driving, but it was beginning to change. In the seventies, outdoor sorts of places like Central Oregon were beginning to appeal to a lot of people from places like the Valley and the coastal cities of California—people who talked about getting out of the rat race or finding a slower pace of life or trading some income for convenience to a wilderness trail and a mountain lake. A number of people who had passed through Sisters on their way to ski on a nearby mountain or to camp in one of the national forests started thinking about moving there. It's practically inside the Deschutes National Forest. From just about anywhere in town, you can look across pastureland or ponderosa pines and see the snowy peaks of the spectacular mountains known as the Three Sisters. In the mid-seventies, the commercial district of Sisters, which had always consisted of the nondescript hodgepodge of stores customarily found in old western towns, began to take on a look that a lot of visitors found attractive. When Black Butte Ranch, a huge tract of private land that cuts into the national forest about eight miles west of town, was developed into an expensive vacation-home complex, the developer, as an alternative to putting in a shopping center, financed the wooden façades and rough-cedar posts and board-and-batten siding and ersatz balconies that can transform a place from what old western towns usually look like into what people think old western towns ought to look like—a process now known in the West as westernization.

Sooner or later, the shops behind the western façades had names like Cook's Nook and The Hen's Tooth and Nancy's Fancy's and The Elegant Dromedary. Partly because a large ranch just outside town has found some customers right in the area for the exotic and costly beasts it breeds, the animals seen grazing in the pastureland around Sisters include not just the customary Herefords and Black Angus but also llamas. The developer of the Black Butte Ranch complex eventually completed a more modest development on the edge of Sisters called Tollgate—it was named not for a thruway exit but for the nineteenth-century toll operation that provided the money to keep the mountain pass clear—and gave its streets names like Oxbow and Lariat and Saddle Horn and Stagecoach. Some of the old-timers in Sisters have grumbled a bit about the fancying up and the summer tourists and the parking problem. Some people in Sisters like to ask exactly what you'd do with a llama worth twenty thousand dollars. ("You sell it to someone who's willing to pay twenty thousand dollars for a llama.") Still, considering the changes Sisters has seen, it is not a place where people seem to dwell on contention. What they tend to talk about is whether to go cross-country skiing after work or how their dogs did at field-obedience class or when the wilderness trails might be dry enough for horse-packing trips. They talk about the outdoors. When they're asked why they live in Sisters—why they took a pay cut to move from Los Angeles, why they came over from the Valley before they were certain a suitable job was available—they are likely to answer by making a sweeping gesture toward the Cascades and saying something about "the quality of life."

Maintaining the wilderness trails became one of Ed Dyer's responsibilities not long after he began working at the Sisters Ranger Station, and they were his pride. He estimated that, on foot or on horseback, he covered six or seven hundred miles on the trails every year himself. He presided over trail-maintenance crews funded by the Forest Service and whatever government program happened to be in operation—the Comprehensive Employment and Training Act or the Youth Conservation Corps or the Young Adult Conservation Corps. He acted as liaison with equestrian groups that made use of the trails. As a scoutmaster, he was known for organizing and leading "fifty-milers"—weeklong backpacking trips that covered a full fifty miles on the wilderness trails.

After several years in Sisters, the Dyers had moved to the outskirts of Redmond—a much larger, more conventional Central Oregon town twenty miles to the east—so that the children wouldn't have to take a twenty-mile bus ride every morning to get to the nearest high school. Even before the move, though, the entire family was active in the Redmond Mormon church. Both Ed and Tona Dyer taught Sunday school. Ed Dyer had become scoutmaster of the church's Boy Scout Troop 26 within a year of his assignment to Sisters. Dyer had never really left Scouting. Years before his own boys were old enough to be Boy Scouts and years after they had gone on to other things, he went through a constant round of troop meetings and courts of honor and campouts and fifty-milers. It was said around Redmond that Troop 26 did consistently well in amassing merit badges and producing Eagle Scouts. Ed Dyer was given any number of awards. Scouting, in the view of another member of the congregation, was Dyer's "prestige thing, his ego trip."

Being a successful scoutmaster may bring a certain kind of prestige, or at least some community appreciation, in an outdoor sort of place like Central Oregon. There are a lot of places—indoor sorts of places—where it would bring no prestige at all. There are a lot of places—places that value social skills and appearance and sophistication—where Ed Dyer might have had some difficulty fitting in. Even his friends acknowledged that once he had you cornered, he could tell you a lot more about a fifty-mile hike than you wanted to know. The western clothes he wore when he was out of his Forest Service uniform did nothing to disguise the fact that he had put on a lot of weight over the years. He was not thought of as someone who always knew precisely what to say at precisely the right moment. But Ed Dyer was someone who seemed to have found a niche in Central Oregon. Through Scouting and other good works, he had become a valued member of the community. He had his wilderness trails and his hunting and his horseback riding. Behind the Dyers' house, two or three miles toward Sisters on Oregon Route 126, there was a patch of pastureland where he kept a couple of horses. Dyer rode on the trails, and he rode in the Deschutes County Sheriff's Posse. He and his wife—a rather retiring, soft-spoken woman with a strong commitment to the Mormon Church—not only raised four children of their own but occasionally took in children of friends and relatives when help was needed. In Central Oregon, the Dyers had carved out a pretty good life for themselves—except for what was, much later, always referred to as Ed's problem. His problem was pedophilia—homosexual pedophilia. He could not control his sexual desire for young boys.

The Mormon Church does not have a professional ministry. The leader of a Mormon congregation—in Mormon terminology, the leader of a ward—is a layman who is known as the bishop. In 1982, the bishop of the Mormon ward in Redmond got some disturbing news about Ed Dyer. One of the Scouts in Troop 26 had told his parents that Dyer made a sexual advance to him during an overnight camping trip. Dyer's version was that he had inadvertently touched the boy while they were sleeping in a tent together, and the boy had panicked. But it turned out that there were other stories of sexual misconduct concerning Dyer and Scouts in Troop 26. Ed Dyer was asked by the church to resign as scoutmaster.

Aside from that, the church leadership had trouble figuring out exactly what to do about him. The first step was easy. The president of what the Mormons call a stake—a stake is roughly the equivalent of a diocese—has a high council that at times sits as a sort of ecclesiastical court. The court has the power to excommunicate a Mormon. It can also simply reprimand him. In Dyer's case, it took a

middle course—what the Mormons call disfellowship, a sort of probation that is based on a period of repentance and rehabilitation.
The church authorities did not inform the civil authorities of the
allegations against Dyer.

It could be said, of course, that the church was simply trying to
avoid embarrassment, or even lawsuits: if the accusations against
Dyer were true, after all, the Redmond ward had for twelve years
had a pedophile in a position of trust and intimacy with young boys.
The Mormons would offer some other explanations for not having
gone to the police. It was always possible, for instance, that the ac-
cusation by the Boy Scout was untrue or exaggerated; Dyer apparently told some members of the congregation that it was all a mistake
and he was being treated unfairly. It could be argued that the fact
that the inquiry had started within the church gave it the equivalent
of the confidentiality traditional between priest and penitent—
although there is no indication that Ed Dyer confessed to anything.
It was presumably also true that the Mormons had difficulty facing
an issue that a lot of them considered appalling and repugnant. Apparently, those in the ward who came to know about Ed Dyer's
problem rarely discussed it. "It's the sort of subject you avoid because
it's distasteful," one of them said later. "It's something you just don't
want to believe has happened."

For whatever reason, it was about a year before the high-council
court prepared to convene again to consider refellowshipping Dyer.
By that time, though, one high-council member had heard what
seemed to be a corroborating allegation from the time Dyer still
lived in the Valley, and had learned that Dyer had put up notices in
places like gun shops announcing that he was certified to give the
hunting-education course required in Oregon for any hunter under
eighteen—notices that could, of course, be seen as a device to meet
boys. That member was asked by the stake president to undertake an
investigation, a role provided for in church rules. The boys in Troop
26 were reluctant to say anything, but the investigator began calling
around to young men who had been Boy Scouts in Redmond in

the past. He worked just about full-time on the investigation for three weeks, and in the end he gave the stake president a thirty-page dossier, accompanied by tape recordings that, with the permission of his informants, he had made of several telephone conversations. The report indicated that the incident with the Boy Scout in the tent was not an isolated incident but part of a pattern that went back at least twenty-five years.

The stake president did not reconvene the court to consider refellowshipping Dyer, but some time passed before he decided what to do instead. Part of the delay may have been caused by preoccupation with other matters. In August of 1983, one of the Dyers' sons, a young man of nineteen named Lance, was found to have leukemia. The members of the ward rallied around to help the Dyer family through the months of treatment—treatment that turned out to be of no avail. Lance Dyer died of pneumonia in May of 1984. It didn't seem to be the best time to pursue a case against Ed Dyer. Also, according to a member of the church who was familiar with the case, Dyer "kept saying he was going to turn himself in." It had been the high council's understanding that during the disfellowship period, Dyer was going to seek counseling and was going to avoid situations that would put him in the company of young boys. Apparently, the council concluded that Dyer had not complied with that understanding, because when it finally convened as a court, in late 1984, the decision was to excommunicate him. "I stayed away from kids for a long time," Dyer said some time later, when his problem was finally being dealt with in a court of law. "And then Louis came along."

Like Ed Dyer, Susan Birdsell Conner grew up loving the outdoors. She lived on the outskirts of Santa Barbara, California, where her parents owned a beauty parlor and her father dabbled in real estate. From the time Susan and her twin sister, Sharon, were eight or nine, they both knew that they were going to be veterinarians, and they both knew that they were someday going to live in a place where

the horses were back of the house rather than miles away in a boarding stable. Their mother can summon up life with two aspiring veterinarians in one sentence: "We had cages all over." Like many
identical twins, the Birdsell sisters were a lot more comfortable with
each other than with other people. By the time they entered school,
they had used a private language with each other for so long that
they had to be treated for slight speech impediments. They enrolled
together at the University of California, Davis, and in 1967 they
graduated as veterinarians. Both married Davis veterinary students
who planned to practice as equine veterinarians. It was a double
wedding.

Sharon got to Sisters first. She and her husband, Eric Sharpnack,
moved there from Point Reyes, California, in 1978 and took over
the Sisters Veterinary Clinic. She concentrated on small animals; he
treated horses, and on a number of occasions llamas. Susan had been
living in the East with her husband, a racetrack veterinarian named
Edward Conner, and their two sons. She and her husband were divorced in 1976, and after a couple of years she and the boys moved
to Oregon, where she eventually joined the Sharpnacks' practice.
Not long after that, Sharon and Eric Sharpnack were divorced. Seventeen years after the double wedding, the Birdsell twins—both divorced and both with two children—were in practice together as
the sole partners of the Sisters Veterinary Clinic.

They seemed to be among those people who were well suited to
Central Oregon and might have been uncomfortable in a place less
focused on the outdoors. "I don't think they'd even know how to
dress up," a friend says of them. Susan Conner bought a house in
Tollgate—a simple rough-cedar house that had nearly an acre of
ponderosa pines and a paddock in the back. Tollgate, like Black Butte
Ranch, is virtually inside the national forest, and she took great joy
in being able to ride from her own paddock onto the forest's trails
and logging roads. She became particularly active in what is known
locally as wagon driving—leisurely caravans of horse-drawn con-

veyances that might range from sulkies to restored buggies to covered wagons.

Susan had one problem not shared by her sister. Sharon Sharpnack's children were both girls, and their father was still in Sisters. Susan Conner's boys had virtually no contact with their father, who remained in the East. Her younger son, Brian, was an outgoing boy who had adjusted with relative ease to the move to Oregon and life in Sisters. But her older son, Louis, was more diffident than his brother and more obviously in need of a father figure. That was why Susan Conner was so pleased when, during Louis's eighth-grade year at Sisters Junior High School, he met an avuncular outdoorsman from the Forest Service named Ed Dyer.

Louis Conner, who was then fifteen, seemed a couple of years younger than he was—a slim, nice-looking boy with sandy hair and a quick, shy smile. He had his mother's love of animals and the outdoors. He belonged to two 4-H groups—one having to do with horses, the other with dog obedience and showmanship. He was gentle and unassertive, the sort of boy who tends not to register on his classmates in a large school. The adults who came in contact with him—teachers, 4-H leaders, Susan Conner's friends—thought of him as a polite young man, eager to be befriended by them. "Every year, there are boys, and sometimes girls, who adopt you," James Green, Louis's science teacher at Sisters Junior High, has said. "You could tell he wanted to talk to an adult—particularly a man."

In the spring of 1984, just before Easter vacation, Jim Green asked the Forest Service if it was possible to have someone come out and instruct his eighth graders in the proper use of the national forest. The Forest Service sent Ed Dyer. Green and Dyer gave a three-day course on how to exist in the wilderness—how to use a compass, how to read a map, how to pack a horse, how to survive in an emergency. During the visit, Dyer said he was looking for someone to hike the trails with him—to take part in "camping and skiing and different things in the outdoors." As Dyer later recalled it, Louis

Conner "turned around and said, 'I'd like to be your friend and go with you.'"

By that time, as it happened, a member of the Mormon congregation had informed an acquaintance on the Redmond police force that Ed Dyer had been disfellowshipped because of allegations of sexual misconduct with Boy Scouts. The informant suggested that it was a matter the police should investigate, but eventually it became obvious to him that whatever investigation had taken place was not going to lead to an indictment. It may be that the Redmond police had problems with the statute of limitations. It may be that there were problems with jurisdiction; a lot of the crimes that were alleged, after all, had occurred on hikes and encampments far outside the Redmond city limits, in the Central Oregon outdoors. It may be that the police were reluctant to launch a vigorous investigation of good old Ed Dyer, or that, like some members of the church, they were simply unable to face the possibility that what was being said about the man who had been entrusted with so many boys for so many years was true.

Louis worked that summer as a volunteer helping to maintain trails in the national forest. He began to talk about the possibility of making the Forest Service his career. Ed Dyer and Louis did a lot of things that a father and son would do in an outdoor sort of place. They went deer hunting together. Dyer gave Louis a shotgun. When the time came for Louis to buy a horse, Dyer helped him pick one out. Dyer often dropped by the house in Tollgate. He offered to supply the Conners with firewood. He had discussions with Susan Conner about how Louis was doing in school and what sort of friends he should be meeting. The adults who knew Louis—the woman who led his 4-H horse group, for instance—thought it was "really nice that he could have an older friend who was interested in the same things he was." Susan Conner was delighted. She thought that her worries about the absence of a father figure for Louis were over.

Of course, neither Susan Conner nor Louis Conner nor their

friends knew why Ed Dyer had resigned as scoutmaster of Troop 26 two years before he met Louis at Sisters Junior High. They were not Mormons. They knew nothing of the deliberations concerning Ed Dyer in the stake high council. They knew nothing about an investigation by the Redmond police. Sooner or later, though, the Forest Service was told of the information that the police had about Ed Dyer. As a result, the ranger in charge of the Sisters Ranger District walked into Dyer's office in February of 1985, closed the door behind him, and informed Dyer that he would no longer be permitted to work with young people unless other adults were present. The allegations in the hands of the police had not been proved, of course, and the ranger apparently tried to be balanced in responding to them. Recalling the ranger's instructions later, Dyer remarked, "He said, 'Well, just be prudent. Don't put yourself in a situation where you're set up.' And I followed those rules."

Dyer did not interpret the rules as applying to his relationship with Louis Conner. Louis continued to be Dyer's companion in the outdoors—although there were times when he seemed reluctant to go on outings with Dyer, and periods when they didn't see each other at all. Susan Conner thought that Louis might be getting tired of Dyer's stories or that he was beginning to prefer the company of boys his own age. Dyer persisted, though, and eventually Louis would accept one of his invitations. Dyer took him elk hunting. Two or three times Dyer took him to an event called a Mountain Man Rendezvous, a weekend encampment at which men dress in buckskin clothes and hold marksmanship contests with black-powder muskets and drink a lot of modern-day beer. In the summer of 1985, a little more than a year after their meeting in Jim Green's science class, Dyer arranged for Louis to work as a member of the Youth Conservation Corps crew maintaining trails.

Meanwhile, the informant from the Mormon church, having tried both the Redmond police force and the Deschutes County Sheriff's Department with no success, turned to the state police. The state police were interested. They didn't foresee any jurisdic-

tional problems. They weren't troubled by the fact that so many of
the allegations were beyond the statute of limitations; the behavior
pattern of a pedophile tends to be so unvarying, they told their
informant, that incidents within the statute of limitations would
almost certainly be turned up. The case was assigned to Lynn Fredrickson, a state police detective who has a reputation for dealing
sympathetically and effectively with young people. New names of
boys who knew Ed Dyer were not difficult to find. On June 18,
1985, Fredrickson showed up at the Sisters Ranger Station and asked
to speak to a summer Youth Conservation Corps employee named
Louis Conner.

Louis acknowledged nothing, but when Dyer learned of the interview he agreed to talk with Fredrickson. Eventually, Dyer admitted having initiated sexual encounters with Louis. He said that on a
number of occasions he and Louis had engaged in mutual masturbation. When Fredrickson reinterviewed Louis, he gathered that Louis
had felt trapped. When his mother had found him reluctant to accompany Dyer on outings, he hadn't known how to explain his reluctance without telling her what he couldn't bear to say. He had
been worried about displeasing the man who had settled into a role
so much like a father's. He had been worried about his job and his
hope for a career in the Forest Service. Louis's story about what had
happened on the outings matched Dyer's story. Another boy—a boy
named Keith, who had met Dyer at a church supper—told a similar
story. Charges of sexual abuse were filed against Ed Dyer.

For a while, it looked as if prosecuting Dyer might necessitate
Louis's testifying in open court. Louis was obviously reluctant. The
prospect of being labeled a homosexual filled him with dread. "He
wanted to cooperate with the process," a clinical social worker who
saw him at the time has said, "but he wanted to keep it a secret." Still,
both Louis and his mother were determined that he would testify if
that was required to convict Ed Dyer. It turned out not to be necessary. After protracted negotiations, a plea bargain was made: in return for Dyer's guilty plea to two charges of second-degree sexual

abuse, the district attorney of Deschutes County agreed to recommend concurrent sentences and to drop any investigation of similar charges. Instead of a trial, there was a sentencing hearing—in Bend, the seat of Deschutes County—to consider questions of punishment and treatment and restitution.

There was testimony from the mothers of both boys involved. "Before I knew all this had happened, I had said that I thought Ed would be blessed for his interest in my son," Keith's mother said. "But I know now that that's not true, because his interest was selfish. It wasn't to help my son or to love him. He simply used him." Susan Conner answered questions about how much had been spent on counseling for Louis, who still seemed to her depressed. Although the one news item carried in local papers about the case, a tiny item in *The Redmond Spokesman,* had not mentioned the names of the boys involved, she said that some kids at school had brought up the subject with Louis. "He doesn't want to go anywhere on weekends," she said. "He doesn't want to be around other high school kids, because he thinks they're going to talk to him about this, and because of his depression." She had decided, she said, that she was in need of counseling as well: "My son blames me for this, because I encouraged him to go with Ed, because I thought Ed was such a wonderful person."

Most of what the judge heard, though, was mitigating evidence presented by Dyer's lawyer. Tona Dyer, speaking in a soft, sad voice, said that her husband was a kind man and a good father. A couple of men who knew Dyer through the Boy Scouts testified that he was sincere and law-abiding and had made a great sacrifice of his time and energy in the years he spent as scoutmaster of Troop 26. It was brought out that Ed Dyer had already suffered for his crimes. He had, in effect, lost his job—the Forest Service had allowed him to take early retirement—and that job had been the center of his life. ("It meant a lot to me to work in that job," Dyer testified. "I really enjoyed it. It was a way of life. It wasn't just a job.") He had been forced to leave Scouting. He had been excommunicated by his church. Although two of the counselors who met with Dyer had come to the conclusion that he was without remorse—they thought he regretted only that he got caught—Tona Dyer testified that they were mistaken. "He's been very depressed, and he is very remorseful," she said. "He just sits around or lays around. . . . He feels really bad because of what he's done and how people feel toward him. He feels really bad. And he feels bad for the people he's hurt. More than, I think, anyone realizes." Mrs. Dyer said she had known about her husband's problem for years. "It does bother me," she said. "But I feel that you don't always look at the thing that someone does wrong. You look at the other qualities a person has, too. And I think if you care about someone you expect that these people are good and maybe they'll be able to crack this problem. And I do care about him."

Dyer himself was on the stand for some time. He denied that he had used his position as scoutmaster as a way of arranging sexual encounters. "It might be construed that way, but it wasn't intended that way," he said. "That was not my reason for staying in the program." Dyer said that he had always wanted to seek help but had been afraid it would mean arrest and the loss of everything—his job, his family. "Most of the boys that I molested by their terms, by the terms of the law, I really loved," he said. "I didn't want to hurt them." Then he looked at Louis Conner, who was sitting in the courtroom. "I know that Louis back here, sitting there, I know that he probably hates me now, because of the problems I brought on him and his family," Dyer said. "But I truly did love him and enjoyed his company and all the good things we did. And I'm painfully regretful of that problem and that situation. And if there was any way I could erase it, and make his life better, I would sure do it."

Dyer may have been right about Louis's hating him. Louis was angered by a lot of what was said at the sentencing hearing, particularly Dyer's answer to a question about who had initiated the encounters between him and the boys: "It was mutual part of the time and part of the time maybe mostly myself." Partly because of Louis's fear of being labeled a homosexual, the question of who was to blame was terribly important to him—in the words of one counselor, "He needed to be real clear that it was not *his* fault that this happened"—and Dyer, despite his guilty plea, seemed reluctant to accept the blame. Just after the guilty plea, Susan Conner had angrily informed the district attorney's office of a telephone call from Dyer in which he had told her that the encounters had come about by mutual consent, and that Louis would be free to make his own decisions on such matters as soon as he had his eighteenth birthday. Also, Louis, as he sat in the courtroom, knew what he had been afraid and ashamed to tell Detective Fredrickson: on two or three occasions, his sexual contact with Ed Dyer had gone beyond the mutual masturbation that Dyer had admitted. The district attorney's office had eventually learned of those occasions. Presumably, one reason Dyer had finally agreed to plead guilty was the knowledge that if Louis Conner testified, he would be testifying about sodomy.

There was nothing in the judge's decision that might have made Louis feel better about what was happening. Although the presentencing report had recommended a considerable time in jail, Dyer was sentenced to serve only twenty days, more or less at his own convenience. The judge also ruled that Dyer would have to enter a counseling program for sex offenders, would have to be on supervised probation for three years, and would have to avoid associating with boys under eighteen. He was not specifically forbidden to see Louis Conner, even after the prosecutor pointed out that Louis, who may have looked only fifteen or so, would be eighteen before the year was out. "From what all the witnesses have testified to, why you're a fine fellow, with a good work record, who's done a great deal for the community," the judge told Dyer. "If you feel positive about yourself, why these episodes aren't going to mar your life, and you can make the best of it."

Presumably, Louis had been angry even before he got to the hearing. Two nights earlier, he had taken out the shotgun Dyer gave him—a 16-gauge single-shot. He had removed most of the stock.

He had sawed off the barrel about six inches from the trigger. A sawed-off shotgun is, of course, easier to conceal than a full-length shotgun, and is also more maneuverable. For targets more than a few yards away, there is a sacrifice in accuracy and power. A sawed-off shotgun is not an effective weapon for hunting deer. What it is used for is killing someone at close range.

January 22 was a bleak day in Sisters. A cold rain fell intermittently. The stunning view of the Cascades didn't exist. It was a Wednesday, five days after the judge in Bend had pronounced sentence on Ed Dyer. As on any other school morning, Louis Conner climbed onto the bus that took him to high school on the edge of Redmond. He was wearing the blue parka he normally wore to school. Hidden underneath his parka was the sawed-off shotgun. At Redmond High School, Louis got off the bus with the other students, but he didn't go into the school building. He walked back down Route 126 in the direction of Sisters—toward Ed Dyer's house.

Dyer's pickup was not in the driveway. He had gone to a swap shop in Bend to see what he might get for a set of sleigh bells he was ready to part with. On the way back, he stopped in Redmond to chat with a friend. In a cold, driving rain, Louis Conner stood in a field waiting. Two hours later, Dyer still hadn't returned. Finally, Louis, soaked and shivering, knocked on the door and told Tona Dyer that he was there to see her husband. She was concerned by his presence. Her husband, after all, had been instructed by the judge not to associate with boys under eighteen. She asked Louis in, though, and told him to stand next to the woodstove to dry out. Twenty minutes later, Ed Dyer showed up. When he was told that Louis wanted to talk to him, he said he'd have to call his probation officer first. The probation officer told Dyer that he should not talk to Louis. Dyer was instructed to drive Louis back to Redmond High School immediately. Tona Dyer, who didn't drive, was to accompany her husband and Louis, so that they wouldn't be alone. The three of them walked out to the pickup. Ed Dyer and Louis Conner had exchanged hardly a word. At the pickup, Dyer opened the door on the driver's side and then went over to lock what he called his sport shed—the place he kept a lot of his outdoor equipment. As Dyer returned to the truck, Louis stepped out from behind the driver's door, holding the shotgun. Tona Dyer thought she heard her husband say something like "No, Louis!" Louis shot him in the chest.

Dyer was still standing when his wife ran into the house to call an ambulance, but she was certain that he had been mortally wounded. In Redmond, a few miles away, Lynn Fredrickson, the state police detective who had filed charges against Ed Dyer, was eating lunch in his car when he heard the report of a shooting on Route 126. The address sounded familiar, and he asked the dispatcher who lived there. When he was told that it was the home of an Edwin Dyer, he thought he knew what must have happened, and he headed for Dyer's house. Before he got there, an ambulance had arrived, and the crew had seen that there was nothing to be done for Ed Dyer. It was Fredrickson and his partner who found Louis, an hour or so later. He was standing in a field about three-quarters of a mile from the Dyers' house. He offered no resistance.

In Oregon, any sentence imposed by a juvenile court, the court that normally has jurisdiction over everyone under the age of eighteen, expires on the defendant's twenty-first birthday—so a juvenile defendant who is, say, seventeen cannot be locked up for more than four years no matter what he has done. In the case of certain serious felonies, though, a district attorney can move in juvenile court to have a defendant who is fifteen or older remanded to the adult court system, where no such limitation on the sentence exists. The criteria for making the decision include the previous criminal record of the juvenile, the protection required by the community, and the "aggressive, violent, premeditated, or willful manner in which the offense was alleged to have been committed." The district attorney of Deschutes County announced that he would attempt to have Louis Conner remanded to the adult court system and tried for murder.

It was not a popular decision. There were people in Deschutes County who said that there was no reason for any trial at all. For some people, Louis Conner had become a sort of hero; at the very least, he seemed more the victim than the offender. Although the risk would have been too great, it occurred to Louis's lawyers that if they elected to try him in the adult court system, where his fate would be determined by a jury rather than a judge, it was unlikely that any jury would convict Louis, no matter what the evidence. It's possible that there were people in Deschutes County who agreed with the district attorney that Louis was guilty of murder. It's possible that there were people who, whatever their views on how the case should be dealt with legally, were disturbed by indications that in the public mind Louis Conner, the timid boy who dreaded the thought of being labeled a homosexual, had, in the tradition of the Hollywood Old West, transformed himself into a hero with one blast of a gun. If there were such people, they kept their opinions to themselves. In letters to the editor and gossip at the cafés and late-night talk in the bars, the prevailing opinion was that Ed Dyer had got what was coming to him.

In Sisters, at least, that view was often expressed after a qualifying observation about how nobody has a right to take the law into his own hands. Most of the people in Sisters are not the sort of people who condone violence or preach vengeance. It's the sort of place whose response to what had happened included inviting two specialists on the problem of sexual abuse to come to town and conduct a symposium. Still, people in Sisters were disturbed at what seemed to be a disparity in the way the county had treated Ed Dyer and the way it was treating Louis Conner. "I think people don't blame Ed or Louis but the judicial system," Eric Dolson, the editor of the weekly paper in Sisters, said as the remand hearing got under way in Bend. "People like to think that the guilty are punished and the innocent are protected. It's part of our sense of security. If they think there's reason to believe that's not true, it upsets them." By the time the remand hearing began, about two months after Ed Dyer was shot to death, a defense fund for Louis Conner in Sisters had raised more than eight thousand dollars.

The deputy district attorney who represented the state in the remand hearing—Roy Miller, the same deputy district attorney who had prosecuted Ed Dyer—basically argued that the three and a half years until Louis Conner's twenty-first birthday was not enough time for the state to have him in custody, whether the custody was considered treatment or punishment. Miller argued that the crime had, in fact, been premeditated. The shotgun had been sawed off two days before the sentencing hearing that so upset Louis; there was no indication that Dyer had said or done anything to provoke Louis just before the shooting. Louis's lawyer, a former Eugene prosecutor named Stephen Tiktin, said that it was Louis who had been the victim—the victim of "sexual abuse perpetrated by a homosexual predatory pedophile." Louis had been willing even to undergo the embarrassment of testifying in open court in order to bring the man who victimized him to justice, Tiktin said, but the sentencing hearing convinced him that "the system had failed." The state presented witnesses to support its contention that there were facilities in the adult correctional system appropriate for Louis; the defense presented witnesses to support its contention that Louis was a natural victim who would be "fair game as soon as he steps into the bowels of the penitentiary."

The witness who seemed to speak with the most authority was Dr. John Cochran, the senior forensic clinical psychologist for the State of Oregon, who was called by the prosecution but testified in favor of the defense contention that Louis should be treated as a juvenile. Cochran turned out to be a pudgy man with a mustache and a thoughtful expression that made him appear personally concerned even when he happened to be speaking of test results that sounded rather technical. In a way, Cochran's testimony amounted to a retelling of the story of Ed Dyer and Louis Conner, this time in psychological terms. Cochran described Louis as a naïve and passive and dependent boy, less mature socially and emotionally than the average boy his age. More than most boys, Cochran said, Louis had a need for the approval of others, to the point of being willing to subject himself to "abuse or intimidation to avoid rejection or abandonment." In other words, Cochran said, Louis was an easily manipulated boy who was perfect prey for Ed Dyer—"a pedophile extremely experienced at grooming people like Louis." In Cochran's view, the stress Louis was under once the investigation of Dyer began was magnified by Dyer's response to the charge against him. "As the circle began to tighten, instead of protecting his pseudo-child he abandoned him," Cochran said of Dyer. "Once in court, instead of making a clean breast of it he blamed Louis." The result, Cochran said, was "a massive amount of betrayal." According to Cochran's interpretation of the events, Louis had not gone to Dyer's house with the intention of shooting anybody; the shotgun was an "equalizer," a way of making certain that the larger man paid attention. Louis desperately wanted to find out why Dyer had said in court that some of the sexual encounters had been initiated by both of them, Cochran said, and Dyer's adherence to the probation officer's instructions not to talk to Louis was, ironically, the last straw: "The usual coping methods that Louis has were obliterated." Cochran testified that the combination of events required to drive Louis Conner to violence would be unlikely ever to occur again. He was, in Cochran's term, "a situational offender."

To no one's surprise, the judge held that the juvenile court would retain jurisdiction over Louis Conner. In holding for the defense, though, the judge, John M. Copenhaver, was careful to separate himself from the notion that Ed Dyer had got what he deserved—the notion that sexual offenders should be "destroyed like rabid dogs." In announcing his decision, Judge Copenhaver said, "Sexual abuse does not mean that a person's life has no value to us. The loss of any life diminishes the quality of life in our community."

Shortly after the remand hearing, Louis Conner's lawyer sent the tort notices required if he intended to file suits in civil court against the Redmond Police Department and the U.S. Forest Service—suits that would presumably allege negligence that led to Ed Dyer's remaining in the company of boys even after his background was known. There were two more hearings remaining in the criminal case against Louis. From what the judge and the defense had said in court, it seemed clear that they both believed what Louis had done fit the legal definition of manslaughter, but there had to be a hearing on that question. And there had to be a hearing—what juvenile courts call a dispositional hearing—to decide on a sentence. While those hearings were being prepared for, the judge let Louis remain at home. Susan Conner found her son in relatively good spirits. "People expect him to be depressed," she said. "But for the first time he doesn't have the cloud of Ed Dyer hanging over him."

A month after the remand hearing, Judge Copenhaver ruled that the shooting of Ed Dyer had been manslaughter. A couple of months after that, those involved in the case gathered again in Judge Copenhaver's courtroom for the final hearing in what was officially called "In the Matter of Louis Robert Conner, a child"—a hearing to decide what should happen to Louis. Deputy District Attorney Roy Miller was there to argue that Louis should be sent to the MacLaren School—the sort of institution that used to be called a reform school, and, under ordinary circumstances, the place where a juvenile found guilty of something as serious as manslaughter would go. The defense, backed by the counselor who had been treating Louis, argued that he should be sent home. The Deschutes County Juvenile Department, which normally comes to such hearings in agreement with the district attorney, suggested a middle course—a small, unguarded residential facility that emphasized intensive counseling. The Juvenile Department's representative testified that the department would prefer to see Louis go home if the alternative was MacLaren, but that one disadvantage of sending him back to Sisters was that the community "might be too supportive," because "Louis is seen as a hero."

Judge Copenhaver took the middle course. He suspended a sentence to MacLaren and ruled that Louis should instead spend six months at ACCORD, a house in the countryside a few miles from Bend which is a sort of adjunct of a nearby facility called the J Bar J Boys Ranch. The day after the decision, a few people from Sisters were quoted in the Bend paper expressing disappointment that Louis had to serve any time anywhere, but a lot of people thought the judge had made a sensible choice. "I think the decision had as much to do with the community as with Louis," a lawyer who has followed the case said after the dispositional hearing. "Given the nature of the offense, it's sort of hard for a judge to say, 'Well, don't do it again,' and send Louis home. He couldn't give the message to the community, 'Go ahead and shoot these guys.'"

Susan Conner had known that a boy who killed someone was not likely to be sent home, but, partly because she had read of something like that happening in a similar case in California, she had gone to the hearing with her hopes up. "I should be really happy," she said not long after the sentencing. "I guess I am happy." Ordinarily, boys sent to ACCORD or the J Bar J Ranch have done nothing more serious than take a car that didn't happen to belong to them. ACCORD is on a few acres of land; the facilities of J Bar J, just down the road, are available. It's the sort of place that tries to take advantage of its access to the Central Oregon outdoors. There are, of course, horses at J Bar J. To build confidence, the boys do rock climbing and mountaineering. Particularly during school vacations, they're encouraged to work outdoors, for wages. In the summer, they often work for the local parks and recreation department, maintaining trails.

At the Train Bridge

The Upper Peninsula of Michigan

JULY 2009

S cott Johnson sees himself as one of those guys who never caught a break. "Seems like whatever I did was never enough," he told the police in one interview. "It seems like whenever I was almost at the point of obtaining something or getting somewhere, seems like something would happen and take it away. You know, it seems like it's been like that way through my whole life." The people who were affected by the crimes he committed see things differently. One of them has said, "Scott Johnson wanted to blame everyone and everything for his pathetic life." At the time of the crimes, the summer of 2008, Johnson's life would have indeed struck many people as pathetic. At thirty-eight—a healthy and fit and presentable thirty-eight—he was living with his mother in Kingsford, Michigan, having retreated in 2001 from an increasingly unsuccessful decade in Louisiana. Kingsford is just across the Menominee River from northern Wisconsin, at the mainland edge of what people in Michigan call the Upper Peninsula, or UP—a vast, underpopulated, heavily wooded landmass that extends into the Great Lakes. In growing up in Kingsford and in the contiguous city of Iron Mountain, Johnson could claim to have been shortchanged when it came to fathers—his biological father left when Scott was an infant, and his stepfather could apparently be a violent drunk—but his mother seemed devoted to him. Years later, after the crimes, she still talked about his smile and the twinkle in his eye. "I thought I was the luckiest mom alive to have a son like Scott," she said. Johnson actually had some pleasant memories of his childhood, particularly of hunting in the woods and target shooting. "He said that by the age of nine he received his first weapon, a single-shot 20-gauge as a gift from his mother," one of the court-appointed psychologists who examined Johnson reported. "Later, he received from her a 30/30 rifle. He described these gifts as not inconsistent or unusual among his peer group or within the rural culture of upper Michigan."

Johnson got to Louisiana through the Army. Shortly after graduating from Kingsford High School, where he'd finished in the top half of his class, he left for basic training, and he was eventually assigned to Fort Polk. At a Baptist church, he met a young woman named Theresa, whose father was also in the Army, and in 1991 they were married. "That appears to be when everything started to go bad," the judge in Johnson's case later said. You could indeed see Johnson's marriage as the beginning of his problems, or you could see it as a sort of canvas on which his problems became visible. The first year or so was fine, his wife later said, but he became controlling and abusive, particularly after he finished his Army hitch and they moved to Shreveport. By 1994, he'd begun to threaten to kill her. "Mrs. Johnson related that the defendant would constantly remind her of how stupid and worthless that he thought she was," the presentencing report on Scott Johnson said. When Theresa Johnson was five months pregnant with their daughter—their first child, a boy, had been born five years before—he pushed her down because she had failed to mail some Christmas cards when he wanted them mailed. The last straw came in 1999, when she confronted him about leaving their daughter in the backyard alone. According to the report, he got so angry that he threw the family cat against the wall hard enough to render it unconscious. When Theresa Johnson returned from the backyard with their daughter in her arms, he was pointing a rifle at her chest from approximately eight feet away. Although her memory of the incident is almost blank after that moment—she has surmised that she must have been in shock—she remembers one remark by her husband: "Look what you made me do." She and the children left for Ohio, where she had family, and she filed for divorce.

After his discharge, Johnson had held a succession of jobs. He worked in a VA hospital. He worked in a center for troubled adolescents. He worked as a shuttle driver for a Ramada Inn. He worked at a convenience store. His stories about how his various types of employment came to an end tend to involve some sort of altercation brought about by the unfairness of his employer. According to one psychologist, Johnson's stories in general tended to involve "the ways in which he has been mistreated by others and about his own superior assets and virtues." That was true of what he said about the National Guard, which he had joined after his active-duty Army service was over. He'd enrolled in Officer Candidate School but eventually washed out. By his account, he'd taken two days off to attend his grandmother's funeral, and "they got pissed off and fucked with me a lot after that. It was very unprofessional." When his wife divorced him, he was in the final year of a five-year apprentice plumbing program, but he dropped out without getting a plumbing license.

After 2001, he no longer saw his children. By the next year, he had begun skipping child-support payments. Theresa Johnson reported some phone calls threatening violence. He had passed some bad checks at a gun-and-knife show—one of them as payment for a .308 semiautomatic rifle. "I was depressed and drinking a lot and smoking pot," he told one of the psychologists. "I was self-destructing. I quit my job, wrote some bad checks, and ran before they could catch me. . . . I got a passport and planned to leave the country but then I went up to Kingsford to see my mom before I left and then it just got easy to stay in Michigan. . . . I couldn't work because they'd catch me, so I did a couple of little jobs or got money from my mom and brother. I just leeched off of them."

That arrangement lasted for six or seven years. Jobs were not as easy to find as they had once been in the part of the UP that borders

Wisconsin—the iron ore that left names like Iron Mountain and Iron River and Vulcan played out decades ago; the forest-products industry has not been in a boom—but Johnson didn't try. In his view, the way to avoid the burden of child support and the threat of arrest for check-kiting was to "go off the grid." His only form of work was maintenance on his mother's house, a modest bungalow not far from the Menominee River. He stuck to himself, gradually not even eating meals with his mother and an older half brother, who also lived there. He did a lot of exercising. By his estimation, he ran eight to ten miles a day and rode his bicycle thirty miles a day. Sometimes he swam in the Menominee, at a swimming hole known locally as the train bridge.

Less than a mile from Johnson's mother's house, Skidmore Drive begins as a regular street but then turns into a gravel road. At the end of the gravel road, a footpath continues through the woods. After half a mile or so, the path veers sharply toward some railroad tracks that lead to a railroad bridge crossing high over the Menominee River. Side paths lead down to the riverbank. The Menominee is wide and slow there. Tall trees grow on either side, so that someone on the riverbank has a feeling of total isolation. Even by the standards of the UP, where no one lives far from sylvan beauty, it's a gorgeous spot. For generations, people from the Iron Mountain and Kingsford area, particularly young people, have come to the train bridge to swim and to drop into the river from a rope that hangs from the bridge's superstructure and to drink beer in a place where there is nobody asking for your proof of age. On the Wisconsin side, there's another mile or so of woods between the river and the town of Niagara. It was in those woods that, around 2004, Scott Johnson secreted some supplies—a sleeping bag, clothes, a knife. In the fissure of a rock, he hid the rifle he'd bought at the Louisiana gun-and-knife show. To police detectives, he later explained this preparation with a maxim: "If you fail to plan, you can plan on failure."

.   .   .

Johnson's routine was not the sort of routine that led to a lot of contact with women. Shortly after his return, he had lived with a woman briefly, but by the summer of 2008 he had not been with a woman in six years. The previous winter, at the Family Dollar store in Kingsford, he'd met a young woman who lived near him, and they had been in each other's company for several months in a platonic way. ("He knew that I don't even like being touched," she later said.) He stopped at her place now and then to chat or to help her with her garden. They sometimes took walks or bike rides—including a couple to the train bridge, which she had somehow never visited before. Then, on July 30, 2008, he asked her if she wanted to go for a bike ride. They went to the train bridge. "We went for a bike ride together in the evening," the young woman later wrote in a statement to the authorities. "We walked into the woods in East Kingsford and crossed the train bridge into Wisconsin. We were alone. He led me into the woods that was off of one of the trails and that's when he put his hands under my tank top and shoved me to the ground and pulled my pants and underpants off and he forced himself into me. I begged him to stop, but he wouldn't. I said 'NO' several times as he was on me but he wouldn't listen."

Johnson later offered another version of the event—in his version, he did not manage to complete the act—but he didn't deny that a sexual assault had taken place. He has said that, particularly because he didn't consider the young woman in question nearly as attractive as some of the women he'd known when he had a job and money, he became enraged when she rejected his advance. Apparently, he pleaded with her not to phone the police. He said that she could punish him any way that she wanted, including beating him with a baseball bat. As he saw it, if she went to the police, he'd be wanted in Louisiana for passing bad checks and in Ohio for failure to provide child support and in Wisconsin for sexual assault. He dreaded the thought of being sent to jail as a sex offender. That night, he stayed in the woods. When he went by his mother's house the next day, she told him that the police had been by and wanted to speak to him. He said he would straighten everything out after he had something to eat, and asked for ten dollars to go to Subway. "I went and got something to eat so I could sit down and think about it," he later said. "What am I gonna do? Am I gonna turn myself in or do the shoot 'em up thing? What am I gonna do?" By late that afternoon, he was walking over the train bridge, noticing the teenagers who had taken advantage of a beautiful summer day to go swimming in the river below. He walked to his camp, on the Wisconsin side of the river. According to a sentencing memo prepared by Assistant Attorney General Gary Freyberg, the lead prosecutor in Johnson's case, "He put on camouflage pants, a camouflage shirt, and a camouflage floppy-brimmed hat. He exchanged the tennis shoes he was wearing for boots, and placed camouflage field bandages in the pockets of his shirt. He retrieved his disassembled .308 caliber semiautomatic rifle from a gun case stashed in a jagged rock outcropping, put the pieces together, and cleaned the rifle."

Johnson has offered several versions of what was going on in his mind as he settled into a spot that gave him a good view of the teenagers on the Michigan bank of the river. "I'm thinking, do I go out with a bang, you know," he said in one police interview. "I got nothing to lose . . . the only power I have in this life is to take." At times, he seemed to imply that his plan was to shoot people at the train bridge in order to attract police and first responders so that he could kill as many of them as possible. ("My initial plan was to use those people as bait.") At times, he has implied that what he was planning was what is sometimes known as "suicide by cop," by putting "police in a position where they had to put me down." At times, he's said that what he contemplated doing was "balancing the scales," so that people could understand the pain he'd been through. At times, also, he has said that he had doubts that he could "really go through with this," and that he was about to dismantle his weapon when he heard people approaching.

"Tiffany Pohlson, 17, Anthony Spigarelli, 18, Katrina Coates, 17, and Derek Barnes, 18, swam across the river to Wisconsin in order to jump off of a large rock overhanging the river located west of the defendant's firing position," Freyberg's sentencing memo says. "In swimsuits and shorts, they walked barefoot in a staggered line on a rough trail through the woods toward the rock face where the defendant waited with his assault rifle. Anthony Spigarelli was in front chatting with his best friend Derek Barnes. Tiffany Pohlson and her best friend, Katrina Coates, followed closely behind. As he waited in ambush, the defendant heard the teenagers coming toward his position. He could tell by their voices that there were two males and two females. The defendant became afraid that he was 'trapped,' that he would be discovered, and that someone would have a cell phone and he would be 'busted.' When the group was about 15 to 20 feet away, the defendant jumped up from his position. The teenagers were startled and confused by the sight of a man in camouflage and they stopped on the trail. When the defendant raised his rifle and advanced toward them, all four teenagers turned to run. As they fled, the defendant opened fire. Anthony Spigarelli was shot in the back of the head and died instantly. His body rolled down the hill toward the river until its descent was stopped by a small tree. Tiffany Pohlson was holding the hand of Katrina Coates when she was struck by a bullet to the back of her head, killing her instantly."

Johnson fired some shots at the other two teenagers, who were fleeing through the woods. Then he turned his attention to the swimming hole and sprayed bullets at the people who were on the Michigan bank. Bryan Mort, nineteen, was seriously wounded. A teenager who had taken cover at the base of the bridge phoned 911 on his cellphone; as sirens approached, Johnson faded back into the woods. He had fired at least two dozen rounds.

No one knew the identity or the precise whereabouts of the shooter. Soon there were a hundred law-enforcement officers in the vicinity of the train bridge. A perimeter was formed around the woods on either side of the Menominee. Nearby houses were evacuated. It wasn't until eight in the evening that officers were able to reach the bodies of Anthony Spigarelli and Tiffany Pohlson. By then, Bryan Mort had been moved by boat to a ramp that was accessible to an ambulance, but he was pronounced dead at the hospital. Scott Johnson spent the night in the woods. The next morning, he dismantled his rifle, walked out of the woods near Niagara, and surrendered.

Several months later, Lisa Hoffmann, of the Iron Mountain *Daily News,* wrote a series of articles recalling the teenagers Johnson had killed. Tony Spigarelli, an outgoing young man from Iron Mountain who played soccer and hoped to study aeronautics someday, had been three weeks away from entering college. Tiffany Pohlson, who was from Vulcan, about ten miles from Iron Mountain, had been due to start her senior year in high school in the fall; her goal was to become a surgical technician. Bryan Mort, who dreamed of opening an auto shop with his brothers someday, had dropped out of school at seventeen but, after working for a while, had gone back to get his diploma. On the summer day when he happened to go to the train bridge to swim, he was two weeks away from becoming the first member of his family to go to college. The shock caused in the community by the murders of three innocent teenagers—the mixture of disbelief and grief and rage—was intensified by the contrast between the horrific act and the tranquillity of the setting. Almost a year later, Terri Bianco-Spigarelli, as if still finding the events at the train bridge hard to believe, said of her son, "He was just going swimming."

That statement was made during Scott Johnson's sentencing hearing, this spring. Johnson had never expressed any interest in an insanity defense—what he called, in a letter from jail to his mother, "playing the coo-coo card." In one interview with a court-appointed psychologist, he said, "You don't have to be crazy to do what I did, just angry." The specialists who examined him agreed. They were unanimous in believing that he did not lack the capacity to understand the wrongfulness of his actions. In March 2009, Johnson had changed his plea from not guilty to nolo contendere, which has the effect of a guilty plea, and the circuit-court judge, Tim Duket, had scheduled a hearing at which victims as well as Johnson would have an opportunity to speak before a sentence was imposed. No matter what was said, Johnson was expected to be sentenced to life in prison without the possibility of parole, the most severe penalty the State of Wisconsin has to offer.

For the family of Bryan Mort, that wasn't enough. Through a petition signed by local residents and the support of their congressman, the Morts pressed for a federal prosecution of Scott Johnson. Under a federal law passed after 9/11, acts of violence on railroad property—which is where Mort was, since the railroad's right-of-way extends fifty feet on either side of the train bridge—can be prosecuted as acts of terrorism, with sentences that include the death penalty. Four days before the sentencing hearing, friends and family of Bryan Mort gathered at the Iron Mountain cemetery on what would have been his twentieth birthday. In the *Daily News* coverage of the event, the quote from Bryan's father was succinct: "The Bible says 'an eye for an eye.'"

The sentencing hearing was held in the county seat of Marinette County, a city that is also called Marinette, about an hour and a half from the scene of the crimes. The audience sat in a large, paneled room that is ordinarily used for meetings of the county board. In the earlier days of the courthouse, before an annex was built, it had been used for trials—EQUAL JUSTICE FOR ALL is still carved over the door—and it had been temporarily changed back into a courtroom to accommodate those who had a personal stake in the outcome of *State of Wisconsin v. Scott J. Johnson.* Except for lawyers, just about everyone was dressed informally, even those who were there to speak. Two people were wearing T-shirts that said SPIGARELLI EXCAVATING. Five women in one row, including Bryan Mort's mother, Sylvia, were wearing T-shirts that said on the back BRYAN W. MORT 1989–2008 and on the front, under Bryan's picture, ALWAYS IN OUR HEARTS. Judge Duket began by reminding people that they were, in fact, in a courtroom, temporary or not, and that outbursts would not be tolerated.

To back that up, more than a dozen officers from the sheriff's office were stationed around the room. Before the judge began the proceedings, another employee of Marinette County—a woman responsible for the care of crime victims and their families—had handed out boxes of tissues and packages of hard candy.

Nine months had passed since the events at the train bridge, but there was no expectation that the anger felt by the families of those killed by Johnson had dissipated. From the release of documents such as police interviews, it had become clear that he was not inclined to express remorse or to beg their forgiveness. ("What do other guys in my position tell 'em? They're sorry? What does that do for them?") In fact, in a jailhouse interview with the Associated Press, Johnson had said that being upset over the death of the teenagers was like being upset over spilled milk.

Given the anger at Johnson, who sat at the defense table in an orange prison jumpsuit, it was not surprising that a lot of what was said in the Marinette County courtroom seemed designed to wound him rather than to describe the loss and suffering that his crimes had caused. Tiffany Pohlson's uncle called him a "useless piece of garbage." Johnson was regularly reminded that he had failed at everything he'd ever attempted—including even his horrific crime, since he'd apparently intended to kill even more people than he had managed to kill. David Spigarelli, Tony's father, concluded his statement by saying that prison would give Johnson "a chance to finally achieve something for the first time in his life, when his cellmate, Bubba, says 'bend over I'm ready to lay this pipe.' He will finally have achieved his master plumber's status. . . . Me and Tony will be laughing our asses off, Scott Johnson." Most of what Terri Bianco-Spigarelli said, through tears, seemed designed to memorialize her son rather than to excoriate the defendant, but she said that Johnson would burn in hell, because God forgives only the remorseful. "I never hated anybody," she said. "I'm a people lover. I get along with everybody. I hate him, and I could kill him."

Scott Johnson read a prepared speech. At the start, he said that the points he would make were based on a maxim that he'd devised when he was twelve: "The truth of the matter at hand is that the truth doesn't count anymore. It is the quality of the lie that endures." He had any number of complaints to make about police-interrogation quotes being taken out of context or psychologists being biased or the press getting the facts wrong, particularly about whether he had planned the shooting in advance. He reiterated his belief that no purpose would be served by saying that he was sorry for what he'd done. ("If I showed a hint of remorse, what would people say then? 'Oh, he's lying. Oh, he's faking.'") He said what he did regret was that he had to live among people who were liars, gullible, arrogant, and brainwashed. The audience controlled itself through most of the speech, but when Johnson implied that money donated to the victims' families for funeral expenses exceeded the costs of the funerals, there was shouting in the courtroom. Sylvia Mort stood up and, before the judge could react, said, "Let me out of here!" As she stormed out, she said, loudly enough to be heard throughout the room, "Fuckin' piece of shit!" When order had been restored, Johnson finished his remarks, closing by quoting two verses of the Louis Armstrong standard "What a Wonderful World."

"These families have you pegged perfectly," Judge Duket said to Johnson, when it came time to impose a sentence. He portrayed the defendant as someone who blamed others for his constant failures, who thought that he was smarter than everyone else, who craved attention, and who responded to his own problems by murdering innocent children. In addition to the harm Johnson had done to his victims and their families, the judge said, he'd brought great suffering to his own family. Johnson's mother had said, "The pain is so bad I wanted to die. This is like a living death," and the daughter he professed to love, now twelve, was, according to Theresa Johnson, terrified that Scott Johnson would get out of jail and come to Ohio to kill her. "If ever there was a constellation of criminal activities that called out for maximum consecutive sentences this would be the case," Judge Duket said. What the prosecutor had asked for, after

enumerating the cases of murder, attempted murder, and sexual assault, was three life sentences without the possibility of parole, to be
served consecutively, plus two hundred and ninety-five years—a
sentence that sounded as if it required something beyond longevity,
in the direction of reincarnation. On the subject of sentences that
can obviously not be fulfilled, Judge Duket quoted a Wisconsin
Court of Appeals decision holding that such sentences can, among
other things, "properly express the community's outrage." The judge
imposed everything that the prosecutor had asked for. Outside the
courtroom, Sylvia Mort, who vowed to keep pursuing the death
penalty, said of the sentence, "It's a beginning."

Near where the path through the woods to the train bridge begins,
there is now a memorial to the three teenagers killed in what the
inscription calls "a senseless act of violence." A small section of
ground has been bricked over, and on it two benches face each
other, on either side of a rectangular granite monument that con-
tains pictures of Tony Spigarelli and Tiffany Pohlson and Bryan Mort.
The monument is also inscribed with the first verse of a William
Cowper hymn, "God Moves in a Mysterious Way." Other than the
memorial, the train-bridge swimming hole is unchanged from the
time the three teenagers pictured on the monument went there to
swim a year ago. It remains idyllic—a scene that could be a calendar
painting depicting lazy summer days in some bucolic patch of the
upper Midwest.

The young woman who was assaulted by Scott Johnson had
mentioned the beauty of the spot when, to the surprise of everyone
involved, she showed up at the sentencing hearing to deliver a victim's statement about how Johnson had betrayed her with an act that
still haunts her every day. The train bridge was also mentioned in the
speech that Johnson made before he was sentenced. "The train
bridge has been washed in the blood that I spilled," he said. "The
beauty of that place has been cursed by my actions. My memorial is
made of iron and concrete."

Covering the Cops

Miami Florida

FEBRUARY 1986

In the newsroom of the *Miami Herald,* there is some disagreement about which of Edna Buchanan's first paragraphs stands as the classic Edna lead. I line up with the fried-chicken faction. The fried-chicken story was about a rowdy ex-con named Gary Robinson, who late one Sunday night lurched drunkenly into a Church's outlet, shoved his way to the front of the line, and ordered a three-piece box of fried chicken. Persuaded to wait his turn, he reached the counter again five or ten minutes later, only to be told that Church's had run out of fried chicken. The young woman at the counter suggested that he might like chicken nuggets instead. Robinson responded to the suggestion by slugging her in the head. That set off a chain of events that ended with Robinson's being shot dead by a security guard. Edna Buchanan covered the homicide for the *Herald*—there are policemen in Miami who say that it wouldn't be a homicide without her—and her story began with what the fried-chicken faction still regards as the classic Edna lead: "Gary Robinson died hungry."

All connoisseurs would agree, I think, that the classic Edna lead would have to include one staple of crime reporting—the simple, matter-of-fact statement that registers with a jolt. The question is where the jolt should be. There's a lot to be said for starting right out with it. I'm rather partial to the Edna lead on a story last year about a woman set to go on trial for a murder conspiracy: "Bad things hap-

pen to the husbands of Widow Elkin." I can, however, understand
the preference that others have for the device of beginning a crime
story with a more or less conventional sentence or two, then snap-
ping the reader back in his chair with an abbreviated sentence that
is used like a blunt instrument. One student of the form at the *Herald* refers to that device as the Miller Chop. The reference is to Gene
Miller, now a *Herald* editor, who, in a remarkable reporting career
that concentrated on the felonious, won the Pulitzer Prize twice for
stories that resulted in the release of people in prison for murder.
Miller likes short sentences in general—it is sometimes said at the
Herald that he writes as if he were paid by the period—and he particularly likes to use a short sentence after a couple of rather long
ones.

These days, Miller sometimes edits the longer pieces that Edna
Buchanan does for the *Herald,* and she often uses the Miller
Chop—as in a piece about a lovers' spat: "The man she loved slapped
her face. Furious, she says she told him never, ever to do that again.
'What are you going to do, kill me?' he asked, and handed her a gun.
'Here, kill me,' he challenged. She did."

Now that I think of it, that may be the classic Edna lead.

There is no dispute about the classic Edna telephone call to a homicide detective or a desk sergeant she knows: "Hi. This is Edna. What's
going on over there?" There are those at the *Herald* who like to think
that Edna Buchanan knows every policeman and policewoman in
the area—even though Dade County has twenty-seven separate police forces, with a total strength of more than forty-five hundred
officers. "I asked her if by any chance she happened to know this
sergeant," a *Herald* reporter once told me. "And she looked at her
watch and said, 'Yeah, but he got off his shift twenty minutes ago.'"
She does not, in fact, know all the police officers in the area, but they
know her. If the desk sergeant who picks up the phone is someone
Edna has never heard of, she gives her full name and the name of her
paper. But even if she said, "This is Edna," there aren't many cops

who would say, "Edna who?" In Miami, a few figures are regularly discussed by first name among people they have never actually met. One of them is Fidel. Another is Edna.

It's an old-fashioned name. Whoever picks up the phone at homicide when Edna Buchanan calls probably doesn't know any Ednas he might confuse her with. Edna is, as it happens, a rather old-fashioned person. "She should have been working in the twenties or thirties," a detective who has known her for years told me. "She'd have been happy if she had a little press card in her hat." She sometimes says the same sort of thing about herself. She laments the replacement of typewriters at the *Herald* with word processors. She would like to think of her clips stored in a place called a morgue rather than a place called an editorial reference library. She's nostalgic about old-fashioned criminals. As a girl growing up around Paterson, New Jersey, she used to read the New York tabloids out loud to her grandmother—a Polish grandmother who didn't read English—and she still likes to roll out the names of the memorable felons in those stories: names like George Metesky, the Mad Bomber, and Willie Sutton, the man who robbed banks because that's where the money was. She even has a period look about her—something that recalls the period around 1961. She is a very thin woman in her forties who tends to dress in slacks and silk shirts and high heels. She wears her hair in a heavy, blond shoulder-length fall. Her eyes are wide, and her brow is often furrowed in concern. She seems almost permanently anxious about one thing or another. Did she neglect to try the one final approach that would have persuaded the suspect's mother to open the door and have a chat? Will a stray cat that she spotted in the neighborhood meet an unpleasant end? Did she forget to put a quarter in the meter? Despite many years spent among people who often find themselves resorting to rough language—hookers, cocaine cowboys, policemen, newspaper reporters—her own conversation tends to sound like that of a rather demure secretary circa 1952. Her own cats—she has five of them—have names like Misty Blue Eyes and Baby Dear. When she is particularly impressed by a bit of news, she is likely to describe it as "real neat." When she discovers, say, a gruesome turn in a tale that might be pretty gruesome already, she may say, "That's interesting as heck!"

Among newspaper people, Edna's line of work is considered a bit old-fashioned. Daily police reporting—what is sometimes known in the trade as covering the cops—is still associated with that old-timer who had a desk in the station house and didn't have to be told by the sergeant in charge which part of the evening's activities to leave out of the story and thought of himself as more or less a member of the department. Covering the cops is often something a reporter does early in his career—an assignment that can provide him with enough war stories in six months to last him through years on the business page or the city desk. Even Gene Miller, a man with a fondness for illegalities of all kinds, turned rather quickly from covering the cops to doing longer pieces. The *Herald,* which regularly shows up on lists of the country's most distinguished dailies, does take a certain amount of pride in providing the sort of crime coverage that is not typical of newspapers on such lists, but it does not have the sort of single-minded interest in juicy felonies that characterized the New York tabloids Edna used to read to her grandmother. When Edna Buchanan began covering the cops for the *Herald,* in 1973, there hadn't been anyone assigned full-time to the beat in several years.

In the years since, Edna has herself broken the routine now and then to do a long crime piece or a series. But she invariably returns to the daily beat. She still dresses every morning to the sound of a police scanner. Unless she already has a story to do, she still drops by the Miami Beach department and the Miami municipal department and the Metro-Dade department on the way to work. She still flips through the previous night's crime reports and the log. She still calls police officers and says, "Hi. This is Edna. What's going on over there?"

·   ·   ·

Like a lot of old-fashioned reporters, Edna Buchanan seems to operate on the assumption that there are always going to be any number
of people who, for perverse and inexplicable reasons of their own,
will try to impede her in gathering a story that is rightfully hers and
delivering it to where God meant it to be—on the front page of the
Miami Herald, and preferably the front page of the *Miami Herald* on
a Sunday, when the circulation is at its highest. There are shy witnesses who insist that they don't want to get involved. There are
lawyers who advise their clients to hang up if Edna Buchanan calls
to ask whether they really did it. (It could be libelous for a newspaper to call someone a suspect, but the paper can get the same idea
across by quoting his denial of guilt.) There are closemouthed policemen. There are television reporters who require equipment that
gets in the way and who ask the sort of question that makes Edna
impatient. (In her view, television reporters on a murder story are
concerned almost exclusively with whether they're going to be able
to get a picture of the authorities removing the body from the
premises, the only other question that truly engages them being
whether they're going to get the picture in time for the six o'clock
news.) There are editors who want to cut a story even though it was
virtually ordained to run at least sixteen inches. There are editors—
often the same editors—who will try to take an interesting detail
out of the story simply because the detail happens to horrify or ap-
pall them. "One of them kept saying that people read this paper at
breakfast," I was told by Edna, whose own idea of a successful lead is
one that might cause a reader who is having breakfast with his wife
to "spit out his coffee, clutch his chest, and say, 'My God, Martha!
Did you read this!'" When Edna went to Fort Lauderdale one day to
talk about police reporting with some of the young reporters in the
Herald's Broward County bureau, she said, "For sanity and survival,
there are three cardinal rules in the newsroom: never trust an editor,
never trust an editor, and never trust an editor."

Edna likes and admires a lot of policemen, but listening to her talk about policemen, you can get the impression that they spend most of their energy trying to deny her access to information that she is meant to have. Police officers insist on roping off crime scenes. ("The police department has too much yellow rope—they want to rope off the world.") Entire departments switch over to computerized crime reports, which don't accommodate the sort of detailed narrative that Edna used to comb through in the old written reports. Investigators sometimes decline to talk about the case they're working on. (Edna distinguishes degrees of reticence among policemen with remarks such as "He wasn't *quite* as paranoid as the other guy.") Once, the man who was then chief of the Metro-Dade department blocked off the homicide squad with a buzzer-controlled entrance whose function was so apparent that it was commonly referred to as "the Edna Buchanan door." Homicide investigators who arrive at a scene and spot Edna talking intently with someone assume that she has found an eyewitness, and they often snatch him away with cautioning words about the errors of talking to the press rather than to the legally constituted authorities. Edna discusses the prevalence of witnessnapping among police detectives in the tone of voice a member of the Citizens Commission on Crime might reserve for talking about an alarming increase in multiple murders.

Once the police arrive at a crime scene in force, Edna often finds it more effective to return to the *Herald* and work by telephone. The alternative could be simply standing behind the yellow rope—an activity she considers fit for television reporters. She may try calling the snatched witness. With a cross-indexed directory, she can phone neighbors who might have seen what happened and then ducked back into their own house for a bolstering drink. She will try to phone the victim's next of kin. "I thought you'd like to say something," she'll say to someone's bereaved wife or daughter. "People care what he was like." Most reporters would sooner cover thirty weeks of water-commission hearings than call a murder victim's next of kin, but Edna tries to look on the positive side. "For some people, it's like a catharsis," she told me one day. "They want to talk about what kind of person their husband was, or their father. Also, it's probably the only time his name is going to be in the paper. It's their last shot. They want to give him a good send-off."

There are people, of course, who are willing to forgo the send-off just to be left alone. Some of them respond to Edna's call by shouting at her for having the gall to trouble them at such a time, and then slamming down the telephone. Edna has a standard procedure for dealing with that. She waits sixty seconds and then phones back. "This is Edna Buchanan at the *Miami Herald,*" she says, using her full name and identification for civilians. "I think we were cut off." In sixty seconds, she figures, whoever answered the phone might reconsider. Someone else in the room might say, "You should have talked to that reporter." Someone else in the room might decide to spare the upset party the pain of answering the phone the next time it rings, and might be a person who is more willing to talk. Edna once called the home of a TV-repair-shop operator in his sixties who had been killed in a robbery attempt—a crime she had already managed to separate from the run-of-the-mill armed-robbery murder. ("On New Year's Eve Charles Curzio stayed later than planned at his small TV repair shop to make sure customers would have their sets in time to watch the King Orange Jamboree Parade," Edna's lead began. "His kindness cost his life.") One of Curzio's sons answered and, upon learning who it was, angrily hung up. "Boy, did I hate dialing the second time," Edna told me. "But if I hadn't, I might have lost them for good." This time, the phone was answered by another of Curzio's sons, and he was willing to talk. He had some eloquent things to say about his father and about capital punishment. ("My father got no trial, no stay of execution, no Supreme Court hearing, nothing. Just some maniac who smashed his brains in with a rifle butt.") If the second call hadn't been productive, Edna told me, she would have given up: "The third call would be harassment."

. . .

When Edna is looking for information, slamming down the phone must sometimes seem the only way of ending the conversation. She is not an easy person to say goodbye to. Once she begins asking questions, she may pause occasionally, as if the interrogation were finally over, but then, in the sort of silence that in conventional conversations is ended with someone's saying "Well, OK" or "Well, thanks for your help," she asks another question. The questioning may not even concern a story she's working on. I was once present when Edna began chatting with a Metro-Dade homicide detective about an old murder case that he had never managed to solve—the apparently motiveless shooting of a restaurant proprietor and his wife, both along in years, as they were about to enter their house. Edna would ask a question and the detective would shake his head, explaining that he had checked out that angle without result. Then, after a pause long enough to make me think that they were about to go on to another case, she would ask another question. Could it have been a mistake in the address? Did homicide check out the people who lived in the equivalent house on the next block? Did the restaurant have any connection with the mob? How about an ex-employee? What about a bad son-in-law? Over the years, Edna has come across any number of bad sons-in-law.

Earlier in the day, I had heard her use the same tone to question a young policewoman who was watching over the front desk at Miami Beach headquarters. "What do you think the rest of Bo's secret is?" Edna said as she skimmed log notations about policemen being called to a loud party or to the scene of a robbery or to a vandalized garage. "Is Kimberly going to get an abortion?" At first, I thought the questions were about cases she was reminded of by the log reports. They turned out to be about *Days of Our Lives,* a soap opera that both Edna and the policewoman are devoted to. Fifteen minutes later, long after I thought the subject had been dropped, Edna was saying, "So is this new character going to be a friend of Jennifer's—the one in the car wreck?"

Bob Swift, a *Herald* columnist who was once Edna's editor at a paper called the *Miami Beach Sun,* told me that he arrived at the *Sun*'s office one day fuming about the fact that somebody had stolen his garbage cans. "I was really mad," he said. "I was saying, 'Who would want to steal two garbage cans!' All of a sudden, I heard Edna say, in that breathless voice, 'Were they empty or full?'"

"Nobody loves a police reporter," Edna sometimes says in speeches. She has been vilified and shouted at and threatened. Perhaps because a female police reporter was something of a rarity when she began, some policemen took pleasure in showing her, say, the corpse of someone who had met a particularly nasty end. ("Sometimes they try to gross you out, but when you're really curious you don't get grossed out. I'm always saying, 'What's this? What's that?'") When Edna was asked by David Finkel, who did a story about her for the *St. Petersburg Times,* why she endured the rigors of covering the cops, she replied, "It's better than working in a coat factory in Paterson, New Jersey." Working in the coat factory was one of several part-time jobs that she had as a schoolgirl to help her mother out. Aside from the pleasures Edna associates with reading crime stories to her Polish grandmother, she doesn't have many happy memories of Paterson. Her other grandmother—her mother's mother—was a member of the Daughters of the American Revolution; Edna still has the membership certificate to prove it. That grandmother, in the view of her DAR family, married beneath her—her husband was a Paterson schoolteacher—and her own daughter, Edna's mother, did even worse. She married a Polish factory worker who apparently had some local renown as a drinker and carouser, and he walked out when Edna was seven. As soon as Edna finished high school, an institution she loathed, she joined her mother in wiring switchboards at the Western Electric plant. Eventually, she transferred to an office job at Western Electric—still hardly the career path that normally leads to a reporting job on the *Miami Herald.*

The enormous change in Edna's life came partly because a clotheshorse friend who wanted to take a course in millinery design persuaded her to come along to evening classes at Montclair State Teachers College. Edna, who had been interested in writing as a child, decided to take a course in creative writing. She remembers the instructor as a thin, poetic-looking man who traveled to New Jersey every week from Greenwich Village. He may have had a limp—a war wound, perhaps. She is much clearer about what happened when he handed back the first short stories the students had written. First, he described one he had particularly liked, and it was Edna's—a sort of psychological thriller about a young woman who thought she was being followed. Edna can still recall what the teacher said about the story—about what a rare pleasure it was for a teacher to come across such writing, about how one section reminded him of early Tennessee Williams. It was the one radiant New Jersey moment. The teacher told her about writers she should read. He told her about paragraphing; the first story she turned in was "just one long paragraph." She decided that she could be a writer. Years later, a novelist who had been hanging around with Edna for a while to learn about crime reporting recognized the teacher from Edna's description and provided his telephone number. She phoned him to tell him how much his encouragement had meant to her. He was pleasant enough, Edna told me, but he didn't remember her or her short story.

Not long after the writing course, Edna and her mother decided to take their vacation in Miami Beach, and Edna says that as she walked off the plane she knew she was not going to spend the rest of her life in Paterson, New Jersey. "The instant I breathed the air, it was like coming home," she told me. "I loved it. I absolutely loved it. I had been wandering around in a daze up there, like a displaced person. I was always a misfit." Edna and her mother tried to get jobs at the Western Electric plant in South Florida; when they couldn't arrange that, they moved anyway. While taking a course in writing, Edna heard that the *Miami Beach Sun* was looking for reporters. The *Sun,* which is now defunct, was the sort of newspaper that hired people without any reporting experience and gave them a lot of it quickly. Edna wrote society news and local political stories and crime stories and celebrity interviews and movie reviews and, on occasion, the letters to the editor.

Edna Buchanan may be the best-known newspaper reporter in Miami, but sometimes she still sounds as if she can't quite believe that she doesn't work in a factory and doesn't live in Paterson, New Jersey. "I've lived here more than twenty years," she says, "and every day I see the palm trees and the water and the beach, and I'm thrilled with how beautiful it is. I'm really lucky, coming from a place like Paterson, New Jersey. I live on a waterway. I have a house. I almost feel, My God, it's like I'm an impostor!"

When Edna says such things, she sounds grateful—a state that an old newspaper hand would tell you is about as common among reporters as a prolonged, religiously inspired commitment to the temperance movement. Edna can even sound grateful for the opportunity to work the police beat, although in the next sentence she may be talking about how tired she is of hearing policemen gripe or how irritated she gets at editors who live to pulverize her copy. She seems completely lacking in the black humor or irony that reporters often use to cope with even a short hitch covering the cops. When she says something is interesting as heck, she means that it is interesting as heck.

Some years ago, she almost went over to the enemy. A Miami television station offered her a hundred and thirty-seven dollars more a week than she was making at the *Herald,* and she had just about decided to take it. She had some ideas about how crime could be covered on television in a way that did not lean so heavily on pictures of the body being removed from the premises. At the last moment, though, she decided not to accept the offer. One reason, she says, is that she faced the fact that crime could never be covered on local television with the details and the subtleties possible in a newspaper story. Also, she couldn't quite bring herself to leave the *Herald.* "If I had been eighteen, maybe I would have done it," she says. "But the *Herald* is the only security I ever had."

. . .

Even before the appearance of *Miami Vice,* Miami was the setting of choice for tales of flashy violence. Any number of people, some of them current or former *Herald* reporters, have portrayed Miami crime in mystery novels or television shows or Hollywood movies. Some of the show-business types might have been attracted mainly by the palm trees and the beach and the exotica of the Latin drug industry: the opening shots of each *Miami Vice* episode are so glamorous that some local tourism-development people have been quoted in the *Herald* as saying that the overall impact of the series is positive. But the volume and the variety of real crime in Miami have, in fact, been of an order to make any police reporter feel the way a stockbroker might feel at a medical convention: opportunities abound. Like most police reporters, Edna specializes in murder, and, as she might express it in a Miller Chop at the end of the first paragraph, so does Miami.

When Edna began as a reporter, a murder in Miami was an occasion. A woman who worked with Edna at the *Miami Beach Sun* in the days when it was sometimes known as "Bob Swift and his all-girl newspaper" has recalled the stir in the *Sun* newsroom when a body washed up on the beach: "I had a camera, because my husband had given it to me for Christmas. The managing editor said, 'Go take a picture of the body.' I said, 'I'm not taking a picture of a washed-up body!' Then I heard a voice from the other end of the room saying, 'I'll do it, I'll do it.' It was Edna."

In the late seventies, Miami, like other American cities, had a steady increase in the sort of murders that occur when, say, an armed man panics while he is robbing a convenience store. It also had some political bombings and some shooting between outfits that were, depending on your point of view, either running drugs to raise money for fighting Fidel or using the fight against Fidel as a cover for running drugs. At the end of the decade, Dade County's murder rate took an astonishing upturn. Around that time, the Colombians who manufactured the drugs being distributed in Miami by Cubans

decided to eliminate the middleman, and, given a peculiar viciousness in the way they customarily operated, that sometimes meant
eliminating the middleman's wife and whoever else happened to be
around. Within a couple of years after the Colombians began their
campaign to reduce overhead, Miami was hit with the Mariel Boat-
lift refugees. In 1977, there were two hundred and eleven murders in
Dade County. By 1981, the high point of Dade murder, there were
six hundred and twenty-one. That meant, according to one homicide detective I spoke to, that Miami experienced the greatest increase in murders per capita that any city had ever recorded. It also
meant that Miami had the highest murder rate in the country. It also
meant that a police reporter could drive to work in the morning
knowing that there would almost certainly be at least one murder to
write about.

"A personal question," one of the Broward-bureau reporters said
after Edna had finished her talk in Fort Lauderdale. "I hope not to
embarrass you, but I've always heard a rumor that you carried a gun.
Is that true?"

"I don't carry a gun," Edna said. "I own a gun or two." She keeps
one in the house and one in the car—which seems only sensible, she
told the reporters, for someone who lives alone and is often driving
through unpleasant neighborhoods late at night. It also seems only
sensible to spend some time on the shooting range, which she happens to enjoy. ("They let me shoot an Uzi the other day," she once
told me. "It was interesting as heck.") A lot of what Edna says about
her life seems only sensible, but a lot of it turns out to have something to do with violence or crime, the stuff of an Edna story. Talking about her paternal grandfather, she'll say that he was supposed to
have killed or maimed someone in a barroom brawl and that his
children were so frightened of his drunken rages that the first sign
of an eruption would send some of them leaping out of second-
floor windows to escape. As an example of her nearsightedness, she'll
mention some revelations in Paterson that seemed to indicate that

she had been followed for months by a notorious sex criminal without realizing it. When Edna talks about places where she has lived in Miami, she is likely to identify neighbors with observations such as "He lived right across the street from this big dope dealer" or "He was indicted for Medicare fraud but he beat it."

Edna's first marriage, to someone she met while she was working at the *Miami Beach Sun,* could provide any number of classic Edna leads. James Buchanan had some dealings with the anti-Castro community and was close to Frank Sturgis, one of the Watergate burglars. Edna says that for some time she thought her husband was simply a reporter on the Fort Lauderdale *Sun Sentinel* who seemed to be out of town more than absolutely necessary. The story she sometimes tells of how she discovered otherwise could be written with an Edna lead: "James Buchanan seemed to make a lot of unexplained trips. Yesterday, at the supermarket, his wife found out why. Mrs. Buchanan, accompanied by a bag boy who was carrying a large load of groceries, emerged from the supermarket and opened the trunk of her car. It was full of machine guns. 'Just put the groceries in the backseat,' she said."

Edna tried a cop the next time, but that didn't seem to have much effect on the duration or quality of the marriage. Her second husband, Emmett Miller, was on the Miami Beach force for years and was eventually appointed chief. By that time, though, he had another wife, his fifth—a wife who, it turned out, was part owner of what the *Herald* described as "an X-rated Biscayne Boulevard motel and a Beach restaurant alleged to be a center of illegal gambling." The appointment was approved by the Miami Beach City Commission anyway, although one commissioner, who stated that the police chief ought to be "above suspicion," did say, "I don't think we're putting our city in an enviable position when we overlook this."

Since the breakup of her marriage to Miller, Edna has almost never been seen at parties or *Herald* hangouts. "I love to be alone," she says. One of the people closest to her is still her mother, who lives not far from Edna and seems to produce ceramic animals even faster than she once turned out fully wired switchboards. Edna's house is a menagerie of ceramic animals. She also has ceramic planters and a ceramic umbrella holder and a ceramic lighthouse—not to speak of a watercolor and a sketch by Jack (Murph the Surf) Murphy, the Miami beachboy who in 1964 helped steal the Star of India sapphire and the DeLong Star Ruby from the American Museum of Natural History—but ceramic animals are the predominant design element. She has penguins and turtles and horses and seagulls and flamingos and swans and fish and a rabbit and a pelican. She has a ceramic dog that is nearly life-size. She has cats in practically every conceivable pose—a cat with nursing kittens, a cat carrying a kitten in its mouth, a curled-up cat. Edna is fond of some of the ceramic animals, but the fact that her mother's productivity seems to be increasing rather than waning with the passing of the years has given her pause.

All of Edna's live animals are strays. Besides the cats, she has a dog whose best trick is to fall to the floor when Edna points an imaginary gun at him and says, "Bang! You're dead!" Some colleagues at the *Herald* think that a stray animal is about the only thing that can distract Edna from her coverage of the cops. It is assumed at the *Herald* that she takes Mondays and Tuesdays off because the weekend is traditionally a high-crime period. (Edna says that the beaches are less crowded during the week and that working weekends gives her a better chance at the Sunday paper.) Around the *Herald* newsroom, Edna is known for being fiercely proprietary about stories she considers hers—any number of *Herald* reporters, running into her at the scene of some multiple murder or major disaster, have been greeted with an icy "What are *you* doing here?"—and so combative about her copy that a few of the less resilient editors have been reduced almost to the state in which they would fall to the floor if Edna pointed an imaginary gun at them and said, "Bang! You're dead!" Edna's colleagues tend to speak of her not as a pal but as a phenomenon. Their Edna stories are likely to concern her tenacity or her superstitions or the remarkable intensity she maintains after all these

years of covering a beat that quickly strikes many reporters as un-
bearably horrifying or depressing. They often mention the astonishing contrast between her apparent imperviousness to the grisly
sights on the police beat and her overwhelming concern for animals.
While I was in Miami, two or three *Herald* reporters suggested that
I look up some articles in which, as they remembered it, Edna ham-
mered away so mercilessly at a retired French Canadian priest who
had put to death some stray cats that the poor man was run out of
the country. When I later told one of the reporters that I had read
the *Herald*'s coverage of the incident and that almost none of it had
been done by Edna, he said, "I'm not surprised. Probably didn't trust
herself. Too emotionally involved."

Policemen, Edna told the young reporters in Fort Lauderdale, have
an instinctive mistrust of outsiders—"an us-and-them attitude."
Edna can never be certain which category she's in. Any police reporter these days is likely to have a less comfortable relationship
with the police than the one enjoyed by the old-fashioned station-
house reporter who could be counted on to be looking the other
way if the suspect met with an accident while he was being taken
into custody. Since Watergate, reporters all over the country have
been under pressure to cast a more suspicious eye on any institution
they cover. Partly because of the availability of staggering amounts
of drug money, both the Miami and the Metro-Dade departments
have had serious scandals in recent years, making them particularly
sensitive to inspection by critical outsiders. The *Herald* has covered
police misconduct prominently, and it has used Florida's public-
records act aggressively in court to gain access to police documents—
even documents involved in Internal Affairs investigations. A lot of
policemen regard the *Herald* as their adversary and see Edna Buchanan as the embodiment of the *Herald*.

Edna says that she makes every effort to portray cops as human
beings—writing about a police officer who has been charged with
misconduct, she usually manages to find some past commendations

to mention—but it has never occurred to anybody that she might look the other way. Edna broke the story of an attempted cover-up involving a black insurance man named Arthur McDuffie, who died as a result of injuries suffered in an encounter with some Metro-Dade policemen—policemen whose acquittal on manslaughter charges some months later touched off three nights of rioting in Miami's black community. There are moments when Edna seems to be "us" and "them" at the same time. Keeping the picture and the press release sent when someone is named Officer of the Month may give Edna one extra positive sentence to write about a policeman the next time she mentions him; also, as it happens, it is difficult to come by a picture of a cop who gets in trouble, and over the years Edna has found that a cop who gets in trouble and a cop who was named Officer of the Month are often the same person.

"There's a love-hate relationship between the police and the press," Mike Gonzalez, one of Edna's best friends on the Miami municipal force, says. A case that Edna covers prominently is likely to get a lot of attention in the department, which means that someone whose name is attached to it might become a hero or might, as one detective I spoke to put it, "end up in the complaint room of the property bureau." Edna says that the way a reporter is received at police headquarters can depend on "what you wrote the day before—or their perception of what you wrote the day before."

Some police officers in Dade County won't talk to Edna Buchanan about the case they're working on. Some of those who do give her tips—not just on their own cases but on cases being handled by other people, or even other departments—won't admit it. (According to Dr. Joseph Davis, the medical examiner of Dade County, "Every police agency thinks she has a direct pipeline into someone else's agency.") Cops who become known as friends and sources of Edna's are likely to be accused by other cops of showboating or of trying to further their careers through the newspaper. When I mentioned Mike Gonzalez to a Metro-Dade lieutenant I was talking to in Miami, he said, "What Howard Cosell did for Cassius Clay, Edna Buchanan did for Mike Gonzalez."

Gonzalez is aware of such talk and doesn't show much sign of caring about it. He thinks most policemen are nervous about the press because they aren't confident that they can reveal precisely what they find it useful to reveal and no more. Edna's admirers among police investigators—people like Gonzalez and Lloyd Hough, a Metro-Dade homicide detective—tend to admire her for her skill and independence as an investigator. "I'd take her any time as a partner," Hough told me. "Let's put it like this: if I had done something, I wouldn't want Edna investigating me. Internal Affairs I don't care about, but Edna . . ." They also admire her persistence, maddening as it may sometimes be. Hough nearly had her arrested once when she persisted in coming under the yellow rope into a crime scene. "She knows when she's pushed you to the limit, and she'll do that often," Hough told me. "And I say that with the greatest admiration."

A police detective and a police reporter may sound alike as they stand around talking about past cases—recalling the airline pilot who killed the other airline pilot over the stewardess, or exchanging anecdotes about the aggrieved bag boy who cleared a Publix supermarket in a hurry by holding a revolver to the head of the manager—but their interests in a murder case are not necessarily the same. If an armed robber kills a convenience-store clerk, the police are interested in catching him; Edna is interested in distinguishing what happened from other killings of other convenience-store clerks. To write about any murder, Edna is likely to need details that wouldn't help an investigator close the case. "I want to know what movie they saw before they got gunned down," she has said. "What were they wearing? What did they have in their pockets? What was cooking on the stove? What song was playing on the jukebox?" Mike Gonzalez just sighs when he talks about Edna's appetite for irrelevant details. "It infuriates Mike," Edna says. "I always ask what the dog's name is, what the cat's name is." Edna told me that Gonzalez now advises rookie detectives that they might as well gather such details, because otherwise "you're just going to feel stupid when Edna asks you."

There are times when Edna finds herself longing for simpler times on the police beat. When she began, the murders she covered tended to be conventional love triangles or armed robberies. She was often dealing with "an up-front person who happened to have bludgeoned his wife to death." These days, the murders are likely to be Latin drug murders, and a lot fewer of them produce a suspect. Trying to gather information from Cubans and Central Americans, Edna has a problem that goes beyond the language barrier. "They have a Latin love of intrigue," she says. "I had a Cuban informant, and I found that he would sometimes lie to me just to make it more interesting." It is also true that even for a police reporter there can be too many murders. Edna says that she was "a little shell-shocked" four or five years ago, when Dade murders hit their peak. She found that she barely had time to make her rounds in a thorough way. "I used to like to stop at the jail," she has said. "I used to like to browse in the morgue. To make sure who's there."

Edna found that the sheer number of murders overwhelmed each individual murder as the big story. "Dade's murder rate hit new heights this week as a wave of unrelated violence left 14 people dead and five critically hurt within five days," a story bylined Edna Buchanan began in June of 1980. After a couple of paragraphs comparing the current murder figures with those of previous years, the story went on, "In the latest wave of violence, a teenager's throat was cut and her body dumped in a canal. A former airline stewardess was garroted and left with a pair of scissors stuck between her shoulder blades. Four innocent bystanders were shot in a barroom gun battle. An 80-year-old man surprised a burglar who battered him fatally with a hammer. An angry young woman who 'felt used' beat her date to death with the dumbbells he used to keep fit. And an apparent robbery victim was shot dead as he ran away from the robbers." The murder rate has leveled off since 1981, but Edna still sometimes writes what amount to murder-roundup stories. "I feel bad, and even a little guilty, that a murder no longer gets a story, just a paragraph," she says. "It dehumanizes it." A paragraph in a roundup piece is not Edna's idea of a send-off.

On a day I was making the rounds with Edna, there was a police report saying that two Marielitos had begun arguing on the street and the argument had ended with one shooting the other dead. That sounded like a paragraph at most. But Edna had a tip that the victim and the killer had known each other in Cuba and the shooting was actually the settling of an old prison score. That sounded to me more like a murder that stood out a bit from the crowd. Edna thought so, too, but her enthusiasm was limited. "We've already had a couple of those," she told me. Edna has covered a few thousand murders by now, and she's seen a couple of most things. She has done stories about a man who was stabbed to death because he stepped on somebody's toes on his way to a seat in a movie theater and about a two-year-old somebody tried to frame for the murder of a playmate and about an eighty-nine-year-old man who was arrested for beating his former wife to death and about a little boy killed by a crocodile. She has done stories about a woman who committed suicide because she couldn't get her leaky roof fixed and about a newspaper deliveryman who committed suicide because during a petroleum shortage he couldn't get enough gasoline. She has done stories about a man who managed to commit suicide by stabbing himself in the heart *twice* and about a man who threw a severed head at a police officer *twice*. She has done a story about two brothers who killed a third brother because he interrupted a checkers game. ("I thought I had the best-raised children in the world," their mother said.) She has done a story about a father being killed at the surprise birthday party given for him by his thirty children. She has done a story about a man who died because fourteen of the eighty-two double-wrapped condom packages of cocaine he tried to carry into the country inside his stomach began to leak. ("His last meal was worth $30,000 and it killed him.") She has done any number of stories about bodies being discovered in the bay by beachcombers or fishermen or University of Miami scientists doing marine research. ("'It's kind of a nuisance when you plan your day to do research on the reef,' fumed Professor Peter Glynn, of the university's Rosenstiel School of Marine and Atmospheric Science.") Talking to Edna one day about murder cases they had worked on, a Metro-Dade homicide detective said, "In Dade County, there are no surprises left."

Edna would agree that surprises are harder to find in Dade County these days. Still, she finds them. Flipping through page after page of routine police logs, talking to her sources on the telephone, chatting with a homicide detective, she'll come across, say, a shopping-mall murder that might have been done against the background of a new kind of high school gang, or a murderer who seemed to have been imprisoned with his victim for a time by a sophisticated burglar-gate system. Then, a look of concern still on her face, she'll say, "That's interesting as heck."

About the Author

CALVIN TRILLIN has been a staff writer at *The New Yorker* since 1963. His nonfiction includes *About Alice, Remembering Denny,* and *Jackson, 1964.* His humor writing includes books of political verse, comic novels, books on eating, and the collection *Quite Enough of Calvin Trillin.*

About the Type

This book was set in Bembo, a typeface based on an old-style Roman face that was used for Cardinal Pietro Bembo's tract *De Aetna* in 1495. Bembo was cut by Francesco Griffo (1450–1518) in the early sixteenth century for Italian Renaissance printer and publisher Aldus Manutius (1449–1515). The Lanston Monotype Company of Philadelphia brought the well-proportioned letterforms of Bembo to the United States in the 1930s.